The Making of Community Work

The Making of Community Work

David N. Thomas

London
GEORGE ALLEN & UNWIN
Boston   Sydney

George Allen & Unwin (Publishers) Ltd,
40 Museum Street, London WC1A 1LU, UK

George Allen & Unwin (Publishers) Ltd,
Park Lane, Hemel Hempstead, Herts HP2 4TE, UK

Allen & Unwin, Inc.,
9 Winchester Terrace, Winchester, Mass. 01890, USA

George Allen & Unwin Australia Pty Ltd,
8 Napier Street, North Sydney, NSW 2060, Australia

First published in 1983

British Library Cataloguing in Publication Data

Thomas, David N.
  The making of community work.
1. Social group work—Great Britain
2. Community development—Great Britain
I. Title
361.8'0941   HV245
ISBN 0–04–361051–X
ISBN 0–04–361052–8 Pbk

Library of Congress Cataloging in Publication Data

Thomas, David N.
  The making of community work.
Includes bibliographical references and index.
1. Social service. 2. Community
organization—Great Britain. I. Title.
HV245.T48   1983   361.8'0941   83–3761
ISBN 0–04–361051–X
ISBN 0–04–361052–8 (pbk.)

Set in 10 on 11 point Times by
Grove Graphics, Tring, Hertfordshire
and printed in Great Britain by
Biddles Ltd, Guildford, Surrey

Contents

Acknowledgements

Many people have contributed ideas and information to this study, and I am very grateful for all the help they have given. I am indebted to several friends and their families who gave me accommodation on my visits around the country. I have found the support of fellow practitioners and trainers in community work sustaining, and all of you who hailed me in the street or at a meeting with the cry 'And how's the project going?' played a part in keeping me at the task. I am particularly grateful to Charlie McConnell for giving the study such a good start in Scotland.

I owe many thanks to the panel of readers who responded to the first draft of this book, and especially to the following people who provided extensive advice and criticisms: Peter Baldock, Ann Curno, Roger Smith, Jenny Stiles, Marilyn Taylor, Pat Taylor, Paul Waddington and Anne Wright. The panel of readers was extremely useful in the comments it provided but responsibility for what appears in the book is, of course, entirely mine. Several people contributed papers to the study and these will be made available in a separate publication called *Community Work in the Eighties*. Copies may be obtained from the Publications Assistant at the National Institute for Social Work.

My Advisory Committee has given me considerable help and I have appreciated and relied upon Paul Curno, Richard Mills and Sister Mary McAleese for the encouragement and confidence they have shown.

Generous support for the study was provided by the National Institute for Social Work, the Calouste Gulbenkian Foundation, the Nuffield Foundation, and another trust that wishes to be anonymous.

The main burden of reading and advice has fallen on Paul Henderson and David Jones. They have been as unselfish and unstinting in the work they have put into this study as in that they have devoted to many other projects in community work. My thanks go also to Stevie Krayer for her poetry, her commitment and her efforts to develop my ideas and make my writing more felicitous. Daniel, my son, suggested the marvellous title of *Childhood and Neighbourhood;* while I could not use it, Danny and Siân's experiences whilst growing up in an inner-city neighbourhood have helped me understand the practical side of some of the ideas in this book.

My work on this study has taken me away from other responsibilities at the National Institute. My colleagues have shown great patience in having an absentee staff member. It is difficult to express adequately the depth of my gratitude to Paul Henderson who has willingly shouldered extra teaching and administration during the study, and without whose support, knowledge and good sense my efforts would have foundered. His has been a major influence in the development of the study.

Two other colleagues have also been important in bringing the project to fruition. Gloria Bravette and Ruth Page have been responsible for the administration and secretarial sides of the project. They worked wonders in making everything go competently and to schedule, not least because of the personal interest they took in the work and ideas that came their way. They were helped by Rosemary Davis, Priscilla Foley and Jayne Parkin. Gloria, Ruffo and Joel deserve a special mention for noticing that there were theories at the bottom of my jargon.

Charlie Grosser, of Columbia University, New York, was to have helped with the study whilst a Fulbright Fellow at the National Institute. He died at the beginning of his sabbatical; he is missed as a friend and colleague, and this book is dedicated to him.

For Charlie

There is a packing up
In the country, a putting away
Of leaves, for the long sabbatical of summer
Is ending, and dust sheets
Will cover the furrows. Empty fields,
Unheated, gather a boxroom chill
Where no life will stir
For a season. The beechwoods blaze
With tapestry, but now like sighs
Condensed, the leaves lie rusting on the grass.

Such endings are only preludes
Enriching the spring to come
Says reason, but knows
With an ache like frost, this year
Will never come again.

STEVIE KRAYER

Introduction

The idea for a study of community work was first mooted in the autumn of 1979. I had prepared a number of research proposals and had discussed them informally with colleagues and with a number of funders. A study of community work was just one of the possibilities, and although it was the proposal that seemed the most formidable it was the one that caught people's imagination. Two decades of experience had elapsed since the rediscovery of community work at the beginning of the 1960s, and the proposal seemed congruent with a new mood in community work of reflection, of stock-taking, of wondering what would be in store in the coming years.

A draft was submitted to the Calouste Gulbenkian Foundation (and later to another trust) in February 1980 and a formal offer of some funds was made in July of that year. It was agreed that the first phase and draft of the study would be completed by Christmas 1981. I spent September preparing the administration for the project and in calling together a small group to advise me on the process and mechanics of the study and to join a panel of readers.

One of the first jobs was to prepare some information that could be circulated. This said that the study

> will seek to understand some of the directions for community work
> (used in its broadest sense, and including community action,
> community education and community relations) in the 1980s. The
> study will work from an analysis of possible social and economic
> changes that may affect, in the coming years, the development of
> community action, and the use of community workers. It is
> anticipated that the study will indicate future areas of work, and the
> priorities amongst them, in a way that will be helpful to community
> groups and community workers, as well as to employers, funders and
> trainers.

This information sheet asked people to send in their ideas to me, or to participate in the study in a number of different ways described below. The sheet was extensively circulated within community work and other relevant interests.[1] There are costs and benefits to such an approach, and one community worker said that I might have done better by quietly going around the country and talking informally to a few people. A university teacher suggested that all one needs is 'the first dozen or so responses to a study like this, and all the rest you can forget about: they rarely add anything that you don't already know about'. The attention given to the study in these early days may have deterred some possible respondents, and may have been unhelpful in making the study seem far grander than it would actually turn out to be.

By the beginning of October 1980 I was ready to talk with people and agencies. This part of the study to gather material and visit different parts of the country is described below, and lasted until March 1981. I then worked until December of that year to produce the first draft of the study. This was circulated to my panel of readers and I worked two and a half days each week until the autumn of 1982 revising the draft in the light of the readers' comments and my own reflections.

I used a number of methods to gather information for the study. These were interviews; group discussions; attendance at conferences; study groups; and a public invitation to individuals and agencies to prepare written papers.

INTERVIEWS

I did not have the time to see every individual or representative of an agency that I felt I ought to see, as well as those who thought that I ought to see them. I did not believe in the value of, or have the resources for, a scientific selection of workers, trainers and administrators. What I wanted to achieve were interviews in different parts of the country, and I used my contacts in those areas to advise me about those with whom I might talk. My criteria for choosing the people to interview on these visits (which were usually one or two days packed with interviews from dawn to dusk) were:

● to see a mix of workers and trainers, from different settings;
● to talk with people who had been in community work for some time, and had a feel for the decade that had just ended;
● that the person could talk about the city and region in which they were based and thus could think about issues that were outside their own particular patch or interest. I also looked for people who, by virtue of their role, experience, or involvement in national organisations or networks, could also reflect on community work within the United Kingdom.

Using these criteria, I interviewed 121 people in different parts of the country;[2] the interviews, which were usually around two hours long, were sometimes acccompanied by a visit to particular projects or neighbourhoods. At the conclusion of each visit, letters were sent to individuals and projects that had been mentioned by my interviewees but whom I had been unable to see. The letters referred to the study and my visit to the city or town, and asked for written materials on the work they were doing.

GROUP DISCUSSIONS

I met a further 98 people in a number of group discussions around the United Kingdom. The groups were invariably small, ranging from five to eighteen people; they included community workers, trainers, researchers, councillors and community activists. I also met staff from national and regional agencies in the voluntary sector, and those from central government departments (in London, Belfast and Edinburgh) with an interest in community work.

CONFERENCES AND WORKSHOPS

There were three major conferences that I attended whose theme was the development of community work in the 1980s. They were held at Brighton, Dundee and Southampton. I also went to a number of other events dealing with topics of relevance to this study.

STUDY GROUPS

Two groups were set up as part of a consultative exercise that took the shape of a simple 'Delphi' technique. After agreeing to take part, each participant was asked to write a brief paper on the particular topic — this was round one. The papers were circulated within the group, and round two comprised of a further paper from each person, reflecting on their first paper in the light of the other participants' comments, and also reacting to what the others had written. These papers were then distributed. Round three was a review paper from me that took up what I saw as the major issues and ideas in the papers. Finally, the participants met to examine the papers and to continue the discussion in person.

Two Delphi exercises were held: the topic of the first was 'training in community work'. Nineteen people, mostly trainers and student unit supervisors, took part in this exercise which culminated in a two-day residential workshop at Northern College.

The second was called 'research and community work'. A group of fourteen researchers, trainers and workers prepared papers, and met for a one-day workshop in London.

The list of the members in each exercise is given at the end of the book. Thirty-four papers were produced in these exercises and contributed to the writing of Chapters 5 and 7.

WRITTEN SUBMISSIONS

I received from individuals, and from a range of departments and agencies, 21 papers that were prepared and written specially for this study. The other original papers were, of course,the 34 Delphi papers. In addition, there were 66 submissions from individuals and organisations that had not been written for this study but contained material that was of direct relevance.

THE PANEL OF READERS

The primary purpose of this panel was to read and comment critically on the first draft of my report. It was also a means to consult with people who represented a number of interests in the field about some of the main ideas and suggestions in the report. The list of the panel members is included at the end of the report.

Drafts were sent to the readers in December 1981 and they were given some six weeks in which to respond. Where possible panel members were paired up geographically and a list of addresses and telephone numbers prepared so that members might find it easy to meet if they found this useful.

The response to the study from individuals and agencies within and outside community work was generally positive and supportive. There were only 28 letters which said they could not contribute to the study, mainly from local authority departments and largely because they had no time or resources to make a contribution, or these were committed elsewhere. Several organisations, for example, expressed interest in the study but said their priority was to submit evidence to the Barclay Committee on the roles and tasks of social workers. This committee, which was set up after, and which reported before, my study, was also based at the National Institute. There were no formal links between the Barclay Committee and this study, nor was there any exchange of material and ideas. Not only did some agencies choose to give priority to the Barclay Committee, but there were some occasions when it was clear that individuals and organisations confused this study with the Barclay Committee; there was, too, a small number of people who were suspicious of this study because they presumed a connection with the social work inquiry. There was also a handful of people who assumed that my location in an institute concerned with social work would inevitably bias the study towards 'a social work view of community work'; one person wrote as early as February 1981:

> I do not wish to participate in any way since I can already sense the flavour of the final report. Perhaps the most telling signpost for

'community work' in the 80's is that this study is being carried out by the National Institute for Social Work?

A letter in the ACW Bulletin at an earlier point in the study was even more certain about the outcomes of my work; it suggested that I appeared already to have made up my mind about community work, and the letter contained some comments on the sponsorship of the study by the Calouste Gulbenkian Foundation, including the possibility that the money spent on this project might have been better given to field projects.

Another person took almost a contrary view: he was worried that the study had insufficient resources; it was too much to expect one person, with limited administrative support, to take on such a major piece of work; community work itself might be harmed if the report went off at half-cock, so it might be better if it were not done at all than to be done with insufficient resources and time. It was inevitable, too, that 'you will be on a hiding to nothing' because it would be impossible to satisfy all or even most of the different points of view within community work: 'For one person to take on this type of review . . . is extremely brave . . . you must know as well as anyone that any such act of heroism will invite a great deal of criticism.' Resources apart, several people were worried that such a study was being carried out by one person because it could not possibly reflect the diversity of the field.

It was sometimes said to me that no matter how good or bad the content of the report might be it would have a disproportionate influence because of some of the institutions associated with it. The report would be influential, it was suggested, not for what it said or didn't say, but because it was partly funded by the Gulbenkian Foundation; it would be seen as the 'third Gulbenkian report' – the previous two that had appeared in 1968 and 1973 had each sold over 8,000 copies and had been important in the development of community work. The fact that the author was at the National Institute for Social Work might give the report a certain status within the social welfare field, whether or not this status was deserved by the contents. 'Look', said one interviewee, 'imagine your report on community work arrives on the desk of a social services director or chairman of the committee: at the same time, the ACW book on radical practice in community work lands on his desk. Now, which do you think he's most likely to pick up and read and take most notice of?'

This is a complex question; I suspect that the comparison with a book on radical practice indicated a fear that my report could be a down-the-middle, soggy affair, yet another example of 'the con-sensual claustrophobia of a Gulbenkian time-warp'. A few people were apprehensive that I would be ignorant of new or radical developments in the field (ignorant by virtue of being in one of the establishment's ivory towers in London) or prejudiced towards them, as one correspondent suggested:

> You have in fact commented on the sort of work I am involved in in your published materials about CDP and in statements you have made at meetings I have attended. What I do now stems from the kind of analysis put forward by CDP to which you are – as far as I can tell – unsympathetic. If I had misread your attitudes towards such questions as the relevance of CDP's structural analysis to community work practice, the contribution of Marxism to community work, the need to link community and workplace issues and the importance of supporting trade union developments, then I stand to be corrected.

I had asked for a meeting with this community worker but was refused because, the worker wrote, 'I'm not sure I can see any point in us talking. Your views on the sort of work with which I have been associated have been widely published, and don't seem to me to leave much room for discussion.' This correspondence is an example of something that is discussed later in the report. It illustrates the factionalism that has been present in community work in the last decade; a consequence of this factionalism is that discussion is valued only with people with similar views, and the possibility of learning from others (and helping those others also to learn) is dismissed. Dialogue becomes a means not of mutual learning and change but of the confirmation of views and prejudices, and a ritual by which people are recognised as being inside or outside a particular group.

It may be that a reluctance to talk with me reflects some insecurity about exposing one's practice to the critical eye of an outsider. This kind of insecurity was also evident in discussions I had with, for example, some large agencies and some departments of government. Here one often had to struggle to overcome the fear that 'the departmental interest' (particularly vis-à-vis other departments) would be at risk or that the 'departmental record' on community work would not stand up to scrutiny.

The breadth I gave to the original conception of the study was over-ambitious. At the beginning of this chapter I quoted from the early information sheet on the study: the goals I set for myself were not wholly feasible for one person with limited resources, and within a study that needed to report earlier rather than later in the decade. One aspect of the study that is less prominent at its completion than inception is the socio-economic analysis. I have done less on this than I would have liked, partly because of limited resources but largely because these resources had also to be devoted to a part of the study that was not foreseen at its inception. It became clear as I started that I would have to review the development of community work up to the year 1980, and I have given a chapter over to this, beginning with the year 1960. This chapter is not a detailed history but a review of some of the issues and ideas that seem pertinent, though my selection and treatment of these issues has been influenced by the contributions others have made to the study through interviews and submissions.

The study is primarily of the development of community work as an intervention and occupation, though it tries to take into account those salient factors within, for example, social movements and local government that have influenced it. The limited amount of contextual analysis may be seen as a constraint, as one of my readers observed:

> in your analysis of the past, present and future of community work you tend to discuss mainly from the perspective of what community workers have thought and done — but you have neglected to analyse how these 'internal' happenings are in part a response to trends and pressures arising out of changes in the external environment in which community work is sponsored and operates — the social, economic, political, cultural and intellectual environment . . . I realise that you do analyse to some extent those contextual aspects, but I didn't sense an adequate capturing of the reciprocal/dialectical relationship between these 'internal' and 'external' factors.

Certainly this book is not a sociology of community work; I have, however, tried to write about community work as a particular and limited intervention but one that has a place in the development of political awareness and practices. Much of this thinking is presented in Chapters 2 and 3, and throughout the book I interweave considerations of community work as an occupation with certain tasks and skills with those that define its contribution in the evolution of a more participative and politically conscious democracy. This vision of community work led another reader to comment:

> From my viewpoint what you are trying to do is have your cake and eat it, too. On the one hand, you define community work in fairly restrictive terms as an occupation with its own specific functions, skills, etc. On the other hand, you link it with a set of objectives which are in very broad terms political.

I have worked on this study as fairly and objectively as possible, but it still may be construed as an example of what Renato Constantino calls 'partisan scholarship' (1978). This refers to putting forward objective facts and developments within a particular framework and point of view, so that they may serve some useful end. I am prompted to make this comment because one correspondent wrote:

> Do you need to be clearer about your own stance with regard to the study? Do you see yourself as an 'outsider' looking in on community work, a sort of political anthropologist, or as an 'insider' who displays his alignment with the occupation? I think this could be important, because otherwise some of your observations and criticisms will be seen and felt as unsympathetic 'snipes' rather than sympathetic challenges.

I am committed to the development of community work, and I have been particularly partisan in the study in criticising those in government and statutory and voluntary agencies who have used community work for their own professional or administrative purposes whilst denying it the resources it has needed to make an effective impact. I have been equally critical in some chapters of those in social movements and political campaigns who have been riding piggy-back on community work as a source of income and a means of dissemination of ideas whilst openly dismissive of its contribution as an intervention.

My position is, as one colleague put it, as a believer in a cause to which I am committed. Such partisanship is not without its difficulties in presenting material in the study. I have tried to write this report to reflect the ideas presented to me in interviews, conferences, written papers, and so on. I hope the study catches some of the variety of views that are available in community work on particular issues. But some parts of the study may strike the reader as being more of a personal view, though, I hope, one that has been formed through careful consideration of what I have seen and been told, and what I have experienced in my years in community work practice and training.

It is already evident that any benefits of this study go beyond the production and availability of this book. The process of gathering material for the study has helped some workers and agencies to review their involvement in community work for themselves; people who have prepared papers for me have found they have been able to use them in their work and forward planning. This process of participation in the study has contributed in some areas to the development of local networks of workers, trainers and others.

The purpose of this book, as with the whole study, is to stimulate discussion within and about community work; it is a contribution to a longer and more complicated process of clarifying what community work can offer in this decade, and what resources it needs to be given if it is to be at all effective. I hope that the ideas that are put forward will not be regarded as firm and immutable proposals; they are intended to initiate dialogue or to add to that which is already in progress.

The book begins with a review of the 1960s and 1970s; this examines, in particular, the association of community work with education and social work, and the development of community work as a disjointed occupation through the last decade. Chapters 2 and 3 are 'mapping' chapters; they try to define community work as a specific intervention that has a strategic purpose in the development of communities and the conditions which govern the effective use of the franchise. Some of the possible areas of community work practice in the 1980s are discussed in Chapter 4. Chapter 5 deals with training opportunities in community work in colleges and field-based schemes, as well as in-service facilities. It discusses the need to keep community work as an open occupation but also as one in which there has to be a greater emphasis on the skills and knowledge to do the job competently. Chapter 6 looks at some matters to do with the recruitment, auspices and funding of community workers, and in chapter 7 there is consideration of the extent and quality of literature, theory and research in and about community work. The chapter concludes with a discussion of the place within community work of a national body whose functions would include training; research; consultancy; and information clearinghouse. This brief account of the areas covered indicates that the study is a mix of review, analysis and proposals; there is the inevitable danger that none of these three is adequately treated, and I am sure that each could have been improved by giving to them all my time and energy. If this book sometimes falls between the three stools of review, analysis and proposals, then I trust that subsequent discussions will be arranged in such a way that each aspect is given the attention it deserves.

NOTES

1 The information sheet went to national newspapers and to magazines and journals in community work and a large number of related fields; to conferences and workshops; to government departments; to all social services departments and probation offices in Britain; to national welfare agencies and to a large number of agencies in the statutory and voluntary sector with a national, regional, or local interest in community work. It was distributed to funders of community work such as trusts, and to community work trainers and fieldwork supervisors, to the Trades Union Congress and to the National Union of Public Employees and the National Association of Local Government Officers. A copy was sent to 150 individuals in practice or training in community work known to me and they were encouraged to distribute it on their networks. It was also circulated through various local and national news services to community workers, including those of the Association of Community Workers and the Federation of Community Work Training Groups. It went, too, to professional associations such as the British Association of Social Workers, to independent academic institutions such as the Policy Studies Institute and to a selection of government-appointed bodies and quangos such as the Commission for Racial Equality and the Central Council for Education and Training in Social Work.

2   For the purposes of interviews, group discussions and conferences, I visited the following places: Belfast, Birmingham, Brighton, Caerphilly, Cardiff, Coventry, Dundee, Durham, Edinburgh, Gilfach Goch, Glasgow, Leicester, Leeds, London, Middlesbrough, Newcastle, Nottingham, Port Talbot, Sheffield, Southampton, Stockton, Sunderland, Swansea, York. I also interviewed people from other parts of the country whilst they were on visits to London.

1 *Through the Sixties and Seventies*

Only the fool points at his origins with his left hand.
Akan Proverb

Community work is an intervention whose practitioners are, on the whole, well-educated, white middle-class people (with more men than women) and mostly in their 20s and 30s; in more recent years they have been joined by older working-class recruits and by people from ethnic groups, many of whom have previously participated as members of neighbourhood organisations. Most community workers are paid to do their job on a full-time basis, though there are those who do it voluntarily and those who do it part-time. It is a specialist function though its ideas and methods have also influenced practice in other occupations.

Community workers do community work, and I shall attempt later to define what it is, and identify some characteristics which distinguish it from other interventions. It is most certainly an intervention into processes within neighbourhoods and agencies. This study is about that intervention and the workers who are paid to carry it out; it is not primarily about community activities or activism – that which community workers are paid to organise and support according to the felt needs of participants. The social movements that have influenced, and been influenced by, community workers do not provide a main focus for the study; nor do those significant institutional changes which have also occurred during the period when community work was emerging as an occupation. These matters will be discussed where they bear upon analysis of community work, but it was not the purpose of this study to review community activism, social movements and institutional reforms.

There is no value in conflating the roles of community worker and community activist. It is a fiction that they are the same. Community work interventions require a certain degree of experience and training; they offer specific skills and knowledge to a community or agency which are different from (though not inherently better than and often overlapping with) those offered by local residents who take on active roles within community groups. Residents may, of course, become community workers but their tasks and roles will be different from those they fulfilled when they were members of a local group.

There are probably thousands of community workers in the United Kingdom, and even more who do some community work'on the side' as part of another job such as teaching and social work. The size of the population of workers depends on definition and is not known with any exactness; we know little about their characteristics – sex, age, race, education, salaries, their working experience. We are uncertain of the numbers employed in the different departments of local authorities (social services is an exception) and in the different voluntary agencies, and how many are employed by community groups. We know little about their regional distribution within the United Kingdom, or their distribution between different communities – urban and rural, for example. There is little information on the issues with which workers are engaged, with what population groups, or on the ways in which workers seek to help. Our knowledge of their motivations, values and work ambitions is unsatisfactory, as it is about the way they relate to each other, their employers and to colleagues in other and related occupations. We do not know enough about how they think of their work, and use experience, theory and research in making decisions in their day-to-day practice.

The most remarkable fact about these workers is that they have achieved so much – and with little in the way of resources and support. Often working alone in some of the most testing inner city areas in the country, they have organised and sustained a vast number of community groups and agency initiatives. There have been failures, bad practice, inefficiency, wrong priorities, and so on, but what is impressive is the extent and variety of the work stimulated and/or supported by community workers. Such interventions have not always been successful in terms of the material objectives of the groups; but the criteria for success must always include the more intangible developments in people's confidence and competence to assert what they see as their interests. The character of local politics has changed radically over the decade: the link, identified by the Seebohm report and many others, has been forged between popular participation and traditional representative democracy. Much of this grass-roots activism has been supported by community workers who have helped to bring about more participative forms of democracy, the consequences of which are yet too early to assess. Whether through housing campaigns, festivals, or neighbourhood care schemes, community workers have helped residents to learn specific skills and knowledge, and to become more interested in, and understanding of, wider issues. The numbers of such residents may be comparatively small, and it is often a criticism of community workers that their educational role has been limited; but whilst the numbers may be small we must not discount the 'knock-on' effect of neighbourhood organising – creating a climate of confidence and legitimation for asserting felt needs, and modelling how collective action may be undertaken.

This, in the briefest of terms, can be said to be the major part of community workers' contribution. In addition, we find in some authorities that they have helped to bring about innovation in the main-stream services and organisational shape of their agencies (patch teams in social services, for example) and contributed to the development of professional and political policies within the authority. There are, too, examples where community workers have been a source of support and inspiration to colleagues trying to develop the more innovative aspects of their own jobs.

It may not feel at all like this to a neighbourhood worker, struggling alone on a cold, damp housing estate on the outskirts of one of our cities. She may feel frustrated and sceptical about the wider significance of her work in organising tenants around housing, play, traffic, employment, or community care issues, and might agree with one contributor to the study who wrote:

It is true that there have been some important examples of progress towards more community involvement in the 1970's. However, I don't know if this is the greatest truth or if these have been small successes within a decade which has been a disaster for community involvement. Let me give two examples: in Waterloo in 1971 the only locally organised activity were two fathers running football teams for boys, and a church which included a local married couple in important roles in its management. Local people did not protest when bad things happened to their area because they did not believe they could. As a result of community work, there are now numerous local action groups and these are all linked together in a neighbourhood council. There is quite a different attitude and many people feel they have a right to influence public discussions and know how to go about it . . .

But a mile away in Southwark Docklands in 1970 much still remained of one of the strongest working class communities in Britain − based on and united by the work in the docks. The power of the dock workers has now been broken. A very high percentage of people have moved away from Southwark. The area is derelict. Democratic rights have been eroded − the planning authority is the London Docklands Development Corporation (LDDC) whose members are not elected but are appointed by the Minister. LDDC meetings are held in secret. The only way to get to LDDC offices is by car or taxi − they are a mile inside the West India docks.

Which is really the way the country as a whole is going?

Is community work mainly an exercise based on running faster to stay on the same spot?

Do large local authorities, and the erosion of their discretion, and more power to national quangos, and more government power going outside the country to Europe and greater units of commercial power, mean that in everyone's day-to-day experience they have *less* power in 1982 than we had in 1970, and we need more community work as a remedial exercise?

These comments about community work as an *intervention* may be complemented by others that emphasise its development as an *occupation,* and there are a number of factors here that give rise to concern. One of the profound problems of community work in the 1970s was that its practitioners usually worked on their own, pursuing piecemeal interventions without a sense of a wider strategy, without being or *feeling* part of an occupational network, and usually without any team or supervisory/consultancy support within their agency. The members of this occupation have also found it difficult (because of isolation, workload and organisational limits to co-operation, for example) to be caring and supportive of each other and to build up a 'community of community workers'. We have often been competitive and scornful of other workers' goals, values and methods. Even at city and regional levels, networks between workers tend to be tenuous and unstable, though these links in Ulster and Scotland seem to be more firm and valued than in England and Wales. There still seems at the start of the 1980s little feeling of belonging to an occupation which has a national dimension, or which can be said to have some basic purposes, values and methods which are held broadly in common. The lack of occupational identity is reflected in the fact that the majority of community workers do not belong to the Association of Community Workers (ACW), or show much interest in the regional groups of the Federation of Community Work Training Groups (FCWTG). ACW has a membership of less than 400, some of whom are administrators and academics. Community workers already placed on the boundaries of groups and agencies are further marginalised by the difficulties of expressing their belonging to each other. Some of these difficulties include the fact that they are usually employed singly to work on the particular problems of a neighbourhood. There is often an expectation in the agency that they will work with other kinds of staff, rather than other community workers. Many workers are on short-term contracts or funding and this constrains both the awareness of the need to link with other community workers, and the time and energy to do so. Community workers have also been, as a group, critical and suspicious of the conventional nature of occupational affiliation and status, and have thus been unable to decide on how, if at all, to relate to each other, and what kind of a corporate image to present to the rest of the world.

Community workers often feel that their posts are particularly at risk when authorities start cutting their expenditure, and there is growing dissatisfaction with short-term funding of demonstration projects. The insecurity is also explained by the fact that community work has failed to become a main-stream programme in the majority of those departments that took it on board in the early 1970s. There are exceptions in areas such as Sheffield and Strathclyde, but after ten and more years of development it has, on the whole, failed to secure more than a marginal status in the political, professional and financial policies of its sponsors in local authorities.

The reasons for this marginalisation are complex. Established occupations such as social work have largely remained indifferent, and even hostile, to community work, and this had not been helped, first, by community work's own ambivalence to these occupations and, secondly, its failure to explain how, as an intervention, it can help agencies such as social services meet the needs of their users. As an *occupation* community work has tried, and probably successfully, to resist incorporation into established professions and services, and we are still trying at the beginning of the 1980s to establish ourselves in our own right, offering an *intervention* that is relevant within a range of services and settings.

Community work is dependent as much at the end of the decade as at the beginning on having other occupations, particularly social work and youth work, supply much of its training. The difficulties community work has faced in putting forward proposals that would ensure more autonomy in its own training are a consequence partly of low occupational identity and consciousness, and partly of the efforts made to diversify training opportunities through, for example, apprenticeship and accreditation schemes, and the work of regional training groups.

One of the difficulties we face in becoming more identifiable as an occupation, and more credible as an intervention, is that the principal ideas of community work practice are still largely unoperationalised. Little has been done either to clarify, build upon, or replace, principles for practice that were laid down in the 1950s and 1960s. For example, the behaviours associated with non-directiveness or with enabling have not been reviewed in light of our considerable experience in the 1970s. Or again, the importance we give to educational goals is belied by the paucity of any practice theory about the worker's methods in achieving these goals. If the occupation's practice theory is still rudimentary, then its thinking on larger issues shows little development on the various orthodoxies of the late 1960s and early 1970s. We have not greatly extended our understanding of concepts such as community, class, power and deprivation; apart from some CDP publications, the occupation has not offered much to social policy and sociology. One particular example of this is that we have produced very little — in both quantity and quality — on the sociology of community groups, though the books by Hugh Butcher and his colleagues (1980) and that by Alan Twelvetrees (1976) are obvious exceptions.

Much the same can be said of the varied values and ideologies of community workers. It is a pluralistic occupation but one which has generated few substantial accounts of the different value positions and, more importantly, their implications for practice. The very broad grouping of the left in community work has not been able, with the exception of some feminist socialists and the William Temple Foundation Group, to articulate its different ideas about community work; indeed, the debate about value and ideology has been dominated by the former CDP Political Economy Collective, who have been twisting and untwisting their strand of the materialist rope since the mid-1970s. The importance of what became known as the 'CDP analysis' dominated the debate in community work about values and practice, and this did little to encourage community workers to articulate the plurality of values within the occupation. The CDP structuralist analysis had such an impact on community work that it had the effect of creating, for CDP workers, a monopoly of radical views; the effect of this was to inhibit the emergence of alternative socialist and other perspectives within and about community work.

These critical observations, which will be developed later, must be balanced by what practitioners have achieved individually and cumulatively and by the fact that community work is a relatively young occupation; its youthfulness has persisted and at the beginning of the 1980s its identity is still indeterminate and its main ideas and values still in the process of forming. Community work is an incoherent occupation in both senses of the word: there is little organisational or collegiate coherence between its practitioners and there are no central agencies around which they can cohere. The lack of specificity and articulation of values and ideas provides the other meaning of incoherence. The turnover during most of the 1970s of community work staff, the lack of an association or union that embraces most workers and the absence of a common setting and employer confirm the picture of incoherence and diffusion. These characteristics are accentuated by the political differences between various sections in the occupation, and by the emergence in the last few years of caucuses (based on sex and race, for example) which, however necessary for the consciousness and support of their members, serve to point up the incoherence of the occupation. I am not suggesting that the occupation should lose these differences, if that were even possible. On the contrary, its pluralist nature is a strength but we need to create the organisational and conceptual basis around which differences might cohere within a reasonably evident occupational identity.

One of the issues raised by these considerations is the nature of job satisfaction in community work. Financial insecurity, isolation, inadequate support and training, for example, together with the tenuous nature of the links between practitioners (and between them and others such as trainers), will do little to promote job satisfaction. Research by John Holmes for the Consultative Group on Youth and Community Work Training showed that for community workers the greatest fall in job satisfaction came when they had been in their jobs for over two years. This dissatisfaction was particularly linked to lack of support and an apathetic or unsympathetic employer, as well as tensions produced by unsocial hours and the stress of divided loyalties. Holmes comments that 'community workers represent slightly more clearly a somewhat depressing pattern in all forms of people work . . . that job satisfaction often falls if job changes do not occur after a period of about two years and that when job changes do occur they are more often than not as a result of the increasing job dissatisfaction than the attraction of new jobs'.

Job satisfaction is affected by the gap that often exists between workers' expectations and their achievements. Community work also asks its practitioners to accept a degree of self-effacement, for which the worker may need to be supported by a firm faith in what she is doing, and/or a sense of belonging to an occupational group. One contributor to the study wrote:

It did occur to me that within the field of community work you also find many people who are essentially Christian and who find that community work is a very positive and practical expression of the values which they hold. This is not the same thing as saying, as it used to be said in social work textbooks, that social work is based upon a Judeo-Christian set of values. Nor is it the same as saying, as Paulo Friere says, that in the transaction between the development agent or teacher and the local person or learner the former dies in order that the latter may live. And yet there is a kind of self abnegation in the whole idea of community work (when it is not practised by political activists who are treating it as a substitute for political action) which seems to me to require in the community worker either some positive faith which makes that achievement a reward in itself or else a parallel system to which he can belong and from which he can obtain other kinds of reward. Because, you see, only a fool would continue to help other people to do things for themselves which he can do much better without their involvement unless he has a positive reason for doing it. The only other explanation for his behaviour could be that either he has a hidden intention to manipulate the situation, or some other purpose, or he is compelled to work in this way because he has no resources of his own and therefore must depend upon the resources which the people involved are prepared to make available in return for his support.

In reviewing the development of community work, I shall not provide the kind of detail provided by historians such as Peter Baldock or Dame Eileen Younghusband. This is less a history than an attempt to select a few themes and issues that seem pertinent in accounting for what community work is today as an occupation. A brief to look forward to the 1980s determines that the 1970s and 1960s are examined in order to illuminate the present, and expected developments from it.

Community work hardly predates 1960. There are, of course, examples of community action that go back way before this date, but an occupation of community workers had not begun to take shape by 1960. The activities between the two wars and after 1945 of workers such as community centre wardens, development officers on overspill housing estates and some secretaries of councils of social service (CSS) are direct ancestors of the present-day community worker, though their interests, theories and methods of working have little in common with the workers of the late 1970s. The fact that a handful of centre wardens and CSS secretaries were prepared to move away from the traditional conceptions of their work does not allow us to suppose that as a group they were beginning to hand down the basic elements of community work practice and theory. On the contrary, it was not until the second half of the 1950s that these basic elements were first systematically articulated, and thus helped to provide the kind of generic concepts and practice theory that could bind together diverse forms of practice and experiment in a common occupation. I refer, of course, to Murray Ross's book *Community Organisation* 'which captured the imagination of staff in councils of social service because it suggested there was a theoretical basis for their work, and it set up a debate about community work as neighbourhood work . . . and . . . as inter-agency work' (M. Smith, 1979).

These early developments occurred largely within the voluntary sector; they were outside the welfare state and particularly the interests of the various departments providing social work services – children, welfare and mental health. Ross's book was to help to change this – he was writing as a social work educator, familiar with the categorisation in North America of social work as case work, group work and community organisation. The conceptualisation of community work as social work and its subsequent acceptance and confirmation in the influential Younghusband report (1959) is quite remarkable given that so much of the interwar and postwar experience had not been at all connected with social work. But by the early 1960s subsequent books from teachers and from the National Council of Social Service contained few doubts that community work was one of the methods of social work. The process that had been set in motion, and which was to bear fruit in the Seebohm report (1968), was not so much the clarification of community work but its use in the task initiated by the Younghusband report to reform and radicalise social work practice in Great Britain.

2178511

Dame Eileen's thinking on the place of community work within social work had been extensively presented in her 1958 report for the United Nations, where one of her conclusions was that a 'closer working partnership might be of mutual benefit, contributing some more effective working methods to community development and enlarging the horizon of social work by forcing it to apply its knowledge and skills on this broader scale'.

Community work arrived at a time (the Seebohm Committee was set up in 1965) when social work theory and the organisation of services was in need of substantial change, and when conceptualisations of its part in social work arrived conveniently from America; its subsequent development owes much more to the conjunction of these two factors than to the realities of existing practice which were on the whole outside social work and the statutory sector. It was a case of definition occurring not from an analysis of practice but as a result of the importation of ready-made conceptualisations and their congruence with the wider agenda of social work reformers. The reforms in social work and education (including the youth service) and in other areas such as health and planning absorbed community work and proceeded at a pace that did not allow community work to determine its own development from the foundations of practice that were being laid in piecemeal fashion in the 1950s and early 1960s; what happened in the 1960s was an attempt to establish proprietorship over community work between social work and education. This tension, involving the respective administrators and reformers of these two aspiring professions, was to be a major influence in shaping community work. (Something similar had occurred earlier in relation to youth work, which eventually found itself tied securely to education. Two entry routes to youth leadership had evolved during the Second World War, one through education and one through social administration and social work, but it was the former that was to prevail.) A related struggle occurred in the mid-1970s between these two professions and those entering community work from social movements and political groups who saw in community work the opportunity not just to achieve their specific political goals but to reform the traditional practices of their groups in achieving them.

SOCIAL WORK

The 1959 Younghusband report identified community work as one of social work's three methods, 'primarily aimed at helping people within a local community to identify social needs, to consider the most effective ways of meeting these and to set about doing so, insofar as their available resources permit', a definition that was to change very little in the next two decades. The report concluded that neither group work nor community work were being systematically taught or practised in the United Kingdom; 'there is almost no provision for professional training . . . in community work', and one of the functions identified for the national staff college that the report recommended (later set up as the National Institute for Social Work Training) was to 'pioneer training in group work and community organisation'. The reference in the report to community work disposes of the myth that the 1968 Gulbenkian report coined the term. It was also used by Batten in his 1957 and 1965 books, and in the 1963 NCSS report. However, there is a sense in which the occupation (as opposed to certain types of activity) could not exist until someone had firmly fixed a name for it and Gulbenkian's use of the existing term 'community work' made it possible for it to become the name of something definite. In this sense it was an invention.

The Younghusband report was one of the first to legitimise community work in Britain. From then on, administrators and academics set the pace with elaborations of community work, and its potential contribution, that were not supported by the realities of its practice in the early 1960s. Peter Kuenstler's book published in 1960 on community organisation in Great Britain explicitly developed the Younghusband conception of community work as a method of social work, deftly expropriating the work of councils of social service and community associations and centres as 'readily recognisable as social work and have long been accepted as such'. (Peter Kuenstler was also responsible for one of the first training courses in community development at university level begun at Oxford at the end of the 1950s, and until 1963 at the London School of Economics. It is of interest that one of his colleagues at Oxford, teaching public administration, was Peter Brinson, who later was the director of the Calouste Gulbenkian Foundation during much of the period that the Foundation gave considerable support for community work, community relations and community arts.)

There was no discernible resistance to this expropriation from the councils of social service, who, on the contrary, went on further to define community work as part of social work in a series of influential seminars and publications that took place between 1961 and 1965. The books were published by the National Council of Social Service, including one on behalf of the Society of Neighbourhood Workers. The emphasis was on social and recreational issues, and the interaction between groups, agencies and organisations within a planned and co-operative endeavour to meet needs; conflicts of interest were not on the agenda, and the seminars and reports stressed community work as a means to developing community integration and the capacities to use a community's own resources to meet identified needs.

The Ingleby Committee on Children and Young Persons reported in 1960; its recognition of the role of family advice centres, together with the provisions of the 1963 Children and Young Persons Act that made it possible for children's departments to initiate 'preventive work', led to the increase of such centres in local neighbourhoods. They were studied in the mid-1960s by the National Children's Bureau, and a report was published by Aryeh Leissner in 1967. Of the four types found, the detached family advice centres had workers initiating community action on such issues as housing, rents and repairs and play provisions; this type of outposted service, based in a flat or shop front premise, provided the first organisational model from British experience of how community work could be developed within a social work setting. The usefulness of the detached community service was further demonstrated by neighbourhood advice centres set up within the early American poverty programmes; these centres influenced David Jones of the National Institute for Social Work when he worked in America in 1965-6, and were part of the background to the setting up of the Southwark Community Project. The value of a detached project was also being tested out in the North Kensington Family Study Project, started in 1964.

The fact that the detached centre was the first organisational model applied within social work (and one that is being rediscovered today in patch systems) is important. Its emergence in the second half of the 1960s helps us to see better how administrators and trainers concerned to reshape social work had created in the first part of the decade a superstructure of ideas about community work as part of social work that was not supported by what was happening on the ground. Here, community work was being developed more within the education service, through community centres and in experiments with detached youth workers and facilities; and, secondly, in the work of an organisation called the Standing Conference of Housing Estate Community Groups (later the Association of London Housing Estates and now the London Tenants' Organisation). In the statutory sector, community work was slowly developing within the education service, not within the social work departments. Yet it was social work that, at the level of seminars, books and government committees, dominated the world of ideas and discussion; the fact that those working within education failed to achieve a comparable output of ideas and proposals, based on their own experience in this country, was to influence community work adversely.

By the middle of the 1960s community work was tied intellectually to social work, even though the latter's experience of it (particularly within the statutory sector) was extremely limited. It was confined to two special projects (Notting Dale and Bristol), to the development of family advice centres and to work going on in community centres, overspill estates and redevelopment areas. These latter areas can be included if we accept the wider meaning of social work that was developing in the decade as its institutional as opposed to residual function was established. But social work was no homogeneous being: social work in the health and welfare services was separate from that in the child care service, the latter being the responsibility of the Children's Department within the Home Office. The interest of the former services in community work was expressed in the Younghusband report but they had little to show by way of experience in the field; the child care service had pioneered with family advice centres and by 1966 staff in the Children's Department (notably Derek Morrell and Joan Cooper) were preparing proposals that were eventually to lead to the Community Development Projects. The CDP experiment, together with the major stimulus to community work given by the Seebohm Committee, were the two important initiatives of the late 1960s that clinched social work's proprietorship of community work.

The proposals from the Children's Department that were begun in 1966 were first set out for the draft white paper *Children in Trouble* which preceded the Children and Young Persons Act of 1969. Part 3 of this draft was a section on *Prevention*. One of its major proposals was for the designation of Community Development Areas 'coupled with an invitation to local authorities, universities and voluntary bodies to cooperate with Government Departments concerned in organising a joint attack on the social problems arising in the designated areas'. The ideas about Community Development Areas, or CDPs as they were later known, were not published in the final white paper *Children in Trouble.* In April 1967 the Seebohm Committee obtained an undertaking from the Home Office that the proposals on Community Development would be dropped. Furthermore, the Committee obtained a promise from the Home Office in October 1967 that no public announcement on the twelve CDPs would be made until after the Seebohm report was published. (It was presented to Parliament in July 1968.) It must be emphasised that the proposals for CDPs were prepared in 1966, they were designed to aid with the problems of family breakdown and juvenile delinquency (no mention of race or inner-city crises) and their announcement was delayed until late 1968, as a result of the undertaking not to publish the proposals until the Seebohm Committee had reported. These facts, evident from the minutes of the Seebohm Committee, are not without significance for popular conceptions that ascribe the origins of the CDPs wholly to the political controversies surrounding race and inner-city issues sparked off by Enoch Powell's speech in 1968. The development of the CDP in the Home Office after 1968 was affected not only by the death of Derek Morrell but as much by the transfer of the Children's Department to the new Local Authority Social Services Department (LASS) in the Department of Health and Social Security. The CDP was left in the

Home Office without a sound administrative and professional base: what one administrator can set up, others can undo, and this was to be a continuing feature of community work in the 1970s.

Less than six years had elapsed between the conclusion of the Younghusband report that community work was not being systematically taught or practised in the United Kingdom and the emergence of community work (though this term was not used) in a government draft white paper as a major strategy in the prevention of family breakdown and juvenile delinquency. There had been in this period no significant increase either in the numbers or responsibilities of those doing community work, and no evaluative studies that demonstrated its effectiveness; nor had there been since Ross's book any publication widely known in Britain which enhanced understanding of the occupation's principles and methods. Indeed, in 1966 Peter du Sautoy commented:

> Last year I met an Australian university lecturer . . . who said that after four months in Britain he had not yet come across any real examples of 'community development' as internationally understood. He had, however, met excellent examples of community social work, which tended to be erroneously described as community development. Perhaps, however, there are some small schemes of genuine community development of the 'project' type – unheralded and unsung.

How was it possible that such an undeveloped and untested method of intervention could assume such prominence, a prominence that was soon to be confirmed by the Seebohm report? There was, of course, the influence (made possible by Fulbright fellowships and the United Nations European Social Welfare Programme) of the early American experiments with community development, as well as the mounting advocacy for community work that emanated from social work academics and others such as councils of social service. Community development, too, was congruent with the plan and mood of the Wilson government to carry out a transformation of British society. Such factors are not unimportant, but we must add to them one called 'administrative self-expression' – community work offered to administrators in the late 1960s and 1970s the opportunity to experiment. It was ideal as a low-cost and low-risk innovation.

The view taken by Bolger and his colleagues (1981) is that community work was also part of the state's 'community strategy'. This aimed to re-establish a 'credible relationship' between the social democratic state and the working class – 'without it the working class could not be accommodated to the consequences of industrial change *within* the boundaries of capitalist social relationships'. The authors argue that the relationship had become distant and fractured, and that orthodox methods of sustaining the relationship (for example, through the process of representative democracy) had become ineffective. What is missing from this helpful account by Bolger *et al.* is an explanation of the process by which the community strategy was unfolded. I doubt that the community approach and community work were perceived as a 'strategy'; rather, community work developed in a very piecemeal fashion within some sectors of administration and academia, and was as much influenced by aggrandisement and reform in professions like social work as by an overt consciousness about the fragile nature of state–class relationships. There was also a good deal of humanitarianism and social concern, some of which focused on improving relationships within the working class (and other groups for that matter) which, as Prior and Purdy indicate (1980) had themselves become fractured during the material enhancement of lives in the long postwar boom. It was, too, less of a strategy than an incremental development because community work was not a well-formed intervention with articulated values, goals and methods of operation; on the contrary, it was in those days essentially an 'approach' or 'vision' whose theoretical and operational aspects are still being gradually unfolded, segment by segment, through practice, training and theoretical exposition.

The adoption of community work by social work was confirmed by the report of the Seebohm Committee in 1968. The report pressed for a community-orientated family service; it discussed the creation of social development areas, citizen participation, voluntarism, social planning and the community development role of the area social services team. It was an impressive display of support for an intervention whose principles and methods were still relatively unknown, and whose elaboration waited upon the publication later in 1968 of the first Gulbenkian report on community work. Together with the urban aid programme announced in late 1968, the Seebohm report was the most important single event that helped to create the *occupation* of community work. Not only did it give widespread publicity and legitimation for community work within social work, but in recommending the creation of a unified social services department it provided, in the last years of relative prosperity of the long boom, the opportunity for an unprecedented expansion in the numbers of community workers. It signified the place of community work as a public service function within the welfare state; along with the urban aid programme, the CDPs and later the Manpower Services Commission, the Seebohm report was to help to transform community work into an instrument of policy within the statutory sector, with, as Richard Crossman said to the House of Commons in February 1970, the personal social services having 'an important role to play in community development'.

The most remarkable feature of this transformation was that it was achieved with virtually no reference to the specialist post of community worker. The Seebohm report refers only to the *possibility* of such specialists emerging from social work staff, supported by senior consultants at headquarters. The appointment of community workers was not recommended, and such specialists were clearly only one element of that committee's much wider understanding of the process of developing communities. What happened in the 1970s was that specialist community workers became seen as the major, and often only, instrument of development. Both politicians and the officers of the new social services departments found appointing community workers a relatively convenient way of expressing their agency's understanding of what Seebohm meant by a community-oriented service.

By the end of the 1960s community work had been firmly added to existing conceptions of social work; it had not replaced them but had been adopted to fashion a new social work within the United Kingdom. Its connection to social work was also manifest in a number of small events, such as the start of community work training at the National Institute, and the beginning of the Institute's project in Southwark in 1968. The Department of Health and Social Security began funding student units in community work in 1971, and in 1972 the Central Council for Education and Training in Social Work first formed its ideas for a study into the teaching of community work (published in 1974).

EDUCATION

Of the two services, education and social work, the former seems in retrospect to have been the front-runner in the early 1960s to take community work on board. That it failed to do so was to have profound effects on the theory and practice of community work in the 1970s.

There were a number of factors that made education the most likely 'host' for community work. First, community work had as one of its two principal objectives the achievement of educational or process goals. It was seen, both in the colonies and in this country in early books such as Kuenstler's, as an intervention whose ultimate justification lay not in the tangible outcomes that were achieved but in the learning opportunities provided to participants as they strove for their specific objectives. This emphasis on informal or community education made community work a type of intervention that might be appropriate within the education service.

Secondly, departments and institutes concerned with education attracted people skilled in community development who were returning from the former colonies — people such as Reg Batten, Hywel Griffiths and Peter du Sautoy, each of whom were key figures in the *Community Development Journal,* established in 1966 as 'a private venture, sponsored by a group of persons in Britain who have been both active and interested in community development and connected subjects', and provided with an interest-free loan by the Ministry of Overseas Development. They were able to demonstrate the relevance to the United Kingdom of the model of community development spelt out by Batten himself in his book in 1957 and by the Colonial Office's own handbook on community development that appeared a year later. Both UNESCO and the United Nations were trying to spread ideas and practices about group work and community development in Europe, and were seeking to weld social work techniques in America with the much broader developmental work from Asia and Africa. There were three major European seminars – Palermo (1958), Bristol (1959) and Athens (1961). Three of the key British participants were Richard Titmuss, John Spencer and Peter Kuenstler. About the same time Reg Poole returned from a visit to Africa and began to relate ideas from community development programmes there to the work of the Liverpool Council of Social Service.

Thirdly, there was a number of staff who were funded or employed by education departments working in community centres who were well placed to become, with suitable training, the nucleus of the community work occupation. This group comprised 231 full-time and 63 part-time wardens of community centres, though Milligan warns that they had 'no recognised training scheme, no nationally recognised status, and no nationally agreed scale of salaries and conditions of service' (1961). Social work did not have this ready-made group of people to form the basis of its experiments with community work, and was not to have them until the early 1970s.

In addition to this core of staff based in the community, there was an infrastructure which might have supported them, seen to their training needs and pushed on the employment of community workers within the community centre and community association movement. Frank Milligan was himself president of the Society of Neighbourhood Workers; there was the National Federation of Community Associations as well as the long-established National Institute of Adult Education which might have equally well taken on the pioneering work done by the National Institute for Social Work in respect of community work courses and publications. The educational facilities and experience of the Workers' Educational Association and the co-operative movement might also have been harnessed had the education service taken the community work bit. There was, too, some existing government support and understanding of the role of the education service in a community setting. The Ministry of Education and the Scottish Education Department had produced classic texts on community centres as early as 1945 and 1947; at the local level, education authorities were able to build community centres and to grant salaries to their staff. In addition, the Ministry of Education saw the National Federation of Community Associations as a way of developing the non-formal educational aspects of the Education Acts and seconded an officer, Harold Marks, to the Federation. Richard Mills, later of the Calouste Gulbenkian Foundation, was also at the National Federation, and he was committed to the development of community work within the educational camp.

The reasons why the education service failed to build on these foundations are unclear. It was certainly a more established service than social work, and more hierarchical in structure and thinking. It may have been less able to tolerate the open and participative values of community work. For most of the 1960s it was concerned with the dominant educational issues of comprehensive schooling and pre-school provision. Adult education and non-formal education remained the 'poor cousin', with low priority in the allocation of resources. There is, too, the consideration that adult education did not get the stimulus to change that comes from a major review of its work – before the Russell report in 1973, the last major review occurred in 1919.

Whatever the reasons, the education service has failed, despite its early position of strength,[1] to contribute much to the development of community work, apart from a few isolated experiments with community schools and adult education, as in the work associated with Keith Jackson, Tom Lovett and Eric Midwinter in the Educational Priority Areas project. There are two qualifications to this conclusion. The first is to note the development of community work within the Scottish community education departments in the 1970s; the second is the interest in community work shown by the youth service consistently through the last two decades. Here, community work gradually emerged over a long period of time from the concern with the 'unclubbables' in the Albermarle report in 1960, and the setting up of the Youth Service Development Council with its grants for experimental work and special projects. The coffee bar period of the early 1960s led to the period of concern with the 'unattached' and to experiments in the late 1960s with different kinds of outposted and community-based youth workers. By the early 1970s youth work had become youth and community work, inspired largely by the Milson-Fairbairn report of 1969 which set youth work within the context of community development and its contribution towards a more participative democracy. The interests of the National Youth Bureau and the Youth and Community Work courses at Westhill and Goldsmiths confirmed the youth service's interest in community work, and the two colleges played an important part in the 1970s, in training workers for the whole field of community work.

The setting up of the first Gulbenkian study group in 1966 provided the opportunity for the meeting of minds between the educational and social work interests in community work. The Foundation had been approached by Muriel Smith to inquire into 'facilities for training in community development of the non-directive kind'. The Foundation first responded by convening in 1965 a small group to arrange a *conference* on training for community work. The group recommended, however, that it should expand into a working party to study the nature of community work, and to prepare a report. This was not without difficulties, but was accepted by the Foundation in 1966.

The remit of the group was broadened to include a look at 'all of community work's manifestations, including social work which had not yet appeared on the scene in relation to community work' (study group informant). The education interests were strongly represented by members such as Reg Batten, Hywel Griffiths, D. F. Swift, George Wedell and Roger Wilson, as well as Richard Mills whose experience and interests at that time had been influenced by community work within an educational dimension. For social work, there was the chairperson, Eileen Younghusband, together with Peter Hodge, David Jones, Bob Leaper, Reg Wright and Andrew Lochhead. The other two members, Elizabeth Littlejohn and Muriel Smith, had links with both interests, but the latter was considerably influenced by Reg Batten. There was a third grouping that overlapped with the other two: there were the community developers with experience overseas (Batten, Griffiths, Hodge, Leaper and Lochhead), and the influence of this group tended to reinforce the position in discussion of the education interest. It is interesting to speculate how the report might have been different if a suggestion from one of its proposed members had been accepted. He argued for many more people to be on the group from settlements, councils of social services and community councils, and thought that people 'whose experience as teachers of community development in relation to developing countries overseas would not have anything of particular value to contribute to the community needs of urban areas in this country'.

Interestingly enough, Peter du Sautoy was not a member of the study group. He had made his views known much earlier:

> I am greatly concerned . . . that any attempts to introduce 'community development' into this country should not either (*a*) be too attached to existing vested interests in allied fields, such as adult education or social work or (*b*) range so widely into every field dealing with community affairs that we shall (i) distort a term which is beginning to have a more precise significance internationally . . . and (ii) become out of step with international thinking and consensus of view on this subject. (1966)

He argued that community development was both a philosophy of approach and a programme of action and saw considerable problems if there was an 'undue identification with social work, adult education or town planning', or an attempt to introduce community development as a multi-purpose approach into a system of specialised and compartmentalised training and administration. He went on to forecast that 'I do not think that community development will progress very far in Britain until people are prepared to regard it as something in its own right – and not as a useful appendage or tool for other subjects – for which special training and study of an "open-ended" kind is needed'.

The two major issues within the study group were territorial and conceptual. The educationalists tended to argue that education, particularly adult education, should 'own' community work, and that as an intervention it was fundamentally an educational or learning process, in fulfilment of which the use of specialist community workers was only one strategy. The educationalists in the group could point to the growing involvement of the service in community work, as well as to the relative absence of such involvement in professional social work. In addition, the important values of community work seemed to be in conflict with the statutory functions of social work, which Batten in particular criticised as controlling and manipulative.

The report itself, published in 1968, went generic about the role and siting of community workers, and recommended the employment of specialist community workers. It did not come down on the side of the education interests, and to that extent they had lost the day, and indeed, the lead that education had built up over social work in relation to community work practice. The social work interest had succeeded in keeping all the employment and training options open for community work, and these options were to be taken up by social services departments and social work courses as a consequence of the Seebohm report. In short, whilst the Gulbenkian report put forward the strongest case for community work, it was other events such as the Seebohm report which were able to ensure its development within social work as a consequence of the failure of the educationalists to turn the study group their way. It is not quite accurate to suggest, as Peter Baldock has done, that the mood in the Gulbenkian group and in the wider field 'saw the future of community work within a social work context' (1977). There was certainly a mood within the reforming elements of social work to establish community work as its third method, but there was much less certainty amongst those concerned with community work that the future lay with social work, and there was considerable disagreement about this within the Gulbenkian group. It may be that its chairperson, Dame Eileen Younghusband, saw the group as yet a further opportunity as much to reform social work practice and theory as to shape the future direction of community work training. She was, after all, not a member of the Seebohm Committee which was meeting at the same time, and the influence of her thinking can be discerned in a Gulbenkian Foundation minute in September 1966 which said: 'The result of this special training [in community work] will be to widen the range of social work, which has been hitherto concerned solely with casework, i.e. with individuals and families . . . the Working Party represents the first organised attempt to consider the sort of training which would be needed for this new kind of social work . . .'

There was a number of reasons why the educationalists did not succeed. They were unable to develop the idea of community work within education as anything more than a philosophy or an approach, and failed to persuade the group of its status in education as a method. The social work interest, on the other hand, could point, with the background of American experience and literature, to community work as one of three social work methods for which training had already been developed. This was powerfully reinforced by the personal assistance given to the group by Robert Perlman and Arnold Gurin; an early draft of their 1972 book was made available to the study group and Gurin's experience as director of the Curriculum Development Project in the USA helped to indicate the viability of community work within social work training. If the educationalists could not provide the rationale for community work as a method, they were as unconvincing that the education service would provide the employment opportunities for community work; it was not difficult, on the other hand, for the social work interest to guess at the general direction that the Seebohm Committee's proposals would take, and to point with some justification to the proposed social services departments as an obvious place in which community workers could be employed. Finally, the purist views of Batten about the non-directive approach tended to isolate him within the study group, offending both educationalists and social workers, and weakening the case of the former; in addition, the group felt the urgency for community work to respond quickly to the mounting crises of the inner cities, and this worked against seeing community work as a long-term process.

The involvement of formal and adult education services declined thereafter and they contributed little in the 1970s to the practice or theory of community work. The academics who formed the education interest on the Gulbenkian group played little, if any, part in the development of British community work in the last decade. The only exception was Hywel Griffiths who went to the New University of Ulster at Coleraine and made a significant impact on the growth of community work in Northern Ireland. Batten did not develop his ideas on non-directive community work as published in his 1967 book; community work turned against the concept of the non-directive approach, partly because it was misunderstood and misrepresented, but largely because *as a method* it remained unexplained. The social work interest, on the other hand, flourished and continued to influence community work in the 1970s, particularly David Jones, Bob Leaper and Reg Wright, who helped to create CCETSW's positive support for community work training in the first half of the decade. From the first years of the 1970s community work was to expand within social services departments and to find a place, with varying degrees of political and intellectual security, on social work courses; its place as a social work method seemed to be confirmed, much to the consternation of many community workers, by the introduction in mid-decade of unitary conceptions of practice and training.

The most profound effect of the demise of the educational influence was that the process goals of community work were not developed beyond the rudimentary expression they were given in the texts of the 1950s and 1960s. No one took up the task of reaffirming the process of education that was part of community work, or of providing a middle-range account of these educational goals, and one which linked them in theory and practice to product or outcome goals. The consequence was not simply that the educational aspects of the intervention have been neglected but that they have remained rooted in two narrow orthodoxies. The first came from the books of people like Batten and the Biddles whose writings on process goals became associated in the minds of the new practitioners of the 1970s only with changes in individual or personal development. The second orthodoxy was to identify process goals within the rhetoric of 'raising political consciousness'; this narrow expression was limited even further by the understanding that consciousness was being raised in a leftward direction. The educational goals of community work embrace both these orthodoxies (it is about personal development and political understanding) but they are also much wider, and may be put quite generally, as Baldock has:

> He [the community worker] is interested in helping them to critically re-examine the society in which they find themselves, to understand the ways in which various political and administrative systems work, to acquire skills in self-organisation, and also more specific skills that may be very relevant to their self-chosen projects . . . (1974)

Linked to the failure to explain educational goals was the inability to be specific about the *methods* by which workers were to help those participating in community activities to learn and change. The philosophies, tasks and skills of informal educational practice within community work that specified what the worker does and how he does it — the practice theory of informal education — are as undefined today as at the start of the 1970s. (This may be less true of those in community arts and theatre, and those influenced by the French concept and practice of *animation*.)

The lacunae about informal educational goals and methods in community work were the most important consequences of the withdrawal of educationalists from community work in the 1970s. There were also some others:

● the opportunity was lost of developing community work within community centres – an opportunity that could have provided locally managed neighbourhood bases for community workers outside the day-to-day operation of a service-giving, local authority department;

● the definition of community work continued to be tied to the particular issues of the day, or, even worse, to the agendas of the workers involved in the occupation at any given moment. Put another way, we allowed the agenda of community groups to stand for, and be identical with, the goals of the occupation which intervened to organise and help them. Thus in the 1960s community work was defined in terms of the social and recreational needs of residents in housing development areas; in the 1970s it had become identified as protest, conflict and campaigns around a number of inner-city issues. The characteristics of the intervention that remain relatively constant through the changing priorities of groups and workers are still obscure, partly because one of these constants – informal education – was not adequately defined in purpose and method.

A broader way of making this point is to say that from the end of the 1960s community work became more and more focused on the achievement of specific tasks identified by different groups of workers, politicians and administrators. Within planning, housing, social services, community relations, the CDPs and numerous voluntary initiatives such as the YVFF, community work was taken up as a method of achieving certain specified tasks of the agency or an experimental programme. There was generally little awareness that community work was only one method of achieving much more fundamental development goals. Nowhere was this to be more clear than in many social services departments where, Griffiths suggests, community workers 'either had to narrowly limit their objectives to correspond with those of the agency (and these tend still to focus on the pathological) or suffer a degree of isolation and alienation from other professional colleagues' (1979). The isolation of community workers (which was often self-imposed), the confinement of community work to particular tasks within an agency's remit and the imposition of bureaucratic forms of administration are the very opposite of what is needed to pursue an effective strategy for community development or agency change.

The consequences of these specific attempts at reform were, first, that they were carried out without reference to wider social and economic issues (a theoretical omission rectified by some of the CDP analysis of the mid-1970s); and, secondly, that they were implemented without reference to each other and without reference to the longer-term educational/developmental goals of community work. Thus at the regional, city and community level, community work developed without a strategy that linked the various initiatives, without theories that linked these initiatives to more structural factors, and without much sense that the particular objectives (better housing, play facilities, and so on) were not just important goals in themselves but the means of a longer-term attempt at enhancing the interest, competence and participation of marginalised groups in the process of government. It is this more fundamental dimension of community work, one that transcends the particular use of it to achieve specific administrative, political, or welfare goals, that has been inadequately expressed in the last decade. The practice of community work is about specific interventions to help people with particular issues; but both the administrative organisation of these interventions and theories about their purpose need to be related to a wider concept of welfare and political development.

There were few voices to temper the enthusiasm with which community work was taken up to cure all kinds of social and economic ills, and understood as a specific intervention within the remits of particular agencies and departments. Peter du Sautoy had died in late 1967 and few people would have seen, let alone been influenced by, an article in October 1968 written by William Biddle, called 'Deflating the Community Developer', published in the *Community Development Journal*. The paper foreshadows the advent of the radical pessimism that afflicted British community work in the mid-1970s as practitioners became aware of the gap between their ambitions and the small realities of practice. Biddle talks of disillusionment and disappointment among 'knowledgeable community developers' that they had not been as successful as they had hoped; he writes of their exaggerated hopes and unrealistic expectations that community development might be 'a panacea for many of the major ills of mankind'. He offers realistic expectations, drawing attention to the educational function in a way that might have moderated and enhanced the more instrumental atmosphere of the late 1960s and 1970s. He writes:

Community developers should come to look upon themselves not as nation-builders or as economic problem-solvers, but as educators. They are educators who contribute to fundamental learning; they are not instructors. They help people become involved in experiences that will encourage these local citizens to evolve new habits of thought and ways of working — by their own choice. The community developer does not tell the people what their new attitudes and behaviours shall be. These are matters for citizens of a community to work out, with the interested help and advice of the developer. If he is wise, he will admit that often he does not know what the more adequate new ways of living should be. That is, the outcome of the educational experience is not some specific learning from the developer, but a new social creation made by citizen-learners, with help from a developer.

The education then is not a traditional teacher to pupil relationship, but a sharing of backgrounds and experiences in answer to problems. Though there are no curricular items of information to be learned, there are hoped-for educational outcomes — in the acquiring of habits of self-help and co-operation — in achievement of new collective self-confidence. If the process is working properly, citizens become more competent to work together in making a better community. No criticism then is pertinent because people failed to adopt some recommended practice, since no specific practice is recommended. Instead, they are encouraged to adopt some way of behaving from several drawn to their attention, or better still, to create some new practice by combining their traditions with ideas brought by the developer and other outsiders.

The role of the good community developer, however, involves an educational paradox, and one that was neglected in the enthusiasm of the young practitioners to do something about the problems of the inner cities and other urban areas. The paradox is that

He devotes himself to people's learning, but he does not instruct them. He relies upon them to learn from their experiences from which they will mature into habits and attitudes of self-direction. He does not choose or set up these experiences for people. These grow out of community living. He can interpret the experiences so people may learn lessons from them that they would not have learned without his words. He tries to induce them to set up maturing experiences for themselves that they might not have thought of without his influence. He avoids dominating people's learning, but he starts processes of development that would not have occurred except for his self-effacing initiative.

His non-domineering, non-instructional role calls upon him to impose a self-discipline upon himself. He must accept a humble role as a participant in a development process that he may have started and certainly helps to keep going, but deliberately avoids controlling.

For his objective is that people shall mature to be able to choose their own better courses of action.

He should not expect to build nations or economic systems or new cultures. He should not expect to receive credit for having the answers to problems. But he should expect to do something far more important; he should help people become competent to build their own cultures, communities, and nations. Even more significant, he should hope to help them achieve the kind of flexible intelligence people need for an era of change in the unprecedented and unpredictable future.

Given this agenda and role, community developers who seek some community utopia are doomed to disappointment and cynicism. The end to be sought is not 'the perfect community' but, argues Biddle, a community that can contend with and solve more and more complex problems: 'The ultimate end is something that happens in a community . . . but even more it is some changes in the lives of the people who compose that community, that they become better collective problem solvers.' He warns us to be humble in making a contribution to this end-product because (and here again he presages the structuralist debates of the mid-1970s) many forces beyond the control of local people will also help to influence their community and culture. Two important limitations, therefore, should keep a community developer realistic in his thinking about his usefulness:

First, is that his influence is but one of many in the shaping of a community life and in the contribution that community shall make to the total nation. The other is that his responsibility is not to teach ways of living that he or his cultural background have found useful; his task is rather to join with local people in helping them to work out their own cultural life. He is both expediter of their creative thinking and introducer of ideas that stimulate their creative thinking. He has succeeded when they can go on to the creation of solutions to problems without his presence, with the methods of thoughtful problem solving which he has helped them to learn. That is, he brings, not solutions to problems but cultivates people's ability to solve problems on into the future.

But the mood in and about community work at this period, as well as the turbulent political condition of the country, was not sympathetic to the experience of those in community development who had worked in America or in Africa and Asia in the 1950s and 1960s. These included not only established teachers but others such as Nick Derricourt and Marj Mayo who were to become part of the radical stream in community work.[2] One of the lost opportunities of the 1970s was that the channels of dialogue were not established between the new, young entrants to the job and those who had had considerable experience of community work in other countries. The explicit religious and conservative political values of people such as the Biddles, as well as the sanctimonious tone of their writings, detracted from their exposition of the educational basis of community work. However, this wide and heterogeneous group of educationalists, including many who had worked overseas, had much in common with many of the socialist streams in community work in the 1970s. What they had in common with, for example, some of the CDP and feminist writing was the idea that community work was an educational process whose ultimate justification was its contribution to the evolution of democratic practices. But an equally surprising combination of, on the one hand, reformers in social work and, on the other, young radical practitioners concerned with 'getting things done' about urban issues ensured that for most of the 1970s the dominant but incomplete conception of community work was as a welfare and not as an educational or democratic practice.

INTO THE 1970s

It is much harder to write about the 1970s. We are still too close to that decade, and insufficient time has passed to be sure about the significant influences within and upon community work. There was, too, so much more to think about and to evaluate; at least in the 1960s community work had a manageable number of manifestations: it was largely what people wrote and said about it, and about what it ought to be and how it ought to contribute. In the 1970s the volume of reflective thought was maintained and at the same time community work was also the wide range of different ways in which it was practised, as well as its infrastructure of theories, research, training opportunities and employment conditions. Community work is also the bodies which it has developed or have grown around it – the Association of Community Workers, the Federation of Community Work Training Groups. Community work is the thousands of people doing it, and we can make serious errors of judgement if we assume that the characteristics and views of those who write about the occupation in books and articles are also those of the unknown practitioners beavering away in the cities and the countryside.

There has also been an increase in a number of other phenomena associated with community work, but which are largely outside the scope of the study. For example, the permeation of many other occupations by some of the ideas, vocabulary and work methods associated with community work; the upsurge in the early 1970s of what Phil Bryers has called 'spontaneous development' as all kinds of groups formed and organised against some decision, or lack of one, by government;

the emergence of various kinds of social movements (for example, those associated with women and ethnic groups, or with nuclear disarmament); the extraordinary growth, documented in the National Consumer Council's survey (1977), of specialist and general advice and information centres; and the emergence of fields such as community arts and community media. These and many other phenomena took place in a decade of political turmoil both in this country and in the world at large, and of worsening economic performance and dislocation.

Community work itself developed within a context of experimentation, ranging from national programmes to quite small-scale projects, whose work in many cases would have not been known outside their locality but whose significance for the development of community work may over the years prove to be more profound than the innovations of national programmes and organisations. It is too soon to tell what will be of enduring influence, and the danger for the historian of this period is to be ignorant of, or to underestimate, the cumulative impact of the small and the modest, and to be seduced by those who, because of their wider remit and better resources, have managed to appear on national stages. Likewise, there is a danger in giving too much emphasis to innovative projects rather than to the more routinised operation of community work within agencies such as the social services departments of local authorities.

The 1960s came to an end with the new occupation of community worker having been created by the Gulbenkian report's emphasis on the worker as a specialist post − 'a function exercised in its own right, with a professional training that combines the best available knowledge and practice'. The report argued the case for community work, but it was its insistence that it was a job in its own right that represented the radical shift from previous years when the job was largely seen as something that informed, or was appended to, the responsibilities of other posts. The Seebohm report (through the creation of social services departments) and the urban aid programme created the opportunities for the new occupation to grow and diversify, aided by the opportunities offered by settlements and the more innovative councils of social service and community relations committees. When we say that community work was created as an occupation in the conjunction of these two reports and the urban aid programme we are really saying that it was brought into being by those who held power − academics, administrators and politicians. It was created as part of the apparatus of the welfare state, and it is a fiction to believe simply that community work was born out of the grass-roots 'rebellions' of the late 1960s and subsequently co-opted by the state. In fact, the reverse is nearer the truth: having been created in academia and government it was co-opted in the 1970s by fieldworkers, and the story of its development in that decade can be told in terms of the attempts of fieldworkers to shape its independence of government and public service. The growth and viability of the occupation was determined by the responsiveness of many urban communities to the need to organise. There was growing community activism in many cities in the late 1960s, particularly around rent increases and development issues. Local activism was affected (and often supported by student volunteers in inner-city areas such as Notting Hill) by the student rebellions here and abroad, and by the squatting movement, both of which modelled how change could be achieved through organising and direct action. There was, too, a discontent with the growing size and authority of the state as it re-tooled itself through various reforms, reorganisations and its closer management of the economy. Reactions against its authority and intrusion into private and communal lives were stimulated, too, by local authority use of compulsory purchase orders for clearance, redevelopment and planning purposes. At the same time, the power of government was balanced by demonstrations of its vulnerability, and this was especially clear in Paris in 1968, and in the same year in Saigon during the Tet offensive.

There was, however, little interest at this time in community work amongst ultra-left groups such as the International Socialists and Socialist Labour League. Such groups were only much later to move into community organising and through the 1960s their ability to organise within communities was hindered by their belief in the role of a Leninist vanguard, where the role of student members was conceptualised as 'detonators' (Ernest Mandel) and largely confined to selling the group's newspapers outside factory gates. Community work was, however, influenced by the ideas and literature of the New Left and the various elements of the counter-culture of the late 1960s. These ideas, together with examples of grass-roots actions such as the 1967-8 rent rebellions and the 'new' squatting movement, helped to shape the direction community work was to take in the next ten years.

The year in which community work 'took off' in Britain was 1968. As well as the Seebohm and Gulbenkian reports, that year saw the CDPs announced and the urban aid programme launched. The Young Volunteer Force Foundation was established and the Southwark Community Project was opened. The Race Relations Act prepared the way for local community relations councils and in 1968 the Association of Community Workers was formed. On the continent, the European Regional Clearing House for Community Work began operating and at home people started writing: books by Batten, Marris and Rein, Leaper, Goetschius and Thomason were published in the years 1967-9, as well as such influential reports as *The Voluntary Worker in the Social Services, Youth and the Community in the 1970's* and *People and Planning*. In 1968, too, the Oxford University Press, on the initiative of Reg Batten and with funding from the Gulbenkian Foundation, took over the publishing of the *Community Development Journal,* no doubt anticipating the growth to come.

By the early 1970s more and more community workers were being employed in statutory and voluntary agencies but, unfortunately, there are no data that provide a reliable picture of the growth of the occupation. From that which is available there is little reason to think that the increase was as dramatic as it is often supposed. By 1975 there were in social services departments about 276 full-time community workers in England and Wales, though we would have to add those for the other regions and those who were classified under social work posts. Even so, this is not a remarkable increase across the several hundred area teams in the country, and was probably a gradual one, assuming that the number was built up year by year. Moreover, there was a marked regional imbalance, with almost three-quarters of the workers in England employed in the London and north-west regions. So, too, with the urban aid programme: the analysis by Edwards and Batley (1978) indicates that only forty-eight community workers were employed between 1968 and 1973, from a total of 2,929 projects. This is an underestimate because workers would have been employed in other project types such as neighbourhood advice centres (27), other advice centres (28), community centres (81) and general community projects (95). Taking these together with community workers, we have a total of 279 projects. These were largely within London boroughs and county boroughs; and for advice/information and community projects a balance was maintained between local authority and voluntary sponsorship; the percentage differences between the two are small enough to support the view that the urban programme stimulated community work as much in the statutory sector as in the voluntary.

Community work in the voluntary sector was given considerable support in the 1970s by local and national trusts and foundations. One of the most important trusts in this respect was the Calouste Gulbenkian Foundation; its importance was less to do with the amount of money it gave and more with the consistency of its support for community work, as well as its influence over ideas and directions in the field. The amount and recipients of grants given, as well as the policy of the Foundation, are explicitly described in its annual reports. The emphasis on community work and race relations within its whole social welfare programme was first formulated in 1964, and was fully realised as policy by 1975. By this time the Foundation had withdrawn from other areas of social welfare, and its concern with community work and community relations included an emphasis on community education and community arts – the Foundation helped to support the emergence of community arts as a development of the Arts Laboratory movement through its early funding of organisations such as Interaction, Centreprise and the Albany Settlement. In 1978 it concentrated its resources more fully on inner-city issues, to give support to groups and voluntary agencies in the twenty-two partnership aid programme areas. It appointed an inner-cities co-ordinator, set up the Community Resources Unit in 1979, established its own advisory committee to promote discussion and organised an Inner Cities Exhibition programme.

The Gulbenkian Foundation granted £1,940,046 in the years 1970–9 in its social welfare programme, mostly to community work and community relations. The majority of grants (for example, 50 out of 54 grants in 1979) were small grants of less than £5,000; large grants (£10,000 and over) were more common before 1975 but most of these went to interests and projects outside community work; in the second half of the decade large grants became much less common (two in 1979, for example, in the community work and community support programme) and these were mostly given to finance the Foundation's own initiatives and to develop training, support, or research facilities in the field.

The consistency of the Foundation's commitment to community work, and its support for innovative projects, are some of the factors that have made it an influence in the development of community work. This influence was exerted, too, through the two Gulbenkian study groups and their publications, through the advisory committee to the resource centres and community support programme, and through its own initiatives such as the Community Resources Unit, the working party on the future relations of work and leisure and the Community Communications Project. Yet the Foundation's most important contribution to community work may well prove to be its funding of the infrastructure of community work practice; the Foundation was almost alone amongst sponsors in appreciating the value of an infrastructure to support fieldwork; it contributed substantial sums to research, training and similar activities at a time when other funders, notably those in central and local government, had little awareness, if any, of the dangers of developing a field practice that was not adequately supported by a sound research, theoretical and training base. In the period 1970–6 some £458,388 or 37 per cent of the total social welfare[3] budget went to indirect services – that is, to fund things like training, research, surveys, reports, committees and studies as opposed to direct fieldwork projects. In 1977–9 some £454,851 or half of the community work grants[4] offered went to indirect service.

Government was, and continued to be, the primary funder of community work not only directly but through its grant aid to voluntary agencies and to community groups. In the growth of the social services and the urban programme there was a consolidation of community work within local authority departments. The sponsorship of government became more dominant in the decade through the schemes of the Manpower Services Commission, the development of sizeable community work divisions in several social services departments, and the collaboration of voluntary agencies, such as the Community Projects Foundation, in funding projects jointly with local authorities. The 1970s was a period for local government of public learning about community work: we can discern in some authorities innovation and evolution in the numbers, function and management structure for community work, whilst in others community work has not developed, and has occasionally been summarily dispensed with after a brief period of flirtation and experiment. The pace of development was also uneven, and we can see many local authorities and their community workers experiencing the very same difficulties that other, and often neighbouring, departments went through at the beginning of the decade. In much the same way, community work began to learn about itself, building up experience in the field and in training, evolving various kinds of employment arrangements and ways of operating, and becoming a little more confident about the knowledge and skills involved in the work.

Two cameos of the 1970s serve to give some feel for development in that decade. The first is of the early years up to 1974, as community work posts increased in the statutory and voluntary sectors. The workers were, on the whole, untrained (though often well qualified academically), as training facilities themselves were only beginning to be made available. The workers were to be found largely in inner-city neighbourhoods; not only was their previous experience and training limited but they had little to guide them in the way of research and literature; they usually had insufficient support from each other and from their employing organisations. They learned the job as they did it, guided by their own philosophies about social justice and their visions for a better society; these visions, and the atmosphere they generated in community work, were heady and often messianic, relating more to the euphoria of the 'student revolutions' of the late 1960s and the urban violence of the early 1970s than to the small gains of locality organising. Community work was linked with social movements; it offered an extension of the life-style and the politics of student life, and the opportunity to flee the constraints of more established occupations. It offered the chance to be paid to do full-time what many were doing for nothing in the evenings as part of their commitment to political groups and ideas. Organisations such as Student Community Action, Task Force and the Young Volunteer Force Foundation were initiated in part to harness the student interest in community activities and provided an initiation and training ground for many of the early entrants to community work.

The workers of this period were on the whole successful, and they helped to organise a large number of varied community campaigns and services that gave previously powerless people the opportunity to turn government decisions their way. The mood of many of the communities in which they organised was ready for action; it was not as difficult in those days as it was to be in the early 1980s to mobilise people and only marginally more difficult to win concessions and resources from local authorities.[5] The lack of skills and training, the painful process of learning on the job, were not obvious or harmful to community groups: only the most unlucky or unsuitable workers could fail to organise because organising campaigns where the local authority was the target, and had the resources to distribute, was, whilst difficult enough, amongst the least demanding forms of community work.

The second cameo is of the last few years of the 1970s and the early 1980s; the autonomy and finance of local authorities had been diminished by public expenditure cuts. Local democracy, suggested one correspondent, had also been diminished 'by this conservative government . . . one can't participate in the decision-making of the state if state power is all in the corridors of Whitehall. It is a very impoverished world if people can only participate in private decision-making, not in public decisions.' The honeymoon period for community work was long over; the growth of development and experimentation had slowed down, and community workers themselves were more realistic about what their work could achieve. They were finding it more and more difficult to involve local people in community activities even though, paradoxically, all sorts of people were more ready than was apparent at the beginning of the 1970s to see community action as a normal way of dealing with things. Strategies had shifted from public demonstrations to include, for example, more effective use of the law and the courts in pressing a group's claims. The campaign or oppositional ethic had been supplemented by an awareness of the need for structural change – this word had come to mean not only changes in the way in which society created and distributed wealth, privilege and opportunity but also the need to change the policies, procedures and services of those agencies that bear so heavily upon the lives of working-class communities.

More workers had had some rudimentary pre-job training and had acquired more on the job, and they were in agencies where their colleagues and managers were more knowledgeable about community work than their counterparts were at the beginning of the decade. Experience and knowledge had accumulated within the occupation, and was reflected in the range and quality of literature being produced. But the irony was that the experience and knowledge had been developed largely within neighbourhood work, and around campaigns for resources from the local authority. Workers were less prepared, by way of skills and attitudes, to deal with far more complex issues (structural unemployment, for example) that were less amenable, if at all, to resolution by campaign-type activities at the local level. They were ill prepared, too, for growth in the importance of inter-organisational work (both between agencies and between neighbourhood groups in city-wide federations) and the need for much harder technical abilities in research and planning.

The atmosphere at the end of the 1970s and early 1980s was one of insecurity and frustration. There was insecurity because of the threats to community work in public expenditure cuts; the absence of solidarity amongst workers that might have been a support in moments of difficulty; and the absence of a sense of occupational purpose to replace the grand ideas of the early 1970s about societal change that had been deflated through the decade.

There was frustration because not only was the rhetoric of the early 1970s sounding less and less credible but the purpose of locally based work *seemed* to be in doubt: could community work survive the erosion of local councils' authority and resources? These doubts, of course, were real only if one saw community work simply as campaign-based activities seeking to wrest resources away from the local state. If one's vision of community work was so narrow then there could be little escape from feeling that one's work was becoming not just more difficult to carry out but also more pointless. There was the temptation for many people to turn aside from community work, to consign it to the dustbin of interesting but short-lived experimentation, and to turn instead to the social movements of the 1980s – life-style politics, liberation movements, environment and peace issues, radicalising the trade unions, and so on. Just as they had provided the wave on which many people entered community work at the start of the 1970s, social movements offered them the opportunity to leave at the end.

The development of community work in the 1970s was very much like a race between a firework rocket and a pedestrian; the early period saw a whoosh of national experiments, such as the CDP, and less well-known local projects funded through the urban programme. These experiments took off with great energy and noise, often attracting national attention; but they were doomed to splutter out as their funding came to the end of its period. As they did so, they let off final bursts of light, like all expensive rockets, in the form of books and articles that illuminated the darkness around them. Whilst all this was going on, there was a more pedestrian development of community work within the established budgets and routines of statutory and voluntary agencies, a development that was to outlive the more flashy demonstration projects and experiments. Nowhere was this more the case than in social services departments which became the largest single employer of community workers.

The experience of community work in these departments has been conveyed in two research reports (Thomas and Warburton, 1975; Davies and Crousaz, 1982), though by the end of the 1970s there was enough variation between departments to warrant caution in generalising. There were some, for example, that had large teams of community workers, drawing support and training from each other, and working with some sense of strategy and design formulated by themselves, by senior professionals, or by elected members in the department. The more prevalent circumstance of single community workers working in an area team of social workers resulted in isolation, marginality and poor supervision and support; this was often evidence in itself that community work had not been conceived within some strategic understanding of its function within, and in addition to, the social work task. These departments were themselves struggling with their own problems of becoming established and of dealing with the reorganisation of social work services at a time when demands on them were also increasing. The reality of these departments – with what Littlejohn has described as 'their mad rush to obtain qualified staff, the intense competition which has developed within the social work profession, and the inevitable desire to be in the vanguard of progress' (1972) – hindered the considered development of community work, as well as the Seebohm vision of community-based and family-oriented services.

Whilst the new departments were able to provide for the creation of community work posts, they were rarely able, and neither was social work in general, to provide the kind of radical norms or intellectual justification that community workers in the early 1970s had inherited from the experiences of the late 1960s and which they sought to put into practice in the inner cities. Social work provided the bread but not the soul of community work through the decade, and radical community work developed, as Peter Baldock has nicely summarised it, within, but not of, the welfare state, standing on the boundary 'between the world of welfare professions in which they gain the means to live and the movement for change to which they belong' (Baldock, 1980).

What the development of community work within social work offered was the legitimation of community work as a method; it had long been seen in the United States as the third method of social work, and this was confirmed by the development of unitary conceptions of social work in the early and mid-1970s. The legitimation of community work as a method helped toward its expansion in the 1970s, not just within social work but amongst radical social movements; the political parties (especially the Liberals) also discovered community politics and saw community work as a tool to reactivate political interest within the electorate and, more recently, within the trade unions. Community work became seen in a crude utilitarian and instrumental way. This posed considerable difficulties, not least that seen as a tool it could not possibly offer in the short term the kind of achievements that were unrealistically expected of it. Additionally, its main concepts or principles as an intervention remained unelaborated through the 1970s. This was a central paradox at the heart of the development of community work in the 1970s: it was expropriated as an intervention by the state, social movements and political groupings to pursue their own particular interests and goals, but they did so with little knowledge of its methods and principles. Indeed, community workers themselves, restrained by a crude anti-professional ethic, were extremely reluctant to make clear the basis of their expertise and competence. We still need at the beginning of the 1980s to work on this paradox creatively; that is, to develop the basic details of community work as an intervention that can help with specific problems and, at the same time, to assert that community work is far more than just an intervention concerned with specific issues and tasks. To define community work both as an intervention to be used on particular interests and issues *and* as one whose contribution is far broader than the particular intervention for which it is employed is one of the more testing intellectual challenges of the next few years.

The splitting off of community work as an intervention from a wider understanding of its contribution was reflected in a number of different ways in the 1970s, not least in the curious status of neighbourhood work. Neighbourhood work carried out in small geographic areas, often single housing estates, was the most widely practised form of community work, and probably the commonest conception amongst practitioners of what community work was. Yet for most of the 1970s the importance of neighbourhood work did not lead to the development of values and theories about the significance of neighbourhood and community as social, economic and political units. Indeed, the concept of neighbourhood had been debunked by a number of sociologists, notably Norman Dennis, and the value of neighbourhood work itself was critically disputed by John Benington in 1972 and by Harry Specht in 1974 in talks to the annual conference of the Association of Community Workers. Neighbourhood work survived these criticisms but its continuing practice was not accompanied by the emergence of ideas about the meaning and importance of neighbourhood and community. Rather there was a distinct move away from the concepts of localism and far more intellectual energy was given over to the concept of the state (the rather benign and friendly 'council' became the impersonal and remote 'local authority' which in turn became the oppressive and manipulative 'local state'), to the idea of city-wide federations and alliances, and to joint action of community groups with trade unions. This intellectual and ideological flight from the neighbourhood expediently forgot that the posited alternatives (alliances, joint action with unions, resource centres) were highly dependent for their success and credibility on thriving neighbourhood groups. Thus whilst neighbourhood organising remained important (despite the disparaging things being said about it) the rationale and goals for it were articulated as being outside the neighbourhood; with few exceptions, the argument for doing neighbourhood work that emphasised the neighbourhood as a crucial political and social system was rarely put. These few exceptions included initiatives and ideas from people like Michael Young, George Clark and Stephen Hatch who were concerned with neighbourhood democracy and councils, but they were well outside the mainstream of community work thought and practice. An exception, however, that seems to be having more influence in restoring the significance of neighbourhood/community is the move towards greater local self-sufficiency and co-operative endeavour in the production of income. Even here there is the danger that community work will be used as a technique to organise local economic initiatives, without placing these initiatives (and others to do with transport and energy) within a wider process of the development of a community as a social and political system.

The interest in practice theory, and the possibilities of a theory or moral statement about personal relations and networks that was implicit in developments in community enterprise and in some feminist thought, came too late in the 1970s to save community work from a long period of theoretical and ideological desuetude. The need for a theory that was broader than the more limited goals of workers and agencies was met by the political economy literature of some of the CDPs, by work on the local state by Cynthia Cockburn, by socialist feminist writing and by the new urban sociology associated with Castells, though most of this was unintelligible to practitioners and trainers alike. What much of this literature had in common were materialist assumptions and a view of class struggle and class politics; it paid attention to the role of the state and other institutions such as the family in the processes of production and reproduction, and identified the appalling distress of many inner-city areas as a product of decisions (or non-decisions about investment) of national and international business.

The materialist writings of some CDP staff had an impact on workers in the middle of the 1970s, providing them with a model of the usefulness of critical research, and exhorting that the details of day-to-day practice ought to be related to a wider understanding of social and political structures. The point was made that even though one may disagree with a Marxist analysis it was vital to have some kind of larger theory about social problems and issues. The 'CDP analysis' sharpened thought within and about community work in the middle of the decade. This analysis was, of course, not wholly original and was heir to the thinking of revolutionary socialist groups of the late 1960s and early 1970s such as the International Socialists. Some of the CDP concerns were also evident within the labour movement as a whole. Multinationals, for example, were attacked by Harold Wilson at the 1973 Labour Party conference and by other ministers in following years, and the National Enterprise Board was created in 1975 as a way of countering their power.

Community workers responded to the CDP analysis not just on the merits of its argument but because here, at last, was a semblance of a coherent theory that was comprehensible and which served to fill the normative and theoretical vacuum that had developed in community work. But the filling of this vacuum by the CDP materialist analysis was merely an illusion that was to be perpetuated to the end of the 1970s partly because workers and trainers desperately needed some broader rationale for their work. It was an illusion because the analysis was not about community work as an intervention or occupation; it was about the state, about capital, about class conflicts and forces. There was no theory about or of community work, except in the insignificant sense that community work in neighbourhoods was denigrated. Indeed, there have been few attempts to construct extended theoretical statements about community work, and to say how they relate to the details of practice. Amongst the few examples of community work's theories of itself are Cockburn's analysis of community work and urban management (1977), the William Temple Foundation book mentioned earlier (Community Development Group, 1980) and the statements about interjacence of Henderson *et al.* (1980).

The paucity of community work's theories of itself are both a sign and effect of the occupation's continuing dilemma through the decade about the nature of its *identity* and *affiliations.* There is, in addition, the complication that an occupation that does not promote theories of itself is unable to define what its contribution may be to contemporary issues; this contribution may be understood in the broadest terms ('developing a participative democracy'; 'building a more caring society'; 'giving people a say in decision making', and so on) but these are only likely to win resources for that occupation when it is new and experimental and when resources are not in short supply.

The themes of identity and affiliation enable us to see how community work has related to other occupations, and how its practitioners have related to each other, and to others in community work such as trainers, employers and local activists. I want to look at how far community work has *cohered* as an occupation — and I shall look at coherence around such factors as organisation, ideas, values and *job comprehension.* Job comprehension refers to the ability to understand, and to try to act upon, the major purposes or rationale for community work as a job. Job comprehension will clearly vary from rather narrow, partisan, or sectional ideas to those with greater *Gestalt* or complexity, where a number of smaller, sectional ideas and practices can be conceived as part of much larger intellectual (and, one would hope, operational) whole. This latter kind of job comprehension can be called holistic or strategic, but the 1970s was a period in which sectional aspects of job comprehension emerged rather than strategic ones.

By coherence I mean the connections that exist between the various aspects of the occupation – the connections, for example, between practitioner and trainer, between practitioners themselves, between the development of practice and that of ideas and values. We look, too, for coherence within the occupation about what is seen as the nature of its contribution, and coherence about the basis of the expertise of its practitioners. Coherence must not be understood as conformity or homogeneity but rather the intellectual and operational linkages that connect the often disparate and sometimes conflicting elements of an occupation to each other. To ask about coherence is to ask whether or not the various aspects of an occupation – its practitioners, institutions, ideas, and so on – function and develop in some kind of interactive relationship with each other, and with the 'outside world'.

During the 1970s community work developed mostly as a disjointed occupation, showing low coherence andd characterised largely by disjunctures between its various parts; only towards the end of the decade did it begin to show signs of linkages in its development. I want to use the rest of this chapter to explore this suggestion and to say something about the relationship between coherence and the emergence of the identity and self-definition of the occupation.

It is not surprising that community work began the decade as a disjointed occupation – there was a great variety of people who were community workers or who were associated with community work, from many different agencies. Their backgrounds, interests, values and ambitions were varied, as was their remit and their skills for doing the job. Their expectations of community work, and those of their employers, were great whereas what could realistically be achieved was much less, a disjuncture in the motivational world of community workers that was only slowly appreciated but which soon led to some disillusionment and painful reappraisal of the purposes of the job. The diversity of interests, skills and values amongst community workers is a valuable aspect of the occupation because it enables community work to respond to the diversity of issues with which it is asked to help; the value of this diversity amongst practitioners was especially clear in the early 1970s as community work became involved in a wide range of social, economic and political problems; it was an adaptive occupation not just because of the diversity of its practitioners but also because of the openness of its boundaries.

It has been long appreciated that these differences led to many political and personality clashes between workers in projects, but taking the occupation as a whole, Frazer has pointed to 'a slightly spurious impression of unity', particularly before 1974. This was provided by belief in generalised values such as participation, and, suggests Frazer, by a common dislike of injustice and compassion for the victims of society that made it easy for community workers to avoid highlighting their different views and aspirations: 'the state appeared to be on the retreat and community workers generally identified with and were seen as part of the movement for change . . . It was also easier to hide differences when a lot of new things were happening and when resources were readily available to support a variety of creative ideas'(1981*b*). Two other factors supported the spurious sense of unity: the first was the mood of anti-professionalism in the occupation which allowed it to define itself negatively; the second was a false consensus that greeted the structuralist arguments of sections of the left in community work; it was false because fieldworkers in particular found it intimidating to engage in discussion and debate about these issues.

Frazer suggests that after 1974 the state and other powerful institutions 'steadily regained control', and the effect of this was 'to bring into sharper relief the different views and aspirations of workers'. The paper on ideologies given by Jerry Smith at the 1977 ACW conference heralded, and made the way for, a more confident articulation of differences, and the process was confirmed by a number of further papers in the book edited by Paul Curno on political issues and community work (1978). About the same time, anti-professionalism in the occupation was joined by a kind of 'covert professionalism'; whilst the attributes associated with the traditional 'disabling' professions were still repudiated, there was increasing interest in defining community work, the skills and knowledge neceessary to do it, the kinds of training that were available and the processes of certification and accreditation. The other aspects of covert professionalism were the continuing importance of the autonomy of the practitioner, freedom from bureaucratic constraints and accountability to the users of the service.

One way of appreciating the heterogeneity of the community work occupation, and then of the disjointedness that appeared, is to see that there were three major categories of community work through the 1970s. These were:

- Programmatic
- Departmental
- Project

I want to explain these and go on to suggest the low coherence that existed within and between these categories.

Programmatic community work refers to those ambitious experiments characterised by clusters of individual projects working within some overall national aegis. The projects and their workers operated (at least initially) within some kind of framework that led to the setting up of the programmes and the development of community work within them. (This is not to imply there was a coherent strategy and a systematic approach to initiating community work at a local level.) The obvious example is the Community Development Project, but much of the community work carried out within EPAs, the Community Projects Foundation and the network of resource centres has many of the features of programmatic community work.

Departmental community work is that carried out within the auspices of on-going agencies within the broad field of welfare, health, education and, in fewer cases, planning, housing and the chief executive's office. Departmental community work includes not only such obvious examples as community work in social services departments but also that in established voluntary agencies such as councils of social service and community relations committees.

Project community work comprises a vast number of small, self-contained projects that worked on specific neighbourhood issues, and which were not part of any national (or local) programme of community work. The variety of individual projects financed within the urban aid programme and by the Manpower Services Commission fall within this category.

Each of these 'categories' of community work made its own contribution to the disjointedness of the occupation during the decade. Workers within the programmatic stream remained largely aloof from the other two and those in the CDPs were especially seen as an exclusive group. The size and separate organisational structures of these programmes allowed the workers to operate in a relatively self-contained world of ideas and contacts; where relationships were made outside the particular programme they were often not with other community workers but, as in the case of some CDPs, with colleagues in the labour movement. Relationships and coherence amongst workers were comparatively well developed because of common funding, management and programme objectives as well as the emergence of shared views about community work and the nature of urban deprivation. Within community work, workers in the programmatic stream enjoyed status and prestige, good salaries, adequate research and support funds and a national platform from which to influence both community work and social policy.

In contrast, workers in the departmental stream, which formed the largest numerical group of practitioners, were distinctly more local and parochial. They were absorbed within the much larger remit and routines of their employing department and, as with those in social services, struggled on with poor peer support and inadequate resources, and faced the disinterest of many of their colleagues. The work of the departmental community worker was like that of a lonely cyclist pedalling uphill against a strong wind without the support and pace-making of a team to sustain effort and commitment over time. Such workers usually lacked any departmental strategy within which community work was located; there was even less likelihood of a local or city-wide strategy that embraced the community work interests of different departments and agencies. These workers enjoyed a comparative degree of long-term security of appointment and funding, unlike their counterparts within the programmatic and project streams.

The project stream were probably the most varied of all three streams. The effects of the urban aid and MSC programmes was to diversify the occupation of community work, providing opportunities not just for local people but for a wide range of people dissatisfied with their previously chosen occupations. Disaffected planners, social workers, teachers, playground leaders, artists and architects took on posts as community workers within this project stream; radical students from university departments, particularly those from sociology, found the opportunity within neighbourhood projects to avoid the more bureaucratic world of departmental community work and to give practical expression to their commitment to the working class. Project workers enjoyed little security of tenure (three years was about the average time of a project) and had few resources for training, consultancy and peer support. Physical and emotional exhaustion was a characteristic of this group; workers invariably worked alone (in pairs if they were lucky) in shop-front premises in areas where the issues were plentiful and complex; the opportunity to retreat from these demands that was open to departmental workers by escaping into the inaccessible offices and routines of their departments was not available to project workers.

The differences between these three streams should not be exaggerated but they were sufficient to produce a certain lack of coherence within the occupation; the focus of workers in each stream was not the occupation community work but the programme, department, or project in which they were involved. Contacts and relationships between workers in the three streams proved difficult to make and sustain, even at local levels; this also was the case for workers in each stream, though of the three, workers in the programmatic stream, particularly within the CDP, were most effective in working, thinking and publishing collaboratively. The way in which these three streams contributed to incoherence was that they each influenced a different aspect of the occupation, and this produced discontinuities between the development of practice, ideas and policy. The articulation of values and political reasoning was most evident within the programmatic stream; workers in programmes such as CDP made explicit and public their political analyses and, in the absence of statements from other 'positions' in community work (particularly from workers in the departmental stream), dominated the scene to such an extent that it appeared as if they were the only ideologies that were around in community work. The manner in which these ideas were presented served to distance other groups who were less coherent or certain in their views, or who were thinking about theory or research development rather than ideology or political analysis.

In much the same way, the different streams in community work addressed different theoretical interests. The programmatic stream, for example, gave to the field a strong interest in contextual or know-why theory; it offered what it called political economy research that sought to understand, usually from one kind of political analysis, the much larger political and economic framework within which community work operated. Practice theory, on the other hand, was influenced and developed far more by people, institutions and events within the departmental and project streams (the exception is the work of the CPF). It was also these two streams that produced much of the scarcer literature on matters such as the management and supervision of community workers, and the content and structures of pre-job and in-service training and consultancy.

The separation of discussion of values from that of theory, and the compartmentalised emergence of different kinds of theory, was accompanied by incoherence in the development of policies within community work. The arenas for such policy discussion *within the occupation* were the Association of Community Workers, the Federation of Community Work Training Groups and the advisory committees serving the Calouste Gulbenkian Foundation. These arenas were, on the whole, influenced more by people from the programme and project streams than by those from departmentally based community work. One of the consequences of this was that the public image and statements of community work as reflected through, for example, the work of ACW were largely the product of people from the programmatic and project streams; many of those from project-based work not only shared the indifference of their programmatic colleagues to the occupation but also felt (by virtue of their isolated working situation) least part of a network of workers combining together in a common job with broadly similar tasks and methods.

We have, then, an occupation where the gaps within and between different streams of workers were accompanied by discontinuities in the articulation of values, theories and policies. By the end of the 1970s a number of phenomena could be observed. The streaming of community work became less pronounced as programmes such as CDP closed, and as CPF undertook more joint work with local authority departments; project-based work became less diverse and more stable, concentrating around a number of limited issues such as health, unemployment and education, and attracting community workers with experience gained in other projects or in local authority or voluntary agencies. Community work jobs became less easy to find and this resulted in lower turnover and mobility, particularly, I think, within social services departments; this had the effect of forcing workers to develop links with colleagues in their own and other departments, and in projects; this was probably a factor that facilitated the renewed interest in networks and regional training groups that was a feature of the last few years of the decade. The streams became less important as other groupings emerged that cut across the streams — groups based on sex and race, for example — and as some localities developed strategies for community work that provided a framework that held together a number of diverse initiatives in a city or region.

The disjointed development of the occupation was compounded by a number of other factors. The rate of growth in the numbers of workers, the high expectations held by workers and employers alike, as well as the range of employers, added to the elements of incoherence. The absence of local and national strategies for community work, and the uncertain relationships with host professions such as social work, and with social and political movements, were others; nowhere was this source of incoherence more painfully experienced than in the realisation that community work as a liberating force sat side by side with community work as an instrument of state management and planning. Community work developed in the space between working-class groups and the state, and its practitioners were subject to all the contradictory and confusing forces that such an interjacent position made inevitable.

Part of the incoherence of the occupation was that it seemed to have no past, and no future. Few of the practitioners in the early and mid-1970s were aware of the practice and intellectual history of community work that stretched back over many decades; there was little sense of depth, of practitioners being connected to each other through a common past in which the occupation had its roots. On the contrary, if the practitioners of the 1970s felt any roots or traditions they were largely confined to the social and student movements of the 1960s. The mood of the 1970s was living in and for the present, and workers became embroiled in the issues of local communities. There was, too, little connection to the future; indeed, the prevailing philosophies were distinctly terminal: community workers worked to do themselves out of a job, and in the middle of the 1970s the radical pessimism that dismissed community work as marginal and ineffective compounded the identity of an impermanent occupation without any futures. The realities of the work did nothing to alleviate this: community workers felt themselves to be dependent on the goodwill of hosts such as social work and youth work and on the tolerance and largesse of local and central employers whose views about community work could change with an election or a controversial piece of neighbourhood action.

In addition, no career structures or patterns were emerging for community workers, and many anyway rejected them; much movement in the occupation was lateral as workers moved from one practice post to another, a turnover and mobility that did nothing to reduce occupational incoherence. People moved into training posts and other occupations; even by the end of the 1970s the number of workers, particularly in the project stream, who had remained in practice for more than five years could almost be counted on two hands. The occupation was not stable: it was renewing itself annually as people moved in and out for two- or three-year stints; community work was often like a transit camp for certain kinds of people between student life and a more orthodox or established job in one of the related professions. One of the consequences was that experience and ideas in the occupation were not consolidating or being developed cumulatively; and the new, younger entrants learned and kept alive all the old illusions, myths and fantasies about community work. For example, the view that community work could liberate the working class from the inequities of capitalism persisted through the decade not because it was a realistic, cogent proposition but because there were always new entrants to community work who believed it and kept the view alive until their experience showed otherwise and the next wave of recruits appeared.

Where in all this were the holding influences – the ideas, events and institutions that connected the various elements of the occupation? What were the forces that made for coherence? I want now to look at a number of organisations with a national focus or remit and will try to show that these did little to reduce the disjointed development of the occupation and, in some cases added to the incoherence. The most obvious one with which to start is the Association of Community Workers, established in 1968, and committed to a policy of open membership in 1973. It decided against developing as a professional association in the 1970s or as a trade union for its membership. It remained badly placed to provide the occupation with more coherence and identity; its membership comprised only a small proportion of community workers in the country, growing from about 140 in 1969 to about 400 in 1982. Its members (about a third of whom do not renew their membership each year) come largely from urban areas, particularly in London and the south-east with only a handful of workers from Northern Ireland, Wales and, until recently, Scotland. It produced no effective structure of local branches or networks, and clearly suffered from not having any full-time staff, and from the reluctance of many community workers to be 'organised'.

Thus in terms of the number, distribution and organisation of its members ACW was hardly a national or representative organisation; indeed, part of the difficulty was that it did not see itself in this light and explicitly rejected any role or responsibility to speak for community work. It seemed to do little to convince 'outsiders' (including community workers) that, in the words of a former chairman, it was 'not dominated by a self-perpetuating elite'. For most of the decade ACW lacked credibility amongst workers, funders and employers. Probably its most important failure was that it did little to advance the interests of community work amongst government and other supporters and as an organisation contributed little of substance to any of the major discussions about policy in any of the fields closely related to its interests, such as health, education, social welfare and employment. Apart from wanting to assert the separate identity of community work, ACW was imbued with a degree of 'libertarian amateurism' that made it suspicious of established authorities, centralism and structure, and unwilling and, indeed, afraid to exercise influence and to take initiatives. The negative attitude of groups such as ACW to bodies in related occupations and government did much to ensure a jaundiced and unreceptive attitude to community work amongst those bodies later in the decade.

Part of the difficulty for ACW was that community workers were largely concerned with issues in their own localities, and had little interest, time and energy to get involved in a national organisation. We should recognise the difficulties community workers experience in reaching outside their neighbourhood: the job is often isolated, the focus of work is usually very local and workers face more than enough demands to keep them fully occupied. One worker put it as follows:

> I *know* national developments matter. I have tried to do something about them on a number of fronts, but it still feels a drag and a diversion to 'stop' my day-to-day work in order to write a reply to some government consultative paper, to go to talk to the Home Office, or address the problem of some broad issue such as 'accreditation' for community work. I don't exactly understand why community workers don't bother, but I do experience why they don't.

It has also been difficult for ACW to work out a suitable active role for its members; for much of the 1970s it was an organisation that simply presented the opportunity for any person or group with sufficient energy to use it to pursue their own interests. But it was also an organisation that was trying, in the face of considerable difficulties, to develop, going through what one correspondent described as 'a growing period from which the flowers may or may not come in the eighties'.

There was a major role for ACW in relation to training; but with the exception of its publications (which continued to be the most impressive part of its operation) ACW showed little interest (until 1981 when a part-time education officer was appointed) in promoting training events, using the experience and resources of its members in the field and in colleges. It was of little influence, too, in discussions concerning community work training as they occurred in organisations such as CCETSW, DHSS, or DES. The initiatives in training lay largely elsewhere – with staff at CCETSW who supported community work through publications, short courses and research, and the development of community work within social work curricula; with the National Institute for Social Work, through its publications, consultancy and short courses; and with groups of workers in some areas who began to experiment with local support networks based on training and explored the possibilities of apprenticeship and accreditation schemes.

Some government departments such as the Home Office and the Department of the Environment were involved as funders of community work, but the schemes and projects they supported offered little to the more coherent development of the occupation. Programmes followed political interests and expediencies, and there was a plethora of small, time-limited projects that were conceived and operated within no articulated central or local framework. The development of community work in social services departments was not stimulated or informed by the Department of Health and Social Security (except in Northern Ireland and Scotland, where consultants on community work were appointed). Staff at DHSS, perhaps under the influence of the medical tradition that dominated the Department, thought and worked largely in terms of client groups; they may have been intimidated by the difficult experiences that their colleagues in the Home Office had had with the CDPs. The concern in the Department around 1974 with the 'cycle of deprivation' did not result in fieldwork programmes but a number of research studies. This was an aspect of a more general problem through the 1970s: social work reformers had succeeded in using community work to broaden the methods and horizons of social work but social work professionals and administrators were not ready to integrate community work into their thinking about social problems and their approaches to dealing with them.

Programmes such as CDP, and government-backed organisations such as CPF, remained relatively self-contained and remote from general developments within community work. There was, of course, considerable variety of staff, practice and values within CDP but only one image emerged, and that was associated with the Political Economy Collective set up in 1974 as 'a group of CDP staff employed by the state in working-class areas committed to a Marxist perspective on the events and situations with which its members are concerned and to producing accounts and developing action based on that perspective'. The effect of the 'CDP analysis' on community work's coherence as an occupation was, on the whole, adverse: the doctrinaire style in which their ideas were put forward alienated many practitioners and trainers, and produced a climate in community work in which people were reluctant to share their experiences and ideas with one another in an honest manner. This was particularly galling because of the values in community work about openness and participation, and because it occurred in a decade when there was so much to talk about it.[6] The persistent denigration of neighbourhood work was, in the words of one community worker, 'a form of emotional and intellectual knee-capping. It took me a long time to get over this, and to see the value of the work I was doing in my neighbourhood.' Employers and funders were put off community work, even though 'to reject community development *in toto* on the evidence of how workers in CDP's may seem to have operated may be tantamount in music to rejecting the claims of Beethoven on the evidence of the performance of his work by an inexperienced amateur or as evidenced in a faulty recording' (Butterworth *et al.,* 1982). The unyielding references to structural factors affecting local communities, no matter how true, closed our eyes to other influences on the effectiveness and coherence of community work, in particular the training and skills of individual workers, and the resources made available to support them and to continue their training and development.

On these points, historians will deal harshly with the influence of the CDPs on community work as an occupation, as they will, too, with the facts that some of its workers and their colleagues in training posts continued to use community work for a national platform and legitimacy even though their own analyses and practice had led them to dismiss community work.

The irony about the disjointed development of community work is that it occurred despite (or perhaps because of) a powerful concern to preserve the integrity and autonomous identity of community work. We have seen that community work was a product of state policies and funding, as well as enlightened liberalism within the establishment associated most closely, as Baldock has suggested, with the Calouste Gulbenkian Foundation. Anxiety was high in the occupation about the possibilities of absorption; there was a fear that community work would be taken over by the state, or by one of its host occupations such as social work. In the 1970s community work was engaged not just in a process of growth but of finding its independence. The problem was that although the state and the liberal establishment were kept at arm's length (but not so far away that funding was jeopardised), community workers failed to attract, or be influential over, those to whom they saw themselves more closely allied – members of social movements, and those involved in the politics of socialist movements and trade unionism. An organisation like ACW, for example, had no organised constituency of fieldworkers, and no substantial membership or involvement of working-class neighbourhood activists, trade unionists, or social movement members.

The assertion of autonomy was thus rather negative, consisting largely of rejecting what seemed to be external interests and definitions; it lacked an articulation of a more positive and self-generated concept of the occupation's purposes. The intellectual complexity of this task, the political and professional differences between workers (and between them and their employers) and the difficulties of discussing these differences openly, combined to postpone community work's definition of itself. This postponement of self-definition, together with the sources of incoherence in the occupation described above, led inevitably to reducing even further the viability of community work as an occupation to which most practitioners felt committed. Commitments were rather made to departments, projects, or programmes or to the ideologies and activities of movements and political groups from which workers came, and others to which they aspired to move.

The relative ineffectualness of community work as an occupation that could attract commitment and identification might not have mattered so much had a central national organisation emerged which could have held the support and loyalties of practitioners and trainers. We have suggested none did. The future for community work as an occupation is perilous without either practitioner commitment to it, or a central body to hold the occupation together and lobby for its interests and development. Hosts such as youth work and social work are being tempted to produce slim-line versions of themselves that exclude community work, a timid intellectual exercise that is being facilitated by public expenditure cuts. The occupation is at threat from within, too. The sources of incoherence remain, and developments that occurred within community work in the late 1970s can be seen in retrospect to have de-occupationalised it − resource centres, for example, do not necessarily support the idea of the community worker as a skilled interventionist needed to organise and support neighbourhood groups. Community workers themselves are returning to the main-stream work of other occupations (which augurs well for the development of social work, for example), or to join social movements and to work within the Labour Party and trade unions. Administrators and trainers who have long been committed to community work are edging away into other concerns, partly because they share the sense of despair and pessimism about the occupation, and partly because they doubt the capacity in community work to confront the problems it faces, and to discuss them in a manner that is open and supportive of people's efforts and ideas.

The prospect of the disintegration of community work as an occupation based around certain principles and methods comes at a time when what it can offer is, apparently, becoming understood more and more. On every side, there is appreciation of community work as an instrument of social policy, of education, of change and development. Occupations such as social work, for example, are moving into community-based methods of working for which the expertise and experience of community workers will be invaluable. In addition, there is a vast amount of work still to be done in urban and rural areas, and this agenda for community work practice in the 1980s is discussed in a later chapter.

NOTES

1 Interestingly, the Young Volunteer Force Foundation (later CPF) was under the Department of Education and Science until its transfer to the Home Office.
2 It is interesting to note the influence of the 'Greek Connection' particularly within community work in London. Those who worked in Greece include Maria Blackmore, Nick Derricourt, Phil Doran, Patrick Harris, David Matthews, Dudley Savill and Bill Taylor.
3 This includes grants outside community work, though the majority were to community work and community relations.
4 Community work here includes community work and the community support programme grants, as indicated in the 1977–9 annual reports. Grants to community relations and community arts are excluded from this analysis. The large majority of grants in community relations and community arts went to direct practice.
5 A contributor to the study wrote: 'The start of community work's "glory days" coincided in some areas with the onset of clearance programmes – and workers found themselves (middle-class, young, educated, political) in solid working-class communities threatened at a very material level – their houses. Those communities had kinship and neighbourhood networks, and access to skills learnt in trade unions, political parties and workplaces. As clearance processes got rolling, these strengths were shredded, areas lost skills and commitments. A more universally sifted population in council-created ghetto areas was the result.'
6 One correspondent suggested that these, and some other comments, 'do not do justice to radical community workers and their legitimate dilemmas; they're only human after all, and if they strike dogmatic postures that is in part a reflection of the stress of change in an evolving "profession" and a reflection of the intellectual uncertainty of the time'.

2 *Participation in Politics and the Community*

> If political institutions do not meet the needs of the people, if the people finally believe that those institutions do not express their own values, then those institutions must be discarded. It is wasteful and inefficient, not to mention unjust, to continue imposing old forms and ways of doing things on a people who no longer view those forms and ways as functional.
>
> *Stokely Carmichael*

Chapter 1 was about the emergence of community work as an occupation in the period 1960–79. But what is community work? In this chapter I shall write about community work having, first, a distributive dimension; that is, it is involved in the distribution of various resources from, on the whole, the local and central state to community groups. The influence over resources is achieved not only through its contribution to neighbourhood work but also through activities in social planning and community organisation. Secondly, community work has a developmental dimension through two processes that I shall call *franchisal development* and *social development*.

COMMUNITY WORK AS A DISTRIBUTIVE PROCESS

This aspect of community work may be understood in the context of the growth of the local and central state since 1945. I shall use the word 'state' in a specific and limited way, to describe a set of institutions and political and administrative processes concerned mainly with regulation, control and welfare. The state is a structure, as MacIver suggests, built within society 'as a determinate order for the attainment of specific ends'. It is, of course, a matter of political decision and not an act of nature or God, that the state exists as an expression of government, and as an administrative device. Successive governments have pushed forward the development of the state and, in particular, there has been a considerable growth in the size, complexity and power of the departments of local authorities. The institutions of the state exist as an instrument of the will of those elected or appointed to govern, and partly as a means to promote the well-being of the population. These institutions are concerned with the regulation of economic life, the enforcement of laws and the provision of various kinds of welfares. They have become established as large bureaucracies that determine policy and priorities, needs and goals and the distribution of services, through a political process involving elected politicians and an administrative process involving professional staff. The distribution of power and influence between and within these two processes, and the relative hegemony of the one over the other, is an important matter, as is their interpenetration with private enterprise, and the contribution made by: first, public bodies and co-operatives in the economic sphere; secondly, a large number of voluntary associations such as trade unions, professional associations, trade associations, churches, pressure and interest groups; thirdly, the informal network of families, neighbours, workmates, friends, and so on, which may be involved in informal care, and in the processes of socialisation and social control. Much of the writing of the CDPs drew attention to the interdependency of the state with all these and other social, political and economic interests.

The 1970s was a period in which the welfare state (including housing, planning, education as well as health, social services and social security) expanded rapidly consuming increasing amounts of the gross national product. There is a continuing debate about the relationship, and the relative autonomy, of the welfare state to economic interests, and the growth of the welfare state has been criticised both by labour and capital as the fortunes of each have annually deteriorated since around 1974. The growth of the welfare state represents an increase in the cost to both labour and capital of the social wage, and makes it a major sector of the service economy, a matter discussed by John Benington in 'Local government becomes big business' (1975). An issue for the interests of capital is the extent to which control over this major sector (which is also seen as attracting resources away from productive investment) lies outside it in the hands not just of government but also of trade unions, professional associations and, to a strictly limited extent, consumer interests. There are doubts, too, that the welfare state is carrying out its maintenance and reparative functions effectively, and concern that much of its cost is accounted for not by direct services to users but by large bureaucracies of administrative and professional staff. This 'officer class' is just as strongly criticised by the users of the services, the majority of whom are working class, who find local authority departments remote, officious, inefficient and often oppressive.

At the moment, it is possible to discern three main approaches to dealing with the extent and concentration of local authority services, and thus implicitly with the nature of the political relationship between the individual, group, or community on the one hand, and government and administration on the other. The first, favoured by some Conservative councils, is to privatise many local authority services; the second, supported by elements of both right and left in politics and social welfare professions, is to loosen the grip of the state by helping people become more self-supporting and independent; the third, adopted by some Labour councils, is to decentralise services and bring them within the control of their users and/or local community.

People have not passively consumed the decisions made on their behalf, and they have developed the means to influence decisions about the allocation of resources. A number of influential and national pressure groups, as well as the trade union movement, have emerged as not-to-be-disregarded influences in politics and administration. We have seen the development of social movements as well as the emergence of spontaneous citizen activity usually around local issues. Some of these movements and groups have been sustained by the interventions of paid workers, including community workers. But the development of community work as an intervention, and the growth of community action in the early 1970s, was not just a response to the activities of the state; it was also a largely unconscious, self-protective response to the conflict between labour and capital that, along with political violence and terrorism, was a characteristic of the country for most of the last decade. Both these factors created a climate where individuals, groups and communities felt the need to defend their well-being and interests; they did this through community-based collective action and through other forms of self-defence against bureaucracies that boomed throughout the 1970s – consumer associations and advice centres are but two examples. The emergence of protest movements was not confined to the working class. In a study of bourgeois social movements in Britain, Elliot and his colleagues have shown that

> the period following the elections of 1974 was marked by the flourishing of new organisations and diverse forms of social protest by middle-class groups . . . examining middle-class unrest . . . reminds us that some of those who are not manifestly poor or subjugated may yet, from time to time, set themselves against the state, against established authorities, and utilise a wide range of tactics to influence politicians and bureaucrats. (1982)

The process of government in the 1960s and 1970s has thus been in a state of disequilibrium, in which the respective powers and responsibility of the people and the governors have been through a period of appraisal. The activities of community groups have played a part in this. Griffiths suggests that

> In the struggles of these community-action groups we realise that we are witnessing the assertion of rights and responsibilities and the renegotiation of relationships between people and the bureaucracies which serve them in a large and complex democracy. (1974)

The renegotiation of relations has been much wider: Purdy writes of the conflict between different users and uses of declining real output, part of which were the expectations (raised by the prosperity of the postwar long boom) 'of ordinary workers and citizens' about what to expect out of life in terms of private affluence and public provision, and the release of 'inhibitions and restraints on action to realise those standards' (1980).

The trade union movement was at the centre of this renegotiation. They not only pursued what we might call welfare goals about wages and work conditions but were involved in a partnership with successive governments in the early and mid-1970s. Taylor writes that 'at no previous moment in British history has the trade union movement been so intimately involved in the work of government . . . [the movement] which had clambered onto the political stage in the wake of post war full employment policies merely to complain about the price of the seats, suddenly found itself playing Hamlet opposite a rather bemused Ted Heath (as Claudius)' (1980). What Taylor omits to describe in his persuasive account of union involvement in government are the other players on the stage – notably the Confederation of British Industry – who together with the unions formed the key elements in the Heath–Wilson conception of government (especially the management of the economy) as a partnership between politicians, labour and capital. Missing from this idea of partnership was, of course, any consideration of those parts of the community whose interests lay outside the traditional spheres of politics, labour and capital. This is something that is clearly related to the emergence of both middle- and working-class protest groups, who found in collective action a sense of significance and influence that was denied to most people in conventional representative politics at local and national levels. What was particularly significant for many middle-class people was that the Conservative Party was in office for only four years in the period 1964 to 1979. It was thus unable to attend to the interests of many of its traditional supporters who, Elliot argues, felt their political and social influence to be declining, especially as organised labour acquired more 'voice' in the political system. Elliot and his colleagues suggest that the large number of new middle-class organisations

took on, more and more, the character of a *class* response. Class interests were identified, opposition to other classes was specified and efforts were made to mobilise both 'grande' and 'petite' elements of the bourgeoisie. Their efforts were directed against Labour governments, against the 'progressive' elements of the Tory party, against organised labour, against parts of the state apparatus, which meant many of the 'untrustworthy' members of the 'new', the bureaucratised middle-class. (1982)

The primary interest of most working-class groups was nothing so grand as 'partnership in government'; they wanted to achieve specific gains for their constituents through affecting decisions about resources administered by local government and there were three kinds of activity that were important:

- Group Organising
- Administrative Development
- Localising Facilities

(1)   Group Organising

People organised themselves (often with the help of community workers) into groups to participate in political and administrative decisions about resource allocation. These groups engaged in negotiations about such matters as housing, play, planning, health, education and income maintenance.

In broad terms, there have been three ways in which groups have tried to influence the distribution of resources:

ACQUIRING AND IMPROVING RESOURCES

Community activities of these kinds tried to effect changes both in the policies about, and in the actual distribution of, resources to local communities. A successful outcome of such attempts was a shift of resources to the community group and its constituents from resource-holders and possibly at the expense of equally needy groups in another part of the city. Resource acquisition was sometimes referred to as 'smash-and-grab' community work.

REJECTING AND CONSERVING RESOURCES

Here the emphasis was on activities which, rather than implementing changes in resource distribution, actually sought to prevent them. The work of groups in these two areas of resource influence was largely to maintain all or part of the status quo and resist the introduction of new, or the removal of existing, resources in the community.

PROVIDING RESOURCES

In resource provision, the emphasis was more on the management of resources previously acquired by a community group for its constituents or wider neighbourhood, or on the development of community resources outside the formal structure and voluntary services. In both categories, community groups were more concerned with *service provision and delivery,* and less with influencing the policies and stock of resources held by, for instance, local government departments.

(2) Administrative Development

The purpose of this work is to enable change and development amongst the staff who administer agencies and their programmes. The tasks have been to

- develop policies and services that are more relevant and effective for identified needs within the community;
- help staff in agencies to engage in more co-ordinated decision-making;
- shape the attitudes of agency staff to their role, and to the participation of community residents in decisions about the allocation of resources.

(3) Localising Facilities

The emphasis here is on the growth of locally based and accountable resources, that offer a variety of services to residents. These resources were often seen as alternatives to more remote/bureaucratic/controlling agency services; they were often managed by local residents; the staff had no supervisory or regulatory powers; and they served a relatively small geographical area. The development of neighbourhood advice and information centres are a case in point: some cities like Sheffield and Sunderland have a large number of them. The Sunderland centres offer:

- *generalist advice giving* – employment, tax, consumer problems, fuel, housing, social security and supplementary benefits;
- *representation* at various tribunals and hearings;
- *community work*, as in enabling the organisation of groups around specific issues;
- *lobbying and campaigning* on a variety of issues;
- *training and education,* for example, welfare rights courses and information;
- *resource provision* – typing, duplicating, and so on.

The advice centres are only one example of the development of local resources. There were other examples in the health, education and arts fields. The development of neighbourhood resources reflected a criticism of the remoteness and bureaucratisation of some agencies, particularly those within social services and health. The alienation of people from the state's welfare agencies has combined with Shumacherian ideas, and those about local democracy, to produce a climate of experimentation with small-scale neighbourhood resources.

Group organising, administrative development and the localisation of facilities were, and still are, the primary means through which the members of a community are involved with politicians and administrators in influencing decisions about resources. These activities are concerned essentially with the process of politics, and with the meeting of people's day-to-day needs. It must also be noted that part of this activity was not just about wresting resources from the establishment; in so far as it was about freeing 'people from the belief that they must depend on others for benefits', it was about the development of mutual aid and relationships between people and between groups, to satisfy not only welfare and recreational needs but also those for work.

To the extent that community workers are assisting groups with specific issues to do with resources then community work has a distributive aspect. It would be wrong to suggest that community work has been concerned just with the distribution of resources and welfares. Work to achieve the specific goals of groups gave residents the opportunity to *participate* in the political and administrative processes that made decisions about services and facilities. Most government- and community-inspired initiatives regarding participation have been developed in relation to distributive goals; from the community side there is a desire to improve the well-being of people in a neighbourhood or interest group, by acquiring resources and seeking more relevant, accessible and accountable services. The interest of some sections of government in participation encompasses a genuine belief in its value, a regard to the view that decisions participatively taken are more likely to be supported on implementation, as well as the need to incorporate the growing dissent in the 1970s from community-based groups. A participative process is an essential part of the feed-back mechanism to centralised corporate management, as well as a check on what Collins has called the 'bureaucratic hegemony' of local and central agencies.

It must be noted that the involvement of community groups in fighting for resources was a form of decision-making by administrators (priorities established by clamour) and represented a way of rationing and distributing resources between groups. It was, too, a way of legitimising or enabling shifts within welfare provisions, particularly those that formed part of policies of positive discrimination.

Participation has been one of the most enduring of values amongst community workers; 'giving people a say in what affects them' is but one of many phrases that express not simply the importance of participation but of aspiration to a different kind of democracy. It is, however, a value fraught with difficulties, not least because it has engendered more slogans than sustained analysis and little clarification of the means by which the demand for participation can be translated into effective procedures. There are different meanings and approaches to participation that are common in community work, from those that value participation in its own right as a means of enhancing the quality of people's lives to those who have been 'challenging the power of representative bodies and of rejecting all decisions and decision-making processes which are not based upon full collective participation'.

The idea of participation has also been questioned by those who see it as a bourgeois mystification or as an instrument of repressive tolerance. Another critique, not so much of participation but of the ways in which it has been exploited in community work, has been presented by Hywel Griffiths. He suggests that democracy has been given (amongst community workers) 'a purist and doctrinaire interpretation and application' that has enshrined the idea of collective decision-making at the expense of a critical analysis of its utility: it is time consuming and orientated to group support rather than task achievement, and based on the false premise that collective wisdom is more valid than individual genius. More importantly, collective decision-making

> has been betrayed by the motivation of those who have advocated them who, whilst professing the altruistic purpose of offering opportunities of fulfilment to participants, have in fact been working to another agenda which would challenge the authority of those who attempt to exercise responsibility . . . the idealistic commitment to participatory democracy which has characterised many community work ventures of recent years represents a triumph of theory over commonsense and ignores, sometimes arrogantly, the predilection of the majority for private lives . . . the strategy of employing participatory and collaborative practices with disadvantaged groups and informal leadership figures whilst on the same time employing conflict tactics against formal leaders . . . has, not unexpectedly, been singularly unsuccessful in persuading the latter that they should encourage wider participation and agree to a broader sharing of responsibility. (1979)

This brief discussion of participation provides the basis only for pointing up both its core position in community work, and its controversial status. Given this position and status, it is all the more remarkable that community workers (or the small number of sociologists and political scientists whose interest it has aroused) have not adequately defined its contribution to the development of representative and participatory democracy, and from that contribution its tasks, skills and knowledge. But perhaps it is not so remarkable:

the concern with participation amongst community workers may be as significant for its expressive as for its functional values. It has provided a form of comprehensible radicalism which in turn has helped to create a cosmetic unity within the occupation. Generalised statements about participation were, wrote one respondent, 'a sharing, caring form of radicalism, easily transmitted to new workers and to groups, easily excused to local authorities, and politically embarrassing for local authority members and officers to oppose'. Participation became the acceptable face of community work, a reliable means of attracting piecemeal funding and of keeping goals so ambivalent or general that they could later be renegotiated by workers. The difficulty, however, was that the demands for more and better participation, no matter how valid and important, were often undermined by the bearers of the message themselves. It soon became clear to many sponsors of community work that whilst its practitioners used participation to attract funds and other resources they were also cynical about its potentialities; the dilemma was that at an expressive level participation remained a salient value in community work, but the occupation became associated with an anti-state ideology that encouraged local people to realise the system was not workable or working for them, and instead to work outside it.

It may also be possible that community work's concern with participation has suffered in credibility because of its association with life-style rather than survival politics. A contributor to the study suggested that

> participation as an end goal is a middle class or life style species of politics which may be intended for the benefit of the working class and with which they may get involved. But in the hierarchy of needs, I think food, drink, shelter and other biological needs precede expressive needs – and survival politics are concerned with these. A more genuinely local programme would seek the attainment of goals concerned with immediate needs before it sought a structure.

The influence in community work of issues associated with life-style or libertarian politics (the environment, nuclear weapons, co-operatives and even community care are other examples to add to participation) and the development in the late 1970s of federations and alliances may be understood as a reaction, by middle-class interventionists with an impatient desire for social change, to the difficulties experienced in building a locally derived programme for change out of the single-issue community groups that are the bread and butter of neighbourhood work. The turn against neighbourhood work that occurred in the mid-1970s was fuelled in part by the realisation of how difficult it was for workers to establish debate and a programme around genuine local issues (particularly in a period of diminishing state resources) and how much it required from workers in terms of long-term, committed, painstaking and self-effacing involvement.

It is possible to give a more adequate account of participation if we look at government in two ways: first, as a *set of relations* within a population and between it and those elected and appointed to govern them; secondly, as a *set of institutions* ('the state') that exist both as an instrument of the will of those elected to govern, and as a means to promote the general well-being (and regulation) of the population. These institutions are characterised by a *set of administrative and political processes* that determine priorities which direct the distribution of resources. It may be that in community work 'participation' has been narrowly conceived as participation in, and influence over, the set of administrative and political processes of the institutions that have made decisions about resources. We have failed to relate our endeavours with participation around resource issues to, first, the structural nature of democratic relationships, and particularly the conditions under which people exercise the franchise; and, secondly, to the social structures and processes of communities.

The involvement of people in management and political processes about resource allocation is, of course, necessary but it might best be seen as only a part of a more fundamental conception of participation which addresses itself to the evolving nature of democratic mechanisms and assumptions and to the participative or interactive nature of local communities. We might wonder whether our *thinking* has been too concerned with group organising around resource issues and not enough with the structural quality of political relationships and of local communities; perhaps our concern with consensual and combative relations with the private and public sector has helped to compound our neglect of the structural aspect of political and community relationships. This neglect occurred because we thought of community work largely in terms of political and administrative processes; these were of the utmost importance in fulfilling the resource needs of groups and the distributive function of community work, but our mistake was to think that helping groups to fight the state was the end in itself. We have learnt from the 1970s that 'battles with the local state' are relevant for redistributing resources but are also to be seen as only one of the means for strengthening both social structures and processes, and political interests and competence.

This point has been well made by Raymond Pringle in a paper about training for community work in the 1980s. He suggests that community work must 'be rooted in a wider theory and practice of organisation, collective action and politicisation'. He argues that

A further political consequence of our lack of theory has been our parochial preoccupation with the neighbourhood. Community workers have tended to get involved with an endless series of small, local protest groups which focused in a 'non-political' manner upon all kinds of single issues. This kind of community work was ultimately divisive. These groups were rarely organised, either functionally or politically, on any wider basis than the neighbourhood. They were therefore unable to align themselves with any broader movement for social reform or to develop a more strategic opposition to general policy issues. It soon became clear that this kind of community work would simply help populist sectional interests to compete in the local political arena. But this apparent strengthening of local pluralist democracy was a far cry from the grandiose and radical claims of many community workers. This is not to deny that neighbourhood work does achieve small improvements and provides some rudimentary political experiences. However, without an extended theory it is impossible to develop a practice which would relate these groups to any broader political initiative. (1981)

There are, as Pringle indicates, a good many difficulties surrounding community work's distributive function. A dilemma is that this function – helping people improve their material and social circumstances – is crucial to community work but is so full of limitations and contradictions that on its own it is not the strongest possible, or most comfortable, justification for community work as an intervention. We need a broader-based theory or concept for community work, and in the next two sections of this chapter I want to suggest that this can be provided by seeing community work as an aspect of franchisal and social development. The next sections deal with some elements of the overall nature of democratic practice and with the pattern and quality of interactions between people at their place of residence. As far as this latter matter is concerned, I will disagree with Pringle and will argue that whilst community workers have been preoccupied with doing work in the neighbourhood, there has been insufficient concern with *thinking* about the neighbourhood or locality, and thinking about neighbourhoods in a way that provides a strategic framework for the numerous specific interventions that occur within them. This theme will be extended in subsequent chapters with the view that although in the 1970s the neighbourhood became the focus for our practice, this was not accompanied by making it the object of our intellectual endeavours. Rather, the opposite occurred and far more attention was given in our thought and writings to other systems such as the local state or workplace organisations. It was this lack of intellectual attention to the place of residence that made our concerns parochial, not the work itself that was being done in neighbourhoods by community workers.

PROMOTING FRANCHISAL DEVELOPMENT

The extent and quality of relations that exist between those elected to govern and those who elected them may be more or less democratically arranged, and define the exercise of responsibility, authority and accountability within the political system. These relations comprise not simply those between the people and those in government but relations between the people themselves and between them and the agencies of the state. It is suggested here that the evolution of these relationships defines a process of *franchisal development.* By this I mean a process that goes beyond the giving of the right to vote, and includes the creation of those conditions that support and inform participation in electoral and other forms of political decision-making.

The development of the franchise is thus concerned with people's status, influence and knowledge in a set of relationships with elected representatives, labour, private enterprise and with each other not just in political negotiations about resource distribution but in central and local governmental processes that are concerned with matters of programme and policy.

The issue of franchisal status and influence has been important in the last two decades because the interests of many sections of the community were not adequately represented, or taken into account, in the making of government policy at national and local levels. The interests of these sections, particularly of marginal groups, were inadequately represented by elected members, partly because these members' actions were over-influenced by their own party policies and their own political ambitions. The interests of these sections were overshadowed by the influence of the organised labour movement and by pressure groups of private enterprise and other national lobbies. Despite its crudeness as an idea and a slogan the phrase 'power to the people' indicated that many members of the population were alienated from the process of government; 'people power' expressed the intent to find alternative forms of participative democracy as well as the need to create a politically educated electorate. There was dissatisfaction not just with the forms of representative democracy and the power of organised labour and private enterprise but also with the *aptitude* and critical faculties that people were able to bring to bear in thinking about issues of programmes and policy. What has become clearer since the end of the Second World War is that democratic processes and relations include more than mechanisms such as elections, and encompass the capacity of people to use those mechanisms, and to use and develop them to their fullest. This capacity may be something that has to be promoted and 'looked after', a warning given by Laski in 1930 when he wrote that 'however important be the political mechanisms on which liberty depends, they will not work of themselves. They depend for their creativeness upon the presence in any given society of a determination to make them work.'

The process of franchisal development is concerned with sustaining democratic practices by building up the power, knowledge and understanding of the people in their relations with government and implicitly with each other. As such, franchisal development ought to be as effective a constraint on the misuse of executive power as constitutional checks and balances, providing a restraint on executive power when elected politicians see the resistance of people to their proposals and decisions. Democratic practice is thus endangered where government and the state that it sustains become powerful and indifferent to the wishes of the people; and where the knowledge and interest of the people about affairs of government is impoverished with the consequence that they are unable to make the kind of critical appraisal of issues that is necessary to hold elected members and appointed officers to account. Without this knowledge the exercise of power through the ballot box becomes a trivialised and 'de-politicised' act.

It may be that the growth of the state is in itself a factor that works against the development of a knowledgeable community. The awareness that the state will survive in its influence over one's life through changes in the political composition of the executive will undermine interest and involvement in political processes as surely as the awareness that the economic superiority of some groups in society offers them an impact on government that is greater than, and undermines that, of ordinary people as it is exercised through the ballot and the effect of 'public opinion'.

State development in the provision of welfares — jobs, social services, housing, education, and so on — may be seen as the development of a kind of political hegemony that is removed from the processes of representative democracy. It is, in Laski's term, 'an invasion of the personality', creating through its reservoir of discretionary powers, its centralised and bureaucratised nature, and its penetration into most aspects of the lives of particularly the working class, a hold on people that persists through changes within the system of political representation. The culture of dependence sustained by state development, with its associated decline in community networks and responsibilities, may itself be inimical to an alert and critical population. The size, remoteness and complexity of the state apparatus also has a deleterious effect on political participation and awareness because they compound the difficulty that the ordinary citizen faces in getting a response to his or her needs and suggestions.

Towards the end of the 1970s there appeared critiques from left and right of the state as the monopoly provider of welfare services, with consequent proposals for diversifying and making more local these services. There may or may not be advantages to a more pluralist system of welfare but this discussion should help us to ask whether state development has had its most adverse effect on democratic practices and aptitudes, and to see that proposals for welfare pluralism may be as important for the re-invigoration of democratic political life as for the better consumption of welfares. In brief, state development has not helped to make representative democracy more effective and credible; the irony is that governments have extended the state to improve the well-being of the population; in so doing, it has helped to create an acquiescent and de-activised political culture. The critical question is whether so much has occurred to undermine political aptitude that rolling back the state will not in itself bring about an enhancement of this aptitude. Rather, this may now occur only as part of a conscious and deliberate policy of *franchisal development.*

The development of the franchise concerns such matters as the extension of the franchise to groups previously without a vote and the evolution of changes in, for example, electoral methods and procedures. But I have suggested that a policy of franchisal development also embodies a determination to make democratic mechanisms work through creating an informed population that has a justified sense in its own ability to influence the process of government. This aspect of franchisal development which is concerned with the conditions under which the franchise is used I will refer to as the growth of *political responsibility.* The development of political responsibility includes the promotion of political significance and competence. In the remainder of this section, I want to argue that both of these have been jeopardised through neglect, and through the diversification and subordination of political processes. I will then suggest that one of the most important justifications of community work is its contribution to the development of political responsibility, and that this contribution provides part of its strategic purpose.

Political significance refers to a cluster of factors that define the relationship and involvement of participants to the political process (at central and local levels). It is a sense of 'counting', of a sense of worth, of being regarded and valued; it is feeling that the potential to influence politicians and administrators is present, of being able 'to do something about' an issue or a matter affecting oneself, or a friend or neighbour. Political significance includes, too, the capacity to identify with political processes, and to feel some sense of commitment to them and responsibility for their effective functioning. A key to significance is the opportunity to exercise power and responsibility, to feel confident of the ability to affect outcomes.

Political competence refers to a sense of interest in political issues and ways of thinking, to having a politically as well as a sociologically imaginative mind; and to the development of knowledge about issues (local, national, international) as well as the skills that are necessary to take part in decisions about those issues.

I want to look at significance and competence by examining briefly two trends in democratic practices that have emerged in the last two decades. The first is the diversification of political systems and the second, the subordination of the electoral political system.

Diversification

An adequate account of political developments in this country must take into consideration not just

- *electoral politics,* that is, the election of politicians at local and central levels;
  but also
- *industrial politics* – which includes the exercise of influence through trade unions and shop stewards, as well as (*a*) initiatives for involving workers in business decisions, and (*b*) the evolution of co-operative forms of enterprise. It includes, too, the exercise of influence by organised capital.
- *administrative politics* – decision-making by non-elected officers in local and central government, and their influence over the lives of ordinary citizens, an influence that can often be exerted with little accountability to the electoral system.
- *community politics* – which comprises the emergence of community groups, as well as the attempt to fashion more devolved forms of government, for example, neighbourhood councils. It encompasses, too, experiments in 'life-style politics' such as housing and food co-operatives, and attempts to 'bypass' state provisions and to avoid reliance on established political parties and groups. We must take note, too, of the emergence of 'street politics', where a wide variety of causes have used tactics such as marches and mass demonstrations both to publicise their case and to win support for it.

The development of industrial and community politics is in part a cause and effect of the subordination of the electoral system, and of the recognition of the influence of capital and organised labour over government. It is a recognition that the consensualist, pluralist assumptions of electoral politics, particularly at local level, are too simplistic: diversification is in part a consequence of the different interests potentially and actually in conflict within society.

It is not clear what the overall effect of this diversification has been on political significance and competence; the emergence of the other three political systems (as well as a sharper differentiation of ideas and groups within the two main political parties) has rendered government and politics more complex and perhaps less readily comprehensible. Whilst the development of industrial and community politics has offered the opportunity for relatively small numbers of people to acquire more significance and competence, it may be that the complexity of the political process, together with the growth of administrative politics, has tended to reduce the political significance felt by large numbers of the population, particularly those already with little in the way of resources, power and influence. We must consider, too, whether the increase in political competence that diversification necessarily requires has occurred, or whether it, too, has declined.

The picture is made more complex because both political significance and competence have been influenced by the *subordination* of electoral politics, as well as a number of other factors that will be considered later.

Subordination

The electoral system has necessarily become less important as diversification occurred and as people and organisations outside that system (such as those of labour and capital) came more and more to influence, and often dominate, local and central government decision-making. Perhaps the role in government of the CBI and the TUC in the Heath and Wilson administrations of the early 1970s represents the most striking manifestation of both diversification and subordination, reflecting the fact of partnership between electoral and industrial politics, as well as their conflict.

It is a daunting task to review briefly the reasons for the subordination of electoral politics and the related phenomenon of the disaffection of many people from political action and thought, as evidenced, for example, in poor poll turn-outs. First, there has been more awareness that, in the words of one report, representative parliamentary democracy is not the ultimate achievement of political democracy. The extension of state services and agencies (the development of administrative politics) means that men and women must be given 'a say in matters which so influence their lives in the local situation . . . This surely means increasing people's involvement in decision-making in, say, health, education and employment, at the place where they actually live and work' (Community Development Group, William Temple Foundation, 1980).

Secondly, there has been more recognition of some of the limitations of existing mechanisms. The criticisms of the simple majority vote procedure for elections, the relatively closed selection process of candidates, the consolidation of cabinet rather than parliamentary power (and of the party caucus at local level rather than the council) suggest how much existing practices are seen as inadequate. Hindess also has pointed out how 'the vast majority of governmental decisions and appointments are not directly subject to democratic process' (1980).

There is, too, a difficulty with enfranchisement. There is de jure a suffrage that is almost universal but there exists what might be called de facto disenfranchisement, or 'political deprivation'. People are disenfranchised because they have to struggle to survive, and keep their family fed, clothed and housed. Poverty, and the struggle against it, drains away energy and interest, producing disaffection and non-participation. People are de facto disenfranchised when they are not able to acquire the initial and continuing education that makes the casting of votes and participation in decisions a meaningful activity. The Russell report on adult education was quite clear on this:

> The way of democracy is to submit areas of controversy to debate, in the belief that right judgements are built upon knowledge, critical enquiry and rational discussion. Those who lack the knowledge, or the tools of enquiry and expression . . . are effectively disenfranchised. The need for education in social and political understanding . . . will continue to be one of the prime needs of the future. (Great Britain, 1973)

In short, the evidence of enfranchisement cannot be simply the right of adult men and women to vote but must also include the conditions which make those men and women willing and competent to use that vote. Having and using a vote is now to be seen as a necessary but not a sufficient condition of a political democracy. It represents the minimum requirements, and there may be disaffection with electoral politics if little is done to progress beyond the minimum.

Political significance and the capacity to comprehend political processes and issues may depend in some part on the degree of association with, or accessibility to, both one's neighbours, work colleagues, and so on, and those who have been elected. The first is important because (*a*) significance can be achieved through membership of, or support for, an interest group that is trying to affect decisions; and (*b*) political interest may be generated not only through generalised ideals and philosophies but also by the way in which people regard their neighbours and reference groups and from this presence or absence of regard define their responsibilities and obligations. General philosophies may indeed be made concrete and immediate through this process of regarding others. We must be open to the possibility that people who live in communities where relationships are few and weak may have less identification with electoral politics locally and nationally. Thus the creation of strong and overlapping social networks may be a precondition for political significance and competence. Of course, the dilemma is that in areas of greatest stress, the potential for the development of these networks is weakest, even though the need for them is greatest. We seem to know so little about *how* people's political interests and awareness are developed. Much of the writing about this in community work gives the impression that people are simply converted, or are politicised through a sudden flash of inspiration or enlightenment. The process is surely more complex, and what I am suggesting here is that a necessary part of this process may be the capacity to be touched by, and feel responsible for, the lives of those who live and work around us. People's capacity to be motivated by political issues and action may thus be partly dependent on the existence and functioning of social relationships and networks.

The second factor (the degree of association with elected representatives) is perhaps less vague in its manifestations and implications. At the local level, councillors have become removed from their constituents as they assumed more the role of urban managers, taking responsibility for the affairs of a whole city or county rather than those of their constituencies. The amalgamation of authorities, and the centralisation of executive and administrative functions, served to remove physically the politician at a time when the psychological distance was also increasing. In addition, the growth in the number of state agencies and their managers (the development of administrative politics) has had the effect of coming between the politician and those in his constituency.

But the factor which has perhaps been most responsible for the subordination of electoral politics is the perceived inability of national politicians *to manage.* The function of political leadership is to manage boundaries, and the transactions within and across them. It was evident in the 1970s that national politicians were unable to carry out this management task: the ability to manage was compromised by the influence of, for example, the Arab oil states, the International Monetary Fund and the power of the multinationals. For the ordinary person in the street, the vulnerability of the country and its dependence on factors outside the control of the electoral political process were probably clarified by a range of events such as membership of the common market, the terrorist activities of the early 1970s and the extraordinary influence of business and the trade unions in the process of government. The collapse of the Heath government, and its prior declarations of states of emergency and the three-day week, under the pressure of the miners' industrial action, served to confirm in the public mind that electoral politics was now subordinate to a range of other national and international processes.

The period 1970–4 signified the undermining of the consensualist assumptions of government. The authority and integrity of electoral politics was challenged on the shop floor and on the streets − power workers' and miners' strikes, the mass and flying pickets, the Pentonville Five and the Shrewsbury picket trial, the Ulster Workers' Council Strike, the IRA mainland campaign during which forty-four people were killed in 1974, the trial of the Angry Brigade and the violence at street events such as Red Lion Square and the Windsor Park Free Festival. The response of government to these events was legislation – 1971 Industrial Relations Act, Counter-Inflation Act, Pay Board, Prices Commission, Prevention of Terrorism Act – which further undermined the standing of government both by being ineffectual and provoking further conflict and unrest. The subordination of electoral politics was made complete in the period 1974–7 when the politicians' inability to manage the economy was made evident. The crisis began with the quadrupling of oil prices in 1974, and led to rising inflation and un-employment and falling production and industrial investment and, in 1976, the collapse of the pound and the humiliation of massive borrow-ing from the International Monetary Fund. Street violence continued in this period, which saw events such as Grunwick, the West Hendon riot and confrontation at Lewisham and at the Notting Hill Carnival.

The lessons were there to be learnt; in 1979 the country returned the Conservative Party on a platform of stronger (but less) government; in the same year, a workers' inquiry involving four trades councils was initiated. Its report is the clearest exposition of the understanding that electoral politics, particularly because of their subordination to the interests of capital, could not be relied upon to pursue socialist policies. The report called for a transformation of the relationship of workers, unions and the Labour Party and concluded 'that working class people have to build up their own forms of political power based on their material power as producers, as the people on whom the distribution of goods and services depends, and, in the home, as the people who reproduce and service the present and future labour force'. The analysis and conclusion recognises both that socialism does not necessarily occur with simply extending state structures and services (a point of contact here with welfare pluralists) and the potential of industrial and community politics. Experiment and experience in industrial and community politics are valued as goals in their own right but also as a means for transforming parliamentary democracy (Coventry Trades Council, 1980).

There are, of course, a good many other factors that have contributed to the decline of political significance and competence, besides those of the diversification and subordination of our political processes. The withdrawal from politics has been influenced, for example, by the 'privatisation' of family and community life, a turning inwards to enjoy private forms of pleasure and entertainment, made possible by rising levels of income and credit extension, and made inevitable by the power of advertising. For some people the decline in significance has been compensated for, and made tolerable by improved material prosperity and security. Affluence is a compensation, but it is also a cocoon that insulates the beneficiaries, as much as does poverty, from the process of political democracy. The complexity of world events and issues aggravated the problems of significance and competence, as did the ascendency of science, promising much through Wilson's technological revolution in diverse areas such as moon exploration and heart transplants, but in the end threatening micro-chip redundancies and nuclear disaster. People's attitudes to electoral politics were also influenced by the corruption that was exposed, particularly in local government and the crookedness of international figures such as Agnew and Nixon. The problems of significance and competence were compounded by growing cynicism and broken hopes and ideals, and the realisation by the middle of the decade that a primary concern of politicians in managing the economy was to reduce material resources in the form, for example, of jobs, social and health services, and housing and education facilities.

The preceding analysis does not assume that there ever existed a 'golden age of democracy' in which people were able to act with significance and competence in the process of government. On the contrary, it would be wrong to think of democracy or of political responsibility as determinate end-states that either had been achieved in the past or were going to be in the future. Each is best seen as a permanently evolving process, responding to the changing political, social and economic circumstances of the time. As improvements take place through franchisal development, they become seen sooner or later as inadequate in changing circumstances. Thus any assessment of political competence and significance must be carried out not in reference to some ideal or idealised state but in relation to the prevailing agenda of government, the functioning of political systems and the patterns and norms of participation amongst the population. In fact, a real danger to democratic practices and political responsibility is that we come to view them as once-and-for-all states that can be achieved and that can acquire a degree of finish or completeness; the danger is increased when we also reduce them to the mere operation of voting or electoral mechanisms. The existence throughout an entire society of an ideology of attainable and attained democracy will do much to ensure that those aspects of democratic practice and political responsibility that have been achieved will become static and ossified, and will not develop with changing circumstances and times. Such an ideology has become established in the West, partly through expediency (it provided a form of stability that was a useful base from which to launch the pursuit of material prosperity and profit) and partly through the veneration of democratic practices that has been an inevitable outcome of the aggrandisement between the 'free West' and the 'enslaved East' since the end of the Second World War.

The contents of the last few pages may be summarised as follows:

The last decade or so has been characterised by a decline, particularly amongst working-class people and marginal groups, in political significance and competence. A number of factors account for this, amongst which I have included the diversification of political systems and the subordination of electoral politics. A country in which the population is accumulatively being denied significance and competence is at great risk, exposed to authoritarian government and the diminution of democratic practices. People who lack democratic significance and competence come to form a malleable group, and this is, of course, conducive to the pursuit of both non-democratic attempts at power and socially irresponsible policies that are pursued for doctrinaire purposes.

The seeds of renewal are there to be found in the process of decay. The alienation from electoral politics, and the successive extension of the state and the growth of administrative politics, have resulted, at the beginning of the 1980s, in a counter-reaction. Welfare pluralists argue that the welfare society is not achieved simply through the welfare state, and more importance is being given to local forms of welfare; socialists have come to see that socialism is not achieved by simple extensions of state power, and they too argue for political and economic pluralism that emphasise the value of locally organised forms of productive and political power. For both groups the role of elected local and central government is similiar: to provide resources, back-up, co-ordination and some concern with standards and issues of equity and justice.

The initiatives of the 1970s in industrial and community politics are also the seeds of renewal. These initiatives were largely concerned to acquire resources and other services but they were based largely on group organising, and involved the acquisition of skills, knowledge and confidence that are relevant to the development of political significance and competence. Community politics gave, too, the opportunity within a neighbourhood to feel a sense of solidarity with those with whom one lived, as well as the opportunity to recoup a sense of responsibility and power. These neighbourhood actions (playground committees, housing campaigns, care schemes, employment initiatives, advice centres, and so on) may only redistribute resources to a limited number of beneficiaries, and often at the expense of other equally needy groups; they are, too, only a marginal response to the structural inequalities and deprivations experienced by many groups. But to criticise such initiatives because their outcomes are local and are not related to structural causes of poverty and inequality is to miss part of their impact. Their justification lies equally in their cumulative contribution to enhancing political significance and competence and thus, in the long run, to the reinvigoration of electoral politics and the extension of ideas and practices of political democracy. Diversification is an evolving aspect of our democratic practices but we must also deal with the problem of significance and competence and at the same time enhance the functioning of the electoral political system. This enhancement requires more than the kind of improvement in parliamentary and electoral mechanisms suggested by Hindess, and more than the development of non-parliamentary democratic mechanisms; there must in addition be positive action that restores significance and competence within democratic processes.

The development of significance and competence is so fundamental that it cannot be left as something that will emerge spontaneously or as the result of the pursuit of distributive goals. Rather, it must be pursued as a conscious policy in its own right, and I have conceived of this policy as part of the process of franchisal development, which comprises several goals/means. They are:

- to experiment with forms of participative democracy;
- to facilitate aptitude in the process of government through:
  fostering skills in civic and political matters
  building community networks
  providing specialist resources to aid community decision-making;
- to promote more awareness about social, political, and economic issues. The role of formal and informal adult education is crucial here.

It would be misleading to suggest that there has been no progress in the last decade towards franchisal development. There were some direct initiatives taken towards achieving progress in the above three goals/means, and the work of Freire, the women's movement and some of the CDP publications had particular influences on the need to develop political interests and competencies through community based forms of action.

(1) Participative Democracy

Some progress has, of course, been the consequence of community groups wanting to have their 'say' in decisions, and of government initiating various forms of participation at local and central level, both of which I take to fall within community work's distributive functions. More direct experiments include:

- neighbourhood councils, as well as community associations, parish councils and community health councils;
- life-style politics, for example, consumer co-operatives, women's movement;

- producer co-operatives;
- open council meetings;
- the introduction of the referendum into British politics;
- the development of intermediary bodies or 'mediating structures';
- the development of local management of neighbourhood resources.

Attempts at parish and neighbourhood councils are part of an evolving process of devolved, more accountable and participative government. Experiments in housing and employment co-operatives, in industrial democracy and in consumer and client participation as part of this process. They are to be evaluated not just in terms of their immediate success and failure but as contributions to the slowly accumulating significance of community assertiveness. They are part of a learning process whose outcomes may not be apparent for many years.

(2)   Facilitating Aptitude in the Process of Government

The intention here is to encourage and support a process of learning whose main purpose would be to develop the aptitude for involvement in government, and a sense of confidence and legitimacy. This process would have three primary features:

(A)   THE ACQUISITION AND DISSEMINATION OF RELEVANT SKILLS AND KNOWLEDGE

These are typically acquired in group organising activities; the larger question concerns other processes of formal and informal learning that would facilitate a more confident grasp of broad civic skills and knowledge. More direct contributions to fostering these skills and knowledge include training courses for voluntary activists; life skills training as part of, for example, the programmes of the Manpower Services Commission; some kinds of adult literacy schemes that have focused on learning for political understanding and participation, and women's studies courses and health groups.

(B)   BUILDING COMMUNITY NETWORKS

Atomistic relations in communities and competitive bidding for scarce resources between groups may work against community assertiveness and empowerment − this is a pompous expression of the divide and rule thesis, and its validity depends in part on the assumption that a sense of identification, and practical and symbolic linkages between people, will better serve the articulation of community interests in government.

These networks must be conceived more broadly than those which emerge to influence the distribution of resources. They must include the development of caring and support relationships between people, and a sense of responsibility for community functions such as socialisation and social control. They may also develop through leisure and recreation activities, including the work of community centres, festivals and fairs. The move from many political parties and ideologies to shift the responsibility for support, control and socialisation away from the state to local networks must be evaluated as a possible way of enabling the relations necessary for significance and competence in government to grow.

In the same way, work to bring together groups in federations must be construed not just as a means to better influencing resource decisions but as an expression of the kind of community networks needed to facilitate franchisal development. The growth of networks amongst tenants as in some parts of South Wales, and the linkages between tenants in different parts of the country, are also important elements of network-building. We must also take account of those factors which in the long term will make the building of local networks both necessary and feasible. The effects of diminishing supplies and increasing costs of energy, together with economic factors, may force local communities to become more self-reliant; the growing numbers of people who are not in paid work may in the long run produce a revived interest in, and energy for, local forms of socialisation and social control. The effects of these changes are difficult to predict, but they may mean the reaffirmation of the character and values of *Gemeinschaft*.

(C) PROVIDING SPECIALIST RESOURCES

The organisation and articulation of community interests depends in part on access to clerical and reprographic resources, as well as to specialist professionals. These resources are much like those described earlier in relation to neighbourhood advice centres. The provision of such resources has included the development of resource centres, the availability of professionals such as community planners, architects and lawyers and the use of students.

(3) Promoting More Awareness about Issues

The existence of an electorate large sections of which are disinterested, poorly informed and participate only marginally, if at all, in the political process, may be seen as a state which sustains the influence of established political interests such as the major parties, and the organised interest groups of labour and capital. There may be short-term political gains to be made from this state of affairs, but in the long term it is inimical to the development of democratic government and conducive to the imposition of authoritarian centralist government. It is fundamental, therefore, that the well-being of democratic practices, and the capacity for community interests to be taken into account in government, depends in large part in fostering an electorate that is more interested and knowledgeable about social, political and economic issues.

Knowledge about such issues is gained as a result of taking part in community activities and group organising. The development of this knowledge contributes to the 'process' goals of community work. But the numbers of people who learn in this way is necessarily limited, and much of the learning may be confined to local or regional issues. Partly in consequence more direct forms of adult education have emerged within and alongside community work, including training courses for activists, community television and radio, community arts and theatre, investigative journalism and documentary television, and alternative information services such as those associated with the political economy research of the CDPs. These have had, however, an insignificant impact compared with the influence of the traditional media, in which political issues and activity are often made to appear violent and extremist, and in which the issues are often made obscure and difficult to sympathise with.

The acquisition of knowledge and skills, and experiments in participative democracy, comprise the educational aspect of franchisal development. The primary purpose of this educational process is the enhancement of political responsibility. A significant strategy within the educational process is the provision of educational resources and services. These have been provided through institutions like schools, adult education centres and those such as the Workers' Education Association, Northern College and the Federation of Community Work Training Groups engaged in innovative work with training voluntary activists, and through the development of community-based media. The kind of education that will be needed was identified in the Russell report:

(*a*) *role education* – providing the background of knowledge, especially in relation to social change, through which the individual's role can be more responsibly discharged in society, in industry, in voluntary service or in public work of any kind;

(*b*) *social and political education* of very broad kinds, designed to enable the individual to understand and play his part as citizen, voluntary worker and consumer;

(*c*) *community education* – as providing the background of knowledge and understanding upon which effective action for community purpose can be founded;

(*d*) *education for social leadership* – where those with potentialities for leadership . . . can discover themselves and try themselves out . . .

The need for this kind of education was put most forcefully by a recent report on adult education and participation:

> Our representative democracy assumes an informed citizenry, yet we are confronted by the evidence of considerable public ignorance. New forms of participation are being developed, requiring new supportive frameworks of information and education. Critical and complex issues confront our society and demand our democratic attention. There is no refuge in an elite of expertise, not least because the fragmentation of contemporary knowledge demands a collective, democratic response that is capable of linking fact with value. It is scarcely too much to say that at present there is an educational vacuum at the centre of our democratic system; and that we shall fail to fill this vacuum at our peril. By reducing the 'information costs' of participation, by helping to redress the informational imbalance between laymen and professionals, by putting resources at the service of the participation process, and by doing this at different levels, in different ways and in new forms of partnership and collaboration; adult education has an important role to play in a revitalised and participatory democracy. (Groombridge *et al.,* 1982)

It may be that one of the most significant achievements of community work in the 1970s was to enhance the access of working-class people to adult education resources. Community work itself offers opportunities for informal education, but its influence has been such that in many parts of the country adult education resources were turned to the advantage of community groups and activists. (The situation may now be different because public expenditure cuts have hit adult education extremely hard in many parts of the country.) It should already be clear that different kinds of contributions from adult educators are needed, and in this context, developments in the community work training world must be noted with some satisfaction. The training of voluntary activists to be better voluntary activists (as opposed to becoming community workers) is clearly consonant with giving priority to the more direct educational process.

It is possible to overestimate the value of more formal approaches to adult education (not least because direct education on its own would seem most likely to be effective with people who already have a concern or cause and feel the need for more background and training). A central feature of community work is the conviction that people learn by doing, by engaging in collective action on their own behalf. Among other things, community work embodies a reaction to traditional education that teaches people facts and theories, without connecting them to their experience. One correspondent also suggested that community work was particularly a reaction to traditional forms of political education or persuasion – preaching to people or writing articles which seek to convince them:

> I think this underlines an error of the CDP people in going over almost completely to writing and presenting analyses (unless they saw themselves as clarifying for workers in contact with people). They acted as if they were educators only. People don't learn that way. Community work states by definition that people develop political awareness by going through certain experiences and by reflecting on these. To neglect either the experience or the reflection and learning is like leaving out fifty per cent of the job. This is not to say that in the past these educational objectives were met . . . workers often lost sight of them. But this was more often due to getting bogged down and forgetting about community work's long range goals than due to the lack of involvement of the education establishment.

Losing sight of educational objectives, or becoming bogged down in day-to-day matters, was something that was not easy to avoid, given the pressing nature of many of the issues with which community groups were concerned. The usefulness of the correspondent's comments is to remind us that community work is defined in part by the integration of task and process goals.

The specific contribution of community work to franchisal development goes beyond the opportunities for people to build up knowledge and experience around local issues. Whilst the acquisition of resources and participation in decisions about them are of utmost importance, and may be the primary or only reason for local people's involvement, such activities are, for the community worker and interested policy-maker, likely to be equalled, if not exceeded, in importance by the longer-term process of enhancing the organising culture of a community. The word 'culture' is used here in the very specific sense argued by Goodenough – culture consists of 'standards for deciding what is, standards for deciding what can be, standards for deciding how one feels about it, standards for deciding what to do about it, and standards for deciding how to go about it' (1963). Thus community work may be short term in relation to its distributive goals but long term in its developmental aspect, transcends the particular issues of the moment, and is concerned with laying down and sustaining participation, organising, group and individual relations and networks as part of the structural fabric of a community. This idea of an organising culture will now be further explored.

Specific issues are highly relevant to the community worker not only because they will be of prime importance to local residents but they are also what bring people together – and, as Alinsky often pointed out, the more issues there are to focus on, the more people will be involved with a wider range of skills, knowledge and interests. The specific issues (housing, care, employment, road safety, play, and so on) are important, too, because they need to be resolved 'to calm the environment', as one respondent put it. That is, attempts at improving inter-group and interpersonal relations, of enhancing political significance and competence, are unlikely to succeed unless they take into account the material conditions which affect people's well-being, and thus their energy, resolution and incentives to 'get involved'. It is as inappropriate to talk about cultural work without issues as it is to work on issues without reference to the longer-term aims of developing an organising culture. Cultural development is the ultimate justification of issue work, and issue-based work is the means to cultural development. However, issue-based work alone may in some circumstances be an uneconomic educational tool (affecting mainly the activists of a group) and one that may also serve to narrow people's aspirations if the skills, learning and commitment of organising become seen only in terms of the needs and requirements of the immediate issue. The object of community work is to lay the basis in a neighbourhood for the capacity to generalise learnt skills and attitudes to a whole range of considerations (not just resource issues) most of which will be in the future. It is this capacity to hold on to learning, confidence and relationships that was described by one contributor to the study as the need 'to make organising part of the culture, of the learned and socialised behaviour of people'. This behaviour will be in contrast with other behaviours such as scapegoating, resignation, apathy, indifference and dependence on others to do something about particular problems. The behaviour/attitudes are characterised not so much by self-help as by self-determination, which includes the possibilities of self-determining to take action yourself or to let others provide you with resources and services. To the extent that the behaviour and awareness is learnt and has developed from an accretion of experience that goes wider than a few activists engaged on issues, then we can call the predisposition and competence to organise part of the culture of a community. Organisation and participation become part of the norms and legitimised responses within that community.

The idea of an organising culture is broader than particular issues, which can be seen as the forcing points for clarifying and strengthening the standards or capacities for the kinds of decisions identified by Goodenough. It is also broader than organisation and participation in relation to councillors and administrators, and other decision-making bodies. It must include, too, the set of relationships that exist between local people and their attitudes to each other. These relationships include not just those that are established through formal networks or federations of groups, or through membership of a common group, but also the day-to-day informal relations in roles such as friend, neighbour, colleague and helper. These relationships go wider than the frequency and quality of interactions, but include, too, people's perceived responsibilities and obligations to each other. I have argued previously in this section that this regard for other people may be as important in stimulating people to get involved in a particular issue as self-interest or abstract political ideals. Fragmented and atomised relationships, and partialised and differentiated roles, may be as inimical to political understanding and involvement as to community care and mutual aid schemes. It is this issue that I want to address in the next section of this chapter; before doing so, I want to conclude by pointing out that there are other factors besides local people and any community workers that affect the development of political significance and competence and the consolidation of an organising culture. They are the politicians, administrators and professional staff of the agencies who determine the allocation of welfare resources, as well as those responsible for the management of private enterprises. There are also the relations with institutions such as schools and trade unions. It is the orthodoxy in community work at the moment that alliances or partnerships with unions and between community groups, and between them and social movements, are necessary and desirable; it is useful, however, to extend this notion of partnership so that it includes not just allies from welfare professions such as social work or from the labour movement but also the politicians and officers of local authorities.

The long-term nature of developing significance and competence will need to be resourced, in part, by the state within a framework of partnership with groups, community workers and others. This partnership is necessary, too, as a way of influencing the way the politicians and officers respond to community needs and ideas, and develop appropriate services. The development of political significance and competence will not properly occur unless there are also changes in the way politicians and administrators conceive of their own roles and responsibilities; these changes will not necessarily happen simply through conflicts with departments over particular issues, but are largely dependent on an on-going process of learning and adaptation. Such conflicts, however, are part of the process of learning, as one worker suggested to me:

> We are now getting closer to seeing our boundary role. Community work is saddled with the job of giving vested interests a shock — especially locally — about policy and the allocation of resources ... community work is a redistributive mechanism — vested interests won't allocate resources differently or imaginatively ...

It is crucial to remember, however, that such conflicts are not the whole part of learning, or a substitute for it, though they are a necessary part of the partnership approach. This approach is based on the ability of the local state to show an interest in the long-term development process, and to be sensitive to how much it must learn and adapt.

Building up what one worker called 'a whole system of action in the city, a climate amongst officers, politicians and groups about what is and should be happening' is a process that needs time, a diversity of community work approaches and a strategy that combines this diversity into a coherent approach. This strategy must embrace direct work with politicians and administrators. It is plainly absurd to have the development of an organising culture as a goal and then to see councillors only as people with whom one takes issue over particular matters. Put another way, the diversification of political democracy (through innovations in industrial and community politics) and the promotion of significance and competence will be affected, in part, and made more valuable by, the enhancement of electoral politics. Part of the task of working with politicians must be to win acknowledgement that the mandate for community work comes as much from its developmental as its distributive function; its part in the process of franchisal development is fundamental and what is needed, in the words of one correspondent, is a more public and open debate about the type of democracy we wish to create so that 'we can reach the type of consensus that will give community workers a much clearer mandate and perhaps even a much more crucial position in an evolutionary process than they possess at present'.

THE PROCESS OF SOCIAL DEVELOPMENT

In the last section I tried to show why and how community work might broaden its concern with participation within political democratic practices and relationships. I now want to explain why we must also extend our notion of participation so that it goes further than an interest in getting a handful of local people involved in an action group or some other kind of organisation, and that we begin to understand how to look at the totality of relations that exist (or may not exist) in a local area. The concern with participation in community work has been unduly narrow and is usually understood as participation in political and administrative processes. It is equally concerned with promoting participation within the community through a range of neighbourly relations and informal groups. Community work is concerned with 'interaction between people as well as common action by them — with the process of community as well as the process of community action'.

The term social development has not been widely used in British community work; it is associated largely with some ideas and publications of the United Nations, and with work in new towns and other large housing developments. It was used by one correspondent to the study in the following way:

> Community work is a facet, and sometimes a tool, of social development; and I would define social development as the development of the individual within society. Further, I see this as meaning the improvement of the ability of the individual to achieve self-fulfilment through being able to realise his ambitions without prejudice to his obligations to society. This achievement must depend upon the individual being able to clearly formulate his desires and the means of achieving them, as well as being aware of, and responsive to, the people with whom he mixes or who may be affected by his actions. The realisation of his desires will normally require both material and social support, which can only be found within community structures . . . Community work is, therefore, concerned with collective effort to provide that support . . . If this self-help cannot provide sufficient resources then communities should seek to diversify their external support as widely as possible, so that they minimise the constraints of patronage. Communities are in the worst possible situation when they rely entirely on governments who may not only exercise monopoly controls, but may also use other statutory processes as a means of coercion . . . You seem to start from the premise that some sections of our society will always be supported by the State and that the task of community work is to try to temper the relationship between the State and its dependents. In my view, the real objective of community work is to make communities and individuals independent of the State . . .

I use the term 'social development' to refer broadly to the growth and maintenance of networks and relationships in a locality; put another way, the term refers to the development of a community as a social system, and conveys in particular a concern with interactions within that system, and the functioning of its social structures and processes. I have already suggested in the previous section that the emergence of political competence and significance may be partly dependent on progress in social development. Getting people together in groups around specific issues or problems may be seen as one aspect of, or contribution to, the social development of a community; yet there has been a failure within community work to link its interventions on specific issues to a wider strategy regarding the development of a local community as a social system. Practice and discussion in this area has largely been dominated by the ideas of *community* and *class;* each has produced its own ideologies and orthodoxies, and each has contributed in a different, and usually unrelated, way to theory and practice in the occupation. The idea of *community* is associated with some of the early pioneers in community work, concerned with issues of social integration in new towns, overspill estates and the new estates of the inner city in redevelopment areas. The idea of community was sustained by the flourishing school of British sociologists concerned with research into communities, an interest that became institutionalised in the setting up and work of the Bethnal Green Institute of Community Studies. The earlier community workers spoke of community spirit and community relationships, and of the involvement of community groups with authorities in a participative community of decision-making where differences of view and interest could be reconciled and resolved through discussion. The 'community' theorists and practitioners were linked to another major orthodoxy of the 1960s and 1970s – the non-directive approach, associated primarily with the work of Reg Batten. It was an orthodoxy that influenced the training of cohorts of youth and community workers but remains one of unfulfilled promise. Its adherents (with the exception of George Lovell) wrote little after 1970 and non-directiveness remained more as a guiding principle or philosophy than a clearly defined statement of tasks and behaviours. It was, too, an approach that was quickly put aside by the radical new recruits to community work in the 1970s whose concern was more often with class than with community and who were extremely suspicious of the connection of the community and non-directive theorists with colonialism. The idea of community became submerged through most of the 1970s but re-emerged towards the end of the decade with the interest that grew around the notions of community care, and the extreme disrepair of many communities in the inner cities.

By the mid-1970s *class* had become a more central concept in community work, but with it came new orthodoxies about community work and the state. The publications of the Home Office's CDPs swept aside the old consensualist orthodoxies, and examined the nature of class interests in British society. Their record of political economy research stiffened the calibre of the rather conventional assessments of need that had become part and parcel of British community work, and the CDP reports on, for example, the housing, employment and investment markets in the inner cities and other decaying areas were an important contribution to social policy thinking. Together with Harry Specht's ACW paper in 1974, the CDP reports were instrumental in persuading many practitioners that community work could not end disadvantage and exploitation; the problems of the inner city were structurally determined, caused and aggravated by much larger national and international forces.

The assertion of the importance of class was a major contribution of the CDP to British community work, and it was soon followed by the assertion by other groups of ideas about race and gender. The dismissal of community work as an ameliorative factor was an inevitable outcome of a structuralist perspective, and the force of the structuralist argument was such that no one responded to it with the statement 'yes, it is ameliorative, and this is its value'. No theories of amelioration were put forward, and none that held together the ideas of community and class: the absence of theories about community work as an ameliorative factor within the kind of structural constraints defined by CDP created a vacuum in the second part of the 1970s that was sorely felt; this was one reason why students, trainers and workers returned consistently to the two other sources of orthodoxy − the 1968 and 1973 Gulbenkian reports − which continued to be best-sellers right into the 1980s.

The failure of the Marxists in CDP to help community workers integrate their thinking about communities with ideas about class is not a surprise. Many of them turned away from community work as an occupation and moved to other forms of organising and to local politics. Few saw the point in putting time and energy into discussing their ideas in community work in a way that workers would find helpful and supportive of the small realities of their own practice. This lack of concern for fieldworkers is evidenced, for example, in the absence of any attempt to spell out a radical practice that flowed from the radical analysis, and a scarcity in the community work literature, as Marj Mayo has pointed out, of discussion of method from a Marxist perspective (1982). What could be more tragic and destructive than the advent of an idea whose time had come, but whose proponents lacked the commitment to community work and the empathy with, and interest in, its practitioners that were necessary to engage with them in a process of learning?

As a result, the two orthodoxies of class and community were to be established in community work almost as antimonies. There were those in and outside community work who were concerned with the issues of class and who saw community work only through this perspective. The ideas and reality of community were for them a distraction in a double sense: they were relatively unimportant and drew attention away from notions about class. There were those who saw only the community system and, worse still, saw community work only as something that was to do with the solution of a number of tangible problems. There was a disregard for the saliency of class and other factors such as race, age and sex and often an ignorance or disregard of the structural factors that determined the well-being of the community with which they were concerned.

The divide between class and community has helped to perpetuate further unhelpful dichotomies. One example is that between what are crudely called the 'social work or community development' tradition on the one hand, and the 'political action tradition' on the other. The former focused on the community as a social unit or organism, and was concerned with so-called 'soft' issues such as social disorganisation and the need to build up networks and resources. The 'political action tradition' identified the community as a political unit, and emphasised 'hard' issues such as oppression and powerlessness. People associated themselves with each tradition, and each was thought to have its own particular organising styles and methods ('consensual' and 'conflict'). This dichotomising of communities into social organisms and political units, and the consequent cleavages within community work thought and practice, has been most destructive; it has worked against a holistic understanding of communities, and ignored the crucial links between social life and political activity, and how each can contribute to the development of the other. The paradox has been created that community workers, blinkered by a concern with specific groups and issues and blinded by a faith in a particular tradition, have been neglectful of the community as a total system.

Most people live in two worlds – the world of work and the world of residence, though the numbers who have access to the world of work are in decline. Access to, and opportunities in, both these worlds are determined by factors such as class, age, sex and race. Class is the best predictor of position and achievement in such matters as job, income, education, housing and health, and a whole range of fringe and not-so-fringe benefits such as pensions. The working class in this country has the worst in income, housing, education, health and environment. The nature and extent of poverty and deprivation is well documented but it becomes easy to respond to 'poverty and deprivation' as if they were disembodied, not related to people, or as if they were evenly distributed throughout the population. Poverty and deprivation, powerlessness and disadvantage, oppression and exploitation are above all characteristics of sections of the working class. It is the object of prejudice and discrimination that is euphemistically described as 'snobbishness' but were it practised against women or ethnic groups would be illegal today. Some parts of this class such as older people, the disabled, single parents, the unemployed and ethnic minorities are disadvantaged in a number of ways. The British class system, and the inferior status, power and well-being of the working class, is morally opprobrious, and destructive and wasteful of human talents and ambitions.

Facts about the working class's income, health, housing, and so on, and those for other groups of people defined by age or race or handicap, for example, are not to be apprehended merely as statistics or treated as abstractions in ideological discussion. These facts – the objective and real situation of this class – are to be seen in a visible and concrete form in the worlds of work and residence. The world of residence is where people live, where perhaps they will shop and send their children to school and enjoy some part of their leisure and recreation time. Go to an overspill housing estate in a northern town, an inner-city area in London, or an estate of high-rise blocks and there you will see that it is the world of residence – the community – where the facts of disadvantage are most plainly evident and keenly experienced. The importance of the community as an escape from work, as a place of reparation and comfort is now perhaps a reality only for the privileged – those primarily outside the working class many of whose communities are better seen today as places from which to escape by those who still have access to the worlds of work, leisure and schooling. In short, being working class, or black, or disabled is something that is given much of its meaning at the place of residence – within the community – and through roles and experiences that are part of that community – such as tenant, claimant, social work client, friend, neighbour, member of a ward party, volunteer, participant in a soccer club or whatever. (The word 'community' is used here as synonomous with the place of residence; it is a territorial unit, and I am not using it in its normative sense to suggest a particular quality felt by residents to be a feature of the place in which they live.)

The state of many of Britain's communities are in varying stages of disrepair and disorganisation, and the most extreme examples of this are to be found in the inner cities, large housing estates and the more recent developments of high-rise buildings. These are the communities of the working class though in the terraces of the inner cities they are often shared to varying degrees with people from other classes living in rented accommodation or as owner-occupiers. The *material fabric* of these communities has now ceased to be adequate – both old housing stock and the new industrialised, prefabricated developments of the last twenty years are deficient on a number of counts, and we have begun the process of blowing up high-rise blocks that have become unfit for human habitation. The environment of the inner cities and of estates is generally poor, and there are usually inadequacies in facilities such as shopping, transport, schools, health, community and recreation centres. There is even more concern over the social fabric of our urban communities, and the extent to which many are in an extreme state of disrepair is indicated in the recent book by Barry Knight and Ruth Hayes (1981). People in working-class communities, in particular, have withdrawn from communal roles and responsibilities; life has become privatised behind locked and bolted front doors. People venture out with diffidence, and show an increasing reluctance to become involved in community activities. Contact with neighbours and friends is often negligible. Previous networks based on neighbours, friends, family and work colleagues have been disrupted (and not replaced) by urban redevelopment and relocation, and the growing heterogeneity of the urban population, which is in itself unstable because of its mobility.

The design of new estates and high-rise blocks inhibits social interaction, as does the deteriorating aspect of public amenities such as lifts and walkways, and the fear of violence and theft. We have created communities in which high densities of people live increasingly physically closer to each other but with decreasing rates of social contact and interaction. Individuals are having to cope with life crises without, first, adequate financial resources and, secondly, help and support from friends, neighbours and family, within a social system that offers them few rewarding interactions outside their front door. A number of factors operate in their different ways to diminish the roles available for people to fulfil − early retirement and unemployment remove the opportunities within the world of work, and the features described above make the community less of a place where people are able or willing to take on public roles that give satisfaction to themselves and service to others. As social systems, these communities are dysfunctional and in a growing state of crisis.

The diminution of social roles and public interaction has been accompanied by group antagonisms and suspicions, most evident between the young and old and between white and black British people. The privatisation of community life has also been accompanied by an increasing disinterest and subsequent ignorance about the lives of those living around one − a lack of concern and knowledge about other families' achievements and difficulties, about their interests and ideas and so on (this can often lead to people having quite the wrong information about other people and groups − fantasies, gossip, rumour, exaggeration and prejudice will flourish). This lack of concern about one's neighbour is a complex phenomenon; it is a real ignorance produced by the diminution of social contacts and interaction; a socially created indifference and fear; a defence mechanism that has evolved to regulate exchanges between people who, particularly on estates, live so much on top of one another; and an inevitable consequence that so many individuals and families have to devote all their energies to their own survival and well-being. A result of the decline in interest in the 'world outside your front door' is a diminution in feelings of personal responsibility for what occurs, particularly in the public parts of a community such as the streets and walkways. Acts of deviance or unsocial behaviour will go uncorrected, even unnoticed. The social control and regulation functions of community life thus begin to atrophy as much as the informal social welfare ones of mutual understanding and aid. This decline in welfare responsibility must be considered alongside that in political responsibility marked, as was indicated in the last section, by a diminution both in knowledge about political issues and a fall in participation in community and electoral politics.

There is, of course, considerable variation in the situation I have described from community to community; matters are at their gravest in several kinds of working-class communities in urban areas and large housing estates, but the issues are also evident in middle-class and relatively well-off and motivated communities. The situation is, above all, one that involves the working class; although there are many factors to be considered such as the design and environment of flatted estates we cannot fully understand the issues surrounding community until we understand what has been happening in economic, political and cultural terms to the working class since at least the last world war. But likewise this understanding about a class must go beyond analysis and slogans about its relation to the state and capital (a relationship that is fundamental to any thorough understanding), and must include an appreciation of the real life and experience of a class not only at the point of production but at the point of community. It is in and through the varied experiences of community that people are able (or not able) to attach meanings and significance to their roles and fate as members of a particular class or ethnic or age or sexual group. Thus class and community are locked together in a circle of mutual explanation.

The decline in welfare and political responsibility that is most evident in working-class communities is a complex phenomenon attributable to a number of causes. The use of mono-causal explanations will lead us not only to simplistic statements but inappropriate or even unrealistic interventions. I refer to 'intervention' because my assumption is that there are groups of people – politicians, the social welfare professions and residents themselves, for example – who would wish to intervene to bring about change, and who wish to know the contribution of community work within a broader strategy of social development. As I have said earlier, it is necessary but not sufficient to indicate that community work brings people together to work on local issues and problems; it is more fundamental that this coming together is a means towards a larger goal, and unless we appreciate this larger goal then specific interventions in community work will always lack a broader programme of which they are recognised to be a part. This larger goal, I suggest, is conveyed by seeing community work as contributing towards the development of *communal coherence.* This may involve promoting a sense of cohesion, of 'we-feeling', of affiliation, a sense of reference to a social system, if not of belonging. This coherence is compatible with the existence of conflicts and the expression of particular interests within a community; the point about coherence is that despite, or because of, conflicts and differences (as well as things in common) people feel they are members with others of a local social system. The other important aspect of communal coherence is the foster-ing of significance. A sense of significance relates to the availability of roles in a community (and at the place of work) that give people a feeling of contributing something to the larger whole of the community.

I have briefly indicated the state of disrepair of the social fabric of British urban communities in particular. My suggestion is that community work's strategic or programmatic objective is, within social development, the promotion and maintenance of communal coherence – the repair of social networks, the awakening of consciousness and responsibility for others and the creation of roles and functions that provide individual significance and a social service. The promotion of coherence occupies an operational and conceptual middle ground because as a strategy it can be related to a number of quite different grand theories about society – the way people relate to each with knowledge and empathy, and support each other in communal roles is absolutely fundamental to, and must remain invariant between, different forms of intervention associated with different political or social philosophies.

The promotion of communal coherence as part of a larger process of social development means intervening to affect change in three major community variables. They are:

● relationships and networks
● attitudes to others
● availability of roles

It is possible to see these as the basis of a programme of change to which specific interventions are a contribution; these three variables also lend themselves to middle-range theorising that makes sense of specific interventions and which can also relate to larger abstractions. Put another way, these variables can provide a rationale for community work that is something more than the benefits that accrue from specific interventions, and something less than the grand ambitions of much diffuse thinking at the macro level. These variables can constitute an operational and conceptual middle ground between the small realities of local community work and the large hopes of many of its practitioners and theorists.

By *relationships and networks* I refer to those that do or do not exist between residents, in their different roles (relative, neighbour, friend, and so on); between groups; and between residents and groups, on the one hand, and organisations (such as those of local and central government) on the other. Here we are concerned with the pattern and quality of interactions between people; these interactions may be as much about conflict as consensus. It is quite wrong to dismiss a concern with community networks as 'consensualist'; on the contrary, we are interested here as much in the differences between people and groups (and between them and organisations) as in the points of common interest and agreement. The crucial fact is whether networks and relations exist to communicate these differences and agreements.

The second variable is *attitudes to others.* I use this as rather a catch-all phrase to include what people know about each other, and the concern and interest they take in what is happening to people in the community around them. It refers to how responsible people feel for what goes on around them, and the extent to which it is possible for residents to identify and empathise with the fortunes and tribulations of their neighbours, friends and relations in their community.

The third variable is *availability of roles,* by which I mean the extent to which it is possible for residents to take up roles in the community (neighbour, volunteer, party activist, tenants' association chairperson, and so on) that are satisfying and a service to others, and which, in turn, strengthen networks and contribute to people's knowledge of, and interest in, each other.

I see this description of communal coherence as very different from the notions of community spirit that were present in community work's early days. My formulation recognises the presence and need for conflict, and does not presuppose the desirability of consensual methods of problem resolution. I have also defined communal coherence precisely and concretely — interactions and networks; knowledge and identification; and creative roles. These refer both to the world within a locality and to its relations with the 'outside' — in the first half of the 1970s the relationship with, for example, local authorities expressed the need to challenge their procedures and decisions, and to win much-needed resources. By the end of the decade, that relationship was changing as community groups began more to ally with local authorities and with each other in the face of cuts imposed by central government. The greater interest in federations and regional networks of groups at the end of the 1970s indicates a form of relationship between people that was not so important earlier. The point is that we should look behind the particular forms of relations between people, between groups and between them and the local and central state, and recognise that these different forms offer, in a way appropriate in the time and circumstances, the means necessary for creating networks, knowledge and roles.

I believe that part of community work's strategic purpose is to promote communal coherence; that is, to help people know and interact with each other in a variety of roles at the point of residence — which I have called the community. Promoting coherence is a good in itself, and an urgent task in light of the disrepair of the social organisation of most of our urban communities. But this promotion and maintenance is also to be valued as a means to achieving the other part of community work's strategic purpose — that of enhancing what I have referred to as people's sense of political and welfare responsibility — through which they take a more active and responsible part in political processes and in processes of social provision and control.

The extent to which communal coherence is present will vary from community to community, and over time, and it clearly will be affected both by local and national factors. There will be times and communities where nothing need be done about coherence; there will be other occasions (in periods of change, for example) where interventions need to be made to sustain and protect it and other times where positive action needs to be taken to promote it because, for one reason or another, it has disappeared. I have already said enough to indicate that we have in urban communities a crisis of social disorganisation where the qualities of coherence are no longer to be found in quantities sufficient to preserve the integrity of the community as a social system, and to allow the inhabitants to exercise welfare and political responsibilities.

Persons concerned with social welfare and policy must ask: what, if anything, is to be done to promote coherence in these, and other, communities? A necessary, but not a sufficient, first step is to improve the material fabric of these communities, and to redirect on the massive scale that is required resources to provide better housing, employment, health, education and other facilities. This realignment of resources can be seen not only as the first step in repairing urban communities but in making good the depredations on the standard of living of the working class that have proceeded since the ending of the long boom in 1974. I do not believe, however, that this repair and development of the material fabric is on its own sufficient to bring about an improvement in the social fabric of urban communities. The state of disrepair is so profound that a specially directed effort needs to be made on the social fabric; we must also remember that the deterioration of urban communities as social systems took place during the 1960s and early 1970s at a time of relative prosperity, so there is little evidence for the view that material resources alone (no matter how essential they are on other grounds) will be enough to make our urban communities viable social systems. We must stop thinking of 'the community' merely as a milieu or context in which other systems operate and other activities occur; we must recognise it as a system in its own right (just like the individual, family, small group, organisation, and so on) and begin to ask what interventions are needed to sustain the functioning of that system.

When I say that 'a specially directed effort needs to be made on the social fabric' I am referring to a programme of social reconstruction whose primary goal is to restore and maintain communal coherence. But it would be wrong to suppose that this programme of social reconstruction was some marvellous package of new initiatives or formulae that could on application bring people together and open up creative roles for them. On the contrary, a programme of social reconstruction, whilst it will require additional resources to implement, involves nothing more or less than identification of the ways in which relations and roles are created, an awareness of those factors that hinder and facilitate this creative process, and an acknowledgement that some forms of outside intervention may be needed to sustain them. The value of conceiving what needs to be done as a programme is, first, that it is an acknowledgement that these outside interventions may be needed, and, secondly, that they must all be implemented in relation to each other, and in relation to processes naturally occurring in any community.

The creation of coherence is dependent on whether or not residents are willing and able to do certain things − chiefly, to take part in interactions and acts of association with neighbours, friends and relatives; to join sporting, religious, political, leisure and other organisations; and to get together with other residents in groups such as tenants' associations, action groups and neighbourhood care schemes to do something about particular problems. For residents, joining a group to oppose a rent increase or to do something about dampness needs no further justification than the specific benefits or improvements that are aimed at. Some of these specific needs and issues in the inner city − to do with housing, income, education, health, and so on − are so great and immediate that it would be pusillanimous to suggest that the struggle to meet these needs needed any further justification, or that the forms of association between residents required to achieve their specific aims were also instrumental in achieving other goals.

But politicians and social welfare professions in local and central government are obliged to take a broader view. The various forms of association between residents (and the promotion of those forms where they do not exist) must be regarded not only as necessary to achieve certain specific, limited goals but also as instrumental in helping to achieve through their cumulative impact the middle-range programme of communal coherence from which more general welfare and political benefits may flow. We must also ask how, if at all, these 'natural' processes of interaction and association need supporting: what, for example, are the resources that are needed such as shops, community centres, drop-in centres? How does the physical design of a community and the nature of streets and walkways affect how people interact with one another? The provision of resource centres in community work was the consequence of asking about the kinds of resources that community groups needed to sustain their activities. Neighbourhood care schemes (though doubtless motivated by a variety of politically and economically opportune considerations) are a consequence of the need to lend support to the interaction of neighbours in processes of mutual aid. These and a hundred and one initiatives in community work and related fields must be seen not simply as achieving certain specific tasks (important though these may be) but as contributions to the more substantial programme of improving communal coherence.

SUMMARY

There have been, particularly in community work, two major inhibitors of successful intervention. The first I refer to as *specific interventionism;* that is, interventions that are made to correct certain specific problems (for example, vandalism, low welfare rights take-up, dampness – the list is almost endless) without an adequate understanding of (*a*) wider issues that help to determine the nature of the communities being worked with, and (*b*) a developed strategy or programme of change within which specific interventions are a part and to whose objectives they are meant to contribute.

The second inhibitor is the presence of what might be called *diffuse causalism.* This is the tendency to offer explanations of the causes of specific local problems that are located at so many removes from the local that they offer no guidance about what might practically be done. Examples of this in community work are analyses that attribute local problems to the operation of multinational corporations; or the class system; or the lack of community spirit and identification; or the presence of societal alienation and anomie. Again, there are numerous examples of what are usually, though not necessarily, abstract statements that emanate in community work from a number of different political or moral viewpoints. The point is not that these statements are necessarily wrong but they do not help us to specify what interventions are needed in the local situation. When I say 'us' I again refer to those – such as councillors, residents, professional staff in welfare agencies – who have a responsibility to intervene and who can usually do so only within a limited range of authority and resources. Whilst it is correct to draw attention to the role of multinationals or the decline in community spirit, or the enervating effects of consumerism, these are variables which do not directly come within the influence, authority, or resources of those charged with welfare interventions.

The specific interventionists have their noses on the grindstone; the diffuse causalists their heads in the clouds. What each needs is some middle ground, both conceptual and operational. Interventions on specific community issues need (1) to be part of a programme or strategy that incorporates some middle-range thinking about social problems and their causality, and (2) to acknowledge that the solution of particular problems is not just a good in itself (but that is all it needs to be for the beneficiaries) but *also* a means in the achievement of a set of middle-range goals. Likewise, diffuse causalists need, in order to be helpful in the framing of welfare policy, middle-range theories that are made sense of by a higher level of analysis but which in turn make sense of welfare interventions. In the best of all possible worlds, we are looking for a way of anchoring both causal abstractions and specific interventions to variables that are within the authority and influence of those charged to intervene.

I have used the last two sections on franchisal and social development to suggest that this anchor is provided by the concepts of *political responsibility* and *communal coherence.* Political responsibility includes the ideas of political competence and significance; community coherence those of networks, attitudes and roles. I suggested in each section that community work is but one contribution to the promotion of political responsibility and communal coherence, and in the next chapter I shall try to say what distinguishes community work as an intervention within a wider programme to foster political responsibility and communal coherence.

I hope the outcome of this chapter is that we can say that community work has three major aspects:

● First, to help people take action on specific issues of importance to them. These issues will almost invariably involve the influence of resources, either those held, for example, by local authorities, or to be found within communities themselves. I have referred to this as the distributive aspect of community work. It is equivalent to the conventional category of 'product goals' familiar in community work literature. Influence on the distribution of resources will be terminal goals for the people involved, but I have argued that we should see them also as *instrumental* in contributing towards:

● secondly, the development of political responsibility; and

● thirdly, that of communal coherence.

These last two may also be seen as enlarging the conventional concern in community work with 'process goals'. These have been rather narrowly defined in the past, usually including no more than the development of specific skills and knowledge in individuals involved in community activities. The ideas of political responsibility and communal coherence extend our understanding of process goals to include changes in the political culture and social structures and processes of a community. It may be more precise to say that the involvement of community work in specific issues provides its distributive aspect whilst its contribution through this distributive work to a programme designed to foster political responsibility and communal coherence provides its developmental aspect. It is important in the continuing growth of community work that we understand that the form and content of this distributive aspect will change from period to period but that whatever these changes may be they will continue to contribute to community work's developmental aspect. The constancy of this development work is fundamental for it provides the continuing justification for pursuing a programme of community work through all the uncertainties and vicissitudes of its distributive function.

There are, of course, a number of difficulties and tensions between the distributive and developmental functions and they are not unlike some of the value and practical problems identified by Marshall in his article on democracy and welfare capitalism (1972). One of the basic considerations is that working on distributive goals will not in itself necessarily promote, for example, franchisal development. It may just as well work against it where direct action to secure resources may in the long term alienate elected members and narrow their vision about widening the process of government. This is not a criticism of direct action but a statement about the incompatibility that may occur at particular moments between achieving distributive and developmental goals. It might also be useful to note that it is not self-evident that skills and networks developed around self-help and mutual support are any the less relevant or effective towards achieving developmental goals than those acquired in more political negotiations about goods, services and incomes.

Reports such as Seebohm and, to a lesser extent, the two sponsored by the Gulbenkian Foundation served to emphasise community work's distributive functions; this was reinforced by the deployment of large numbers of community workers within social services and youth work departments, and the position that each came to have in promoting basic training opportunities in community work. The perception of community work by employers of community workers was, naturally enough, largely confined to its distributive aspects, and this gave rise to the phenomenon of specific interventionism that I described earlier. There was amongst community workers, however, some understanding of the development functions of the occupation, though these were often partial and limited, confined to vague principles to do with participation, or interwoven in such a way with expressions of their own political preferences and choices that their importance was undermined. Some of these political preferences were articulated in such a way (for example, 'shifting resources towards the deprived') that they had much in common with the distributive concerns of agencies and local people themselves.

Few of us understood the contribution of community work to social development, and the particular importance of strengthening communal coherence and the viability of communities as social systems. We were as caught up as other workers in the 'people-professions', in the idea of welfare as a system of standards and services to be applied from the 'outside' by professional workers to units in the population. This was particularly ironic because community work itself fulfils its welfare or distributive functions through facilitating self-initiated collective action, and thus models alternative concepts of welfare that are congruent with the aims of social development.

When employing agencies and local people assess the credibility of community work as a social intervention they will naturally give much importance to its effectiveness in achieving its distributive goals: the residents of an area want something done about a problem they experience. This is a real difficulty for community work: in periods when resources are plentiful it is easy to forget developmental functions as groups go all out for what they can get and may desperately need in their neighbourhoods. When resources are scarce, and people may be reluctant to get involved in collective action, distributive goals are harder to achieve. In either case, it is important to remember that distributive issues are *also* democratic issues, even though they may not be perceived as such. For example, collective action over motorways, planning, housing conditions, and so forth, is an expression of discontent with the paternalism and authoritarianism of much local government, with the size and power of welfare bureaucracies and with the limited opportunities for people to participate in crucial decisions about their well-being. When people protest or organise to provide services they are not simply to be seen as expressing particular political or welfare preferences; they are, more fundamentally, actors in a process of extending (albeit incrementally and cumulatively) the assumptions and practices of democratic government, as well as their own capabilities to participate in it. In the first half of the 1970s resources were relatively plentiful, and local authorities were able to accede to the requests of action groups simply as if they were wholly distributive matters. The erosion of local authority resources and power in the 1980s has helped to highlight the democratic content of the needs and demands expressed by local groups (that is, a group complaining about an estate's repair services is at the same time expressing something of what it feels to be the relationship between itself and its constituents on the one hand, and officers and elected members of the local state on the other), and this helps to explain the interest in some local authorities for decentralised and more accountable service.

In periods where community work's distributive function is being realised as much through social planning and community organisation as working in neighbourhoods it may be extremely difficult to see the importance of this work for franchisal and social development. Part of the risk of incorporation that this agency-based work entails is that workers will lose their intellectual grasp on the wider, more strategic rationale for their work, and activities like social planning will become reduced to a form of organisational tinkering. The distributive side of social planning and community organisation also poses other questions about democratic and social development. Are proposals, for instance, about the decentralisation of services to be welcomed because they have the potential to support participative democratic practices through cutting bureaucracies down to size and making services more amenable to local influence or control? Or are such proposals a threat to certain democratic values because localised services provide the state with a more effective means of surveillance? These few examples suggest that many aspects of our work (and that of other workers in related professions) that are too often evaluated only on distributive or welfare criteria (or those of management and efficiency) can have a benign or adverse effect both on the ability of our democratic practices to evolve and on the viability of our communities as social systems.

3 The Contribution of Community Work

One of the purposes of the last two chapters was to provide a number of anchor points for an understanding of community work. One such point was an historical appreciation of the emergence of community work as an occupation, and a second was to see community work within franchisal and social development. It was argued that helping people to influence the distribution of resources was to be valued as a way of promoting political responsibility and communal coherence; these provide community work with a middle-range programme through which many of the specific interventions that are carried out as part of the distributive function are given a wider significance. I also suggested that the developmental function of community work could be seen as a constant that survived the inevitable changes in the form and content of the occupation's distributive function.

This chapter will try to show the particular ways in which community work contributes both distributively and developmentally, and to indicate those features of community work that, broadly taken, can be said to distinguish it from other interventions. I do not wish to suggest that in the past various forms of community work and other interventions have been purposefully planned within a set of strategies. That would be nonsense, for much of the criticism of our interventions in the past is that they have not been so conceived. But it may be possible to identify some approaches that have been pursued independently of each other, and within which specific interventions have been carried out largely without reference to each other; and that the cumulative effect of these discrete and usually unco-ordinated efforts has been some influence on the distribution of resources and on political responsibility and communal coherence.

Our experience in the last two decades indicates that community work's distributive and developmental functions have been part of five principal approaches.[1] These are:

Community Action
Community Development
Social Planning
Community Organisation
Service Extension

Activity within each of these has been implemented by some practitioners as their primary task, by others such as clergy, doctors and social workers as a secondary function and by a variety of individuals acting for themselves or as members of a range of political and social groups. On the other hand, it is clear that some activity has been naturally occurring, and this is most evident in the spontaneous participation of people within community action and community development. These five approaches are much broader than community work, and each includes elements of the other; this is particularly true of service extension.

Identifying these five approaches is essentially a way in which we can analyse situations and think about action. It is not suggested that the diverse number of groups and individuals within each approach necessarily conceived of their work in this way, or that there was coherence or homogeneity within each approach. They are only a way of categorising certain methods and activities for the purpose of analysis and discusssion. They are perhaps too broad to be called strategies, a point made by one correspondent who argued that

> Different objectives may be involved and the activities may be working against each other. Nor do they necessarily contribute to the distributive and developmental functions to which you refer. They may be hindering them! They are only strategies in the weak and very general sense that they make certain assumptions or tend towards certain end states. They would only become strategies if the ends and means were much more closely specified.

The use of the word 'strategies' is more helpful in reminding us that in the future community work and other initiatives in these approaches might be more programmatically conceived and implemented.

It has been common in the past to say that these five approaches form the strands that make up community work; this may have been muddle-headed. The correct relationship is that community work is a contribution to each of these approaches and, perhaps far more importantly, we need to be more aware of the range of other contributions that are possible and desirable, and whose value may have been obscured by the attention given to community work. These other contributions have come from related occupations such as social work, adult education, planning, public health, and so on, where individuals and groups have experimented with new 'community-based' services. The work of people in advice centres, community arts, training sessions for local people, community relations, organising volunteers, and so on, are further examples. These innovations have had their own specific goals but we must also see them as a contribution to one or more of the above approaches. When we see that these initiatives are really related to these five approaches then we relieve their practitioners of the conceptual and semantic contortions into which they have entered in the 1970s in trying to establish they were doing some kind of community work. Terms like 'community work orientation to health care' or 'community work planner or adult educator' are examples; it is less confusing to accept that these and other people are not doing community work (which we define later as a specific sort of intervention) but are contributing alongside community workers (with whom they may have much in common in terms of values and methods of work) to the five approaches that I have identified. These contributions are to be given value in their own right and are not to be treated as some variant of community work. (Just as the word 'hoover' has become adopted as a name for vacuum cleaners, whatever their brand name, so 'community work' has been used to label most of the interventions that have contributed to these five approaches, even though it is only one of them.)

This way of looking at things turns on its head the conventional proposition (established firmly in British community work by the Gulbenkian reports) that community work consists of community action, community development, social planning and community organisation, or that these are strands of community work. It seems more accurate and helpful to accept that community work is an intervention which is only one aspect of the five approaches, which may be described in the following way. (I rely here on a paper by Patrick Sills given at the Volunteer Centre in 1980.)

Community Action

This focuses on the organisation of those adversely affected both by decisions, or non-decisions, of public and private bodies and by more general structural characteristics of society. The strategy aims to promote collective action to challenge established socio-political and economic structures and processes, to explore and explain the power realities of people's situations and, through this twin-pronged approach, to develop both critical perspectives of the status quo and alternative bases of power and action. Community action is characterised by: (1) relatively militant attempts at influence by both individuals and federated groups; (2) particular emphasis on links between community and industry based analysis and action (through, for example, trade union councils and campaigns to prevent closure of plants); (3) exploration and interpretation of socio-economic trends in society adversely affecting communities, dissemination of this knowledge to a wide range of activists, the development of collective awareness of the forces underlying such trends and, long term, the radical conscientisation of working-class people; and (4) civil disobedience or direct action like squatting and occupations.

Community Development

The community development strategy emphasises self-help, mutual support, the building up of neighbourhood integration, the development of neighbourhood capacities for problem-solving and self-representation, and the promotion of collective action to bring a community's preferences to the attention of political decision-makers. The strategy has three main sub-types: (1) the promotion and maintenance of mutual support networks, for example, neighbourhood care schemes and elderly people's self-organised clubs; (2) collective self-help in providing material amenities or benefits, for example, the building of a community centre, as in many developing countries, ethnic self-help groups, food co-operatives and credit unions; and (3) the organisation of influence, often involving conflict strategies, on resource-allocating bodies, for example, most tenants' associations and neighbourhood-based action groups most of the time.

Social Planning

This is concerned with the assessment of community needs and problems and the systematic planning of strategies for meeting them. Social planning comprises the analysis of social conditions, social policies and agency services; the setting of goals and priorities; the design of service programmes and the mobilisation of appropriate resources; and the implementation and evaluation of services and programmes. It is concerned with intervening at the level of organisations and institutions, and much of its focus is the well-being of aggregates or segments of a population. Social planning methods emphasise both rational and technical procedures as well as political ones. For example, needs, problems and resources may be explored through surveys using social science-based questionnaire and interview techniques, and through consultation with people likely to be affected, their representatives, or organisations which speak on their behalf. This may involve participative mechanisms like community health councils, planning inquiries and public meetings arranged by the community planning agencies. It is intended that such inquiries and consultations will elicit priorities among problems and suggest preferred solutions; it tends to be assumed that such knowledge will then be rationally converted into enlightened political decision-making.

Community Organisation

This involves the collaboration of separate community or welfare agencies, with or without the additional participation of statutory authorities, in the promotion of joint initiatives. These tend to be service-oriented, but are frequently both pioneering and designed as projects which demonstrate both the degree and kind of existing needs and the value of a particular approach to their solution. In the case of voluntary organisations, the joint bodies perform what Kramer has called the vanguard role, to innovate, pioneer, experiment and demonstrate programmes which may eventually be taken over by government (1979). Examples of community organisation structures are councils of voluntary service and community relations councils, but the approach is also adopted on ad hoc projects, at neighbourhood levels, in the form of alliances and federations, and between departments or sections of statutory agencies.

Service Extension

This strategy seeks to extend agency operations and services by making them more relevant and accessible. This includes extending services into the community, giving these services and the staff who are responsible for them a physical presence in a neighbourhood. Most of the major professions have extended their services in this way during the 1970s, and we have seen the development, for instance, of community medicine, community education, community-based social work and the emergence of multi-service or multi-department centres ('mini town halls') in local communities. Besides the physical decentralisation of facilities, service extension encompasses an interest in more accountability to consumers, the use of indigenous resources and a desire to view social problems on an aggregative as well as on an individual basis. The motives for service extension are quite diverse, and often not sufficiently differentiated, ranging from an interest in more efficient service delivery to various ideological commitments, for example, to demunicipalise welfare, to enhance community control, to reinvigorate political systems and, influenced by Schumacherian ideals, to reduce centralised and bureaucratic structures.

Community work's distributive function involves these approaches, and it is likely to be effective in achieving substantial progress in its developmental function only if they are implemented together and in relation to each other. Yet in the United Kingdom there have been attempts to suggest that one approach is more effective, or 'proper', than others. Community action has been preoccupied with wrestling over resources that have been largely to do with the production, distribution and consumption of goods and services, and with income maintenance. Much of it has been informed by short-term political thinking that has been confined to reflections on combative or liberating conflicts with the state over resources, with little attention (except within some sections of the left in community work) to the more fundamental and long-term issues to do with political responsibility and communal coherence. Community development, too, has been largely concerned with welfare resources and that part of it has been despised that sought to meet welfare needs, not only through the state but also through local forms of self-help and co-operation. Until the influence of socialist feminism in the late 1970s, there had been little thought about how such networks are relevant to political responsibility and communal coherence. Social planning and community organisation, too, have been regarded with suspicion, and their utility as strategies has been appraised only in relation to, first, community work's distributive function (and then rather poorly at that) and, secondly, the building of federations of groups and other interests. Although community workers have a part to play (both as specialists and as consultants to other staff) in implementing policies of service extension, they have, on the whole, not been involved either in the practice of, or the thinking about, service extension. The lead here has been taken by other fields – notably by academics in social work and social policy and by councillors in some socialist local authorities. There has been no one (with the possible exceptions of Peter Beresford and Aryeh Leissner) associated with community work practice or teaching who has contributed publicly to discussion about alternative structures and services for such fields as social welfare, education and health care.

It is not suggested that these five approaches comprehensively define all the activities that have occurred in relation either to distributive goals, or to franchisal and social development. Neither is it the case that each approach predicts a particular outcome. For example, the outcome of a change in an agency's services (for example, making them more relevant or accessible to users) may be achieved just as well through community action or development as through community organisation or social planning. Likewise, the work of a neighbourhood group to analyse employment patterns in a region, and consider alternative sources of work, may be as much community action or development as social planning.

Not all activities within these approaches will count as community work. Developing mutual aid networks, forms of direct action over resources, planning and co-ordinative mechanisms between agencies will count as community work only if the work is done in a certain way. It is especially inappropriate to claim that social planning and community organisation are per se community work, because there are people and agencies involved in those activities who have quite different methods to those that would be adopted by community workers. Work with groups of agency staff must be no less informed by certain salient principles than work with neighbourhood residents; that would be the distinctive contribution of community work to community organisation and planning. We must also be clear that a distinguishing mark of community workers and others in these two areas is not just the principles by which they work but also the concern to promote political responsibility and communal coherence. Thus the community worker will be working with agencies to improve the quality of services, and whilst this improvement will be the end goal for the agency and its customers, the worker will also be concerned that such improvements do as much as they can to support, rather than undermine, political responsibility and communal coherence. The question that faces each of us in local and central government, in various professions and organisations, is: how can we carry out our work in a way that better supports aspects of franchisal and social development?

This discussion of social planning and community organisation is intended to emphasise the point that initiatives and practical work undertaken within each of the five approaches can be realised through means other than community work methods and community workers. This fact (which is as evident in community action and community development where there has been considerable activity which has not been supported by community workers) was appreciated by du Sautoy in 1966 in the *Community Development Journal:*

> It should be remembered that there is much very useful work in the development of communities which is not community development in the more precise current use of the term − and a certain amount of work called 'community development' which isn't.

Community workers must come to realise that they are not just doing community work, helping people to make material and educational improvements, but they are also contributing to the five approaches, which are much broader than community work, and potentially of far greater significance, particularly in the development of political responsibility and communal coherence.

The point that community work is only one contribution is conveyed in Figure 3.1. These contributions to the five approaches are given only as examples and, of course, the diagram does not distinguish between actions and activities which contribute towards development and those that hinder it; it is always open to question whether a particular activity within, say, social work or social movements contributes to development. It is not a complete description and the task remains to give a further picture of alternatives that developed in the 1970s and to suggest what other interventions, besides community work, might become important in the 1980s. Ideas and innovations from social work and adult education, for example, must be analysed not just in terms of their relationship to community work but in their contribution, if

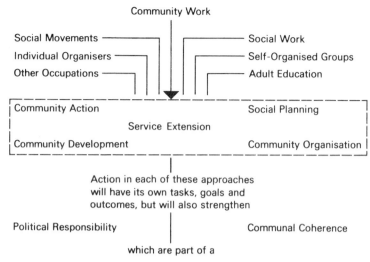

Figure 3.1 Community work and the five approaches.

any, to the five approaches and thus to the promotion of political responsibility and communal coherence. In addition to asking what are the other activities within the five approaches besides that of community work, we should also inquire about the relative efficacy of community work and its costs and benefits compared with other interventions.

The way in which community workers intervene is different and requires particular skills and knowledge of the worker. But whether organising a group to take part in a rent strike or engaged in some form of community development, an objective that will be, or should be, held in common is the strengthening of political responsibility and the extension of networks and opportunities to carry out various roles and functions. The value of the contribution to political responsibility and communal coherence will depend on the extent to which resources are committed programmatically; the single community worker working alone on a high-rise estate in developing a small tenants' organisation is unlikely to make much impact on political responsibility and communal coherence unless, at the same time, there are other initiatives being taken on the estate to create other opportunities for tenant interaction, identification and the fulfilment of roles.

The realisation that the raison d'être of community work is its contribution to the five approaches relieves the occupation of several self-inflicted burdens and expectations. The development of responsibility and coherence provides the deeper meaning and rationale for the 'small realities' of community work practice; it provides, too, a bridge between this practice and grander ideals and theories concerned with social justice and equity. When we see community work as just a part of the five approaches, we have a new flavour to the old chestnut of whether it is a profession or social movement, or, if it is both, which of these two attributes is in the ascendant at any particular point in its development. Community work is an intervention (to be defined later); its practitioners form an occupation, and whether that occupation becomes a profession, and what kind of profession, is an issue that will become clearer in time. Many social movements have influenced its growth and development, and their members have much in common with community workers. These social movements, as well as the work of unaffiliated working-class activists and middle-class reticulists, are better seen not as a 'part' of community work, or a definition of it, but as making their own distinctive contribution to the five approaches – though naturally enough such movements will have their own specific ends and may not be willing to conceive of their activities within the broader framework of political responsibility and communal coherence. The point is not whether community work is a social movement or profession but that the five approaches involve social movements, as well as some professions, and some occupations such as community work.

It is also a relief no longer to be burdened with our own and other people's expectations that community work will 'crack the urban problem' – as well, of course, as eliminate poverty and disadvantage, restore civil and welfare rights and reform local and central government! Community work can on its own do no more to solve the urban crisis than any other single intervention; but in combination with these interventions, and accompanied by attention to the material fabric of communities, it can make a crucial contribution to the five approaches. I say a crucial, if only one, contribution because as an intervention community work has the potential to be the most salient of all the interventions needed as part of a programme of social and political reconstruction. Community work will be defined later in this chapter but now I want only to say briefly why it can play a major part in the improvement of political responsibility and communal coherence. It is, first, an intervention carried out on a full-time basis, and where the goals of bringing people together and extending their capabilities in a variety of roles is a main-line concern. Its values stress the autonomy and self-direction of the group; because of this and the way the worker handles his relationship with the group, involvement for participants may be a process of growth and learning in a number of different roles and functions. Other values emphasise the accountability of such groups to their constituencies, the need to ensure that they are participative in their working and the identification of problems as being collectively experienced; these and other values are central to the concern of strengthening networks and relations, and of building up an interest in, and identification with, other people in the community. The system with which community work is primarily concerned is 'the community' whilst other occupations who contribute to the five approaches are primarily focused on other systems such as the individual, family and small group, though, of course, they need to be aware and knowledgeable about how these systems are affected by the community of which they are a part. This primary concern with 'the community' as a social system implies that community work might be expected to have (and to be able to formulate) an overview of how, in a particular community, various interventions combine in implementation of the five approaches. This can be put another way: of the contributions, we may see community work as *primus inter pares,* not least because it is a specialist intervention in preparation for which we are becoming better able to provide proper training. As a consequence its contribution is not confined to carrying out its own specialist interventions, but also, first, in influencing other occupations, groups, individuals, movements, and so forth, to carry out their remits in ways that support political responsibility and communal coherence; and, secondly, in being able to formulate how all these contributions cohere within a purposeful programme of development.

A factor that confirms community work's special position within this programme is the fact that it alone will contribute to all of the approaches. Other contributions will be *partial* in the sense that they will feed into one or perhaps two of the approaches but not all of them. A social movement, for example, is likely to confine itself to community action. Such contributions will be partial as the result of a number of factors including ideology, expertise, preference, priorities, resources and remit. As an occupation, community work has the remit to contribute to each of the five approaches, though to date it has not contributed equally to each or with the same degree of expertise and interest.

What I have written about community work's own specific goals (for example, organising tenants into an association) as well as its contribution to the five approaches may seem strange to a community worker working on her own on an estate in north London, or an overspill development outside Huddersfield. The reality for such workers is likely to be that of working in isolation, facing indifference or hostility from other professions in the area (who certainly show no sign of being part of a developmental programme to enhance political responsibility and communal coherence) and where it is difficult enough to convince oneself and residents that it is worthwhile organising a summer festival let alone having a vision about anything broader. It is equally likely that she feels isolated from other practitioners in the occupation, and she may have no sense of being with them as part of an occupation that, despite the many local variations of goals and methods and the diversity of values and attitudes, is engaged in a common endeavour. I say 'despite' but it is also the case that it is precisely the heterogeneity of the occupation that allows it to contribute to each of the five approaches; if community work here were to become a narrowly based practice this would be to the detriment of its ability to make this all-round contribution. The value of this heterogeneity is, however, limited at present by two factors: first, different interests or theories in community work strain against each other, as each asserts the merits of its views or way of working; and secondly, the cumulative impact of the work done by community workers and others will be more haphazard than purposeful, more diffuse than concentrated, unless we develop a conception (that is operationalised in each local area as a programme of interventions) of how all the various elements in community work and other occupations and movements combine to effect improvements that are far broader and more important than the specific goals of each particular intervention.

The isolation of workers, and the low sense of occupational identification and attachment, must be put right through better forms of local and regional support, and the assignment of community workers to community work teams or to multi-disciplinary ones. But the other side of the feeling of isolation is a degree of autonomy and self-direction for the community worker. The framework provided by the five approaches, and the local programmes of intervention that they may give rise to, are not necessarily incompatible with this degree of autonomy, though team working does inevitably impose its own disciplines. The diversity amongst community workers in their goals and priorities must be sustained, and it will be inevitable that some workers will be committed only to their own specific agenda, whilst others will appreciate the broader framework provided by the ideas of political responsibility and communal coherence. The important matter is not that any worker or project agrees with the view of community work as but one contributor to the five approaches (or, if they do agree, that they necessarily think of their day-to-day practice along these lines) but that this view informs the thinking of those, at local and central levels, who make policy in relation to community work, and allocate resources. Put more broadly, there needs to be greater awareness of how the various occupations, social movements and administrative developments (for example, patch systems) can be put to greater effect in fostering political responsibility and communal coherence, at the same time that they seek to achieve the goals for which they were designed.

This is not to say that any particular piece of community work must be directed towards all five approaches. The idea that community work is a contribution to these refers to the occupation as a whole; individual workers and projects will be involved in one of the approaches more than the others, or will mix, say, community action and/or community development with social planning. Which of the five approaches is emphasised is likely to vary with time, with the views of residents and the authorities, and with the interests and mandate of workers and agencies. The responsibilities and opportunities given to community work will likewise vary. It is probably the case that if any impact is to be made on the dysfunctioning of communities then all five approaches must be implemented in a long-term programme that combines (with resources for the material fabric) community work and other initiatives.

DEFINING COMMUNITY WORK

In this last section, I shall try to put forward the basis of a working definition of community work. Definitions are problematic, and a word of caution is needed. The consequence of a definition is to include some, and exclude other, activities and people, and to win acceptance and resources for those that fall within the boundaries of the definition. As such, it is not purely a rational, analytic exercise but one that is also informed by values and vested interests, and is in its consequences an attempt to exercise influence. Definitions, too, are prone to rigidify a field of activity, unless they are exposed to continuing revision; such a hardening of boundaries may not be possible in such a fluid field as community work, nor desirable in a young occupation that has a good way to go before establishing an empirical and theoretical base that is secure enough to support generalisations about its practitioners, their purposes and their roles. Openness of definition and flexibility in practice may be necessary to encourage the development of community work, particularly because it is an activity that has to be sensitive to the opportunities of the moment and the varying needs of people and organisations. On the other hand, concrete definitions of tasks, skills and knowledge are equally necessary if community work is to have the credibility, the resources and the trust to seize opportunities offered by residents and agencies.

Perhaps the least satisfactory aspect of the process of definition is that it tends to reduce complex ideas, and to lose the variety and richness of the activities concerned. This is a particularly difficult problem in community work, not least because it has its points of origin and development in a number of different parts of the social welfare and educational services, as well as in a heterogeneous range of social and political movements, each with their own philosophies and goals. It is difficult to think there is an 'essence' or a core at the heart of community work which, once identified, could be seen to transcend the particular associations with other occupations and movements.

Whilst this book is concerned with community work only as an intervention/occupation, it has a number of other and wider meanings for people engaged in its practice and training. First, it has been identified as an *attitude* that defines a more participative and egalitarian set of relations between the givers of services and those who consume them. It is an attitude that moves decisions about resources out of the realm of administrative imposition and professional expertise.

Secondly, community work is associated with a particular kind of *critique* of existing arrangements of power and resources; it is often used as a shorthand for 'radical', though the elastic meaning of that word in community work often renders it useless as an analytic concept.

Thirdly, it is used as a *principle* of service delivery; here the phrase suggests a particular way of organising services that makes them more local, relevant, accessible and accountable to their users and the community.

Fourthly, community work is used as a *frame of reference* and identification for a broad alliance of like-minded people. These will include community workers but also others (for example, planners, residential workers) who do not use community work as a method of intervention but subscribe to the broad radical church in community work and thus prefer to identify with community work rather than with their own profession. Some of these will have been influenced by the permeation of their own professional training by community work ideas, and others by their involvement in social movements or political parties. Their activities play an important part in the much larger process of development, to which community work as an intervention is only one contribution.

And lastly, community work has been used to describe a *work-site*. Professionals doing their job from a community base (rather than an office, for example) have been described as community workers by virtue of being 'in' the community, though what they do may have very little in common with community work as an intervention.

The remit of this study has been to review community work as an occupation, which derives its legitimacy from the particularity and the expertise of its interventions. What can we say about it that helps to distinguish its contribution as an intervention from those made by other occupations, social movements and community activists? We need to look for some things held in common by those who practise community work, but it is not sufficient to accept what people *say* or *think* in common because such contingent and evolving matters can hardly be the basis for defining an intervention. The ingredients that are sufficiently dispersed amongst practitioners to bring them all together as practitioners of a particular kind of intervention must be found essentially in their practice rather than in their visions and ambitions.

An explanation of community work as an intervention must also be able to relate to the kinds of goals described for community work within the processes of franchisal and social development. The task of promoting political responsibility and communal coherence are the strategic goals or programme for community work, and are not part of its definition as an intervention. The relation of the intervention to these broader based strategies within society necessitates a degree of comprehensiveness in a definition; but it must retain some concreteness, and avoid being so elastic that the definition loses its meaning and usefulness.

Any attempt at definition must also recognise that community work is an evolving practice; a definition must, therefore, be not only necessarily 'incomplete' but be open enough to allow for modification as community work develops in its practice, research and theory. Whilst definitions will be influenced by the current moment, they should also be able to convey the 'enduring factors' of the practice – factors that will be modified and shaped by the current moment, will reappear in different guises from era to era (for example, the concern with learning changes its vocabulary from period to period, and we now talk of 'consciousness-raising') but will be essentially the same. As we progress, new elements will enter the definition, as we learn more about community work, and as we are able better to appreciate the past, and refine our perceptions and concepts.

It is well to say what community work is not, since there are so many misconceptions that are fostered by the proliferation of the word 'community'. David Jones has helpfully suggested that

People often talk as though any kind of helping activity or service is community work. But an activity is even more likely to be considered community work if it is provided off the agency's premises; if the enterprise is under non-statutory auspices; and if it involves volunteers, especially young volunteers who are more 'community' than other volunteers.

Much of what is identified as community work in this loose way may be very desirable in its own right and, in appropriate circumstances, community work may have these characteristics. But to use the term community work so broadly is pointless . . .

Caring for people in the community as contrasted with institutional care is not community work. Community work can make an important contribution to the development of community care services just as it can to the development of residential care. Thus, while development of community care services logically requires the use of community work methods, community care and community work are not synonymous.

In recent years, social workers and others working in the social services have become increasingly concerned with collective social problems and questions of social policy. As citizens they have become involved in social action on matters affecting them personally; as employees they have become concerned with modifying and developing the practices and policies of the agencies in which they work; as members of professional associations they are attempting to make an impact on social policy.

These are all perfectly appropriate and desirable activities and relevant to the consideration of community work. But to regard them as the equivalent of community work merely confuses the matter.

People in a variety of positions − from publicans to policemen, from company directors to caretakers − may on occasion, either intentionally or spontaneously, act as community change agents. Whilst this activity may be socially useful and desirable, it is not the case that such activity makes them community workers. (1977)

Community service, community arts and education, community relations and community-based service provision are not synonymous with community work, though they may often employ community workers or make some use of community work values and techniques. Those 'working in the community', offering locally-relevant services and subscribing to many of the goals of community work, are not necessarily doing community work, which is a particular kind of intervention different from that made by the community-based and community-minded teacher, social worker, policeman, or what have you. For example, the fact that an adult education centre has staff who subscribe to modes of analysis and values associated with community work and, further, ensure that the centre is not operating traditionally or like other centres, does not make those staff community workers or the centre outside the genus of adult education centres. We must find a more appropriate label for them, and resist the temptation to label them 'community work' simply because their ways of thinking and service are outside the main-stream of their own occupation. The indiscriminate use of the word 'community' has confused the particularity of quite different kinds of interventions, is only broadly descriptive and does not give any precise indication of the entity with which the worker is concerned nor to the particular nature of his intervention.

Community work is not synonymous with community politics, although it is concerned to intervene in the process of community politics to start and sustain groups and relationships where this does not appear to be happening spontaneously. Community work is not a social movement, though it has been influenced by many and its practitioners will continue to be in sympathy with many movements, and to support them locally where this is appropriate. The processes, methods, techniques and objectives of social movement organisers have much in common with community work; indeed, in some cases it is hard to draw any sharp dividing line. But, as David Jones has argued, 'for the purposes of discussion it is necessary to make a distinction, not in terms of the desirability of the activities, but in terms of the position of the worker in relation to the issues involved and to the people being worked with'. He suggests that 'the movement organiser is personally committed to the specific objectives being pursued, adopts a leadership position in relation to those being worked with and sees the individuals and groups being organised as instrumental to his own or his group's purposes'. The community worker, on the other hand, is not necessarily personally committed to the specific objectives, adopts an enabling, supporting role rather than a leadership one and sees the individuals and groups being organised as ends rather than means.

There are a number of fallacies that inhibit an adequate definition of community work, and it is perhaps just as well to get these out of the way. These are:

Athene Fallacy

This is the view (first mentioned by Peter Baldock) that community work 'sprang into being fully grown . . . All of a sudden there was a lot of it about.' The error of this view is that it ignores the process of development of community work; it leads one to believe that community work is defined by the activities and interests only of the era in which it suddenly sprang into public view; and leads one to commit the:

Temporal Fallacy

This fallacy occurs when viewing community work only as the product of a particular historical period. It would be wrong, for example, to suppose that community development has meaning only in relation to its use in the colonies or in relation to leisure activities in New Towns. The process and utility of community development is far wider than any particular historical application. Those who commit this fallacy confuse substance with application at particular moments in time. The activities and issues of the early 1970s do not define community work, any more than it was defined by the quite different events and climate of the early 1960s. We must keep open the possibility that such orthodoxies as the 'community action model' were evolved from the special circumstances of the 1970s and, as one correspondent put it, 'were infected by the ideological pre-occupations of groups of community workers at that time'. These orthodoxies are thus contingent matters.

Imperial Fallacy

This happens when particular institutions or professions (for example, social work) or specific strategies (such as community development) strive for and appear to take over community work and to own it. Community work then becomes wrongly identified with those institutions, and the fallacy is to suppose that community work is equivalent to those institutions and their priorities. It is fallacious to suggest that community work is synonymous with the use it is put to by particular agencies. A definition of community work should establish only what kind of intervention it is; the use to which that intervention will be put will then be affected by 'the climate of the time' but essentially by local needs, and the priorities and resources of group, worker and his agency. It has much in common with the *overlap fallacy,* where community work's intimate and perhaps inseparable association with other areas of activity (for example, adult education), and a corresponding overlap in knowledge, skills and goals, leads one fallaciously to suppose that community work and those areas are one and the same thing. A variation of the imperial fallacy is the *articulation fallacy.* This occurs where community work is identified with a particular profession, merely because that profession happens to have available a readily understandable and, at the time, acceptable rationale for taking community work under its wing.

Partial Abstraction Fallacy

The fallacy is to define the whole process of community work by reference only to part of it. People abstract elements of community work and try to suggest they are the only ones.

Functional Area Fallacy

This is probably the most widespread fallacy in attempts to define community work. It arises from saying that community work consists of neighbourhood work, or agency development. These, of course, are the areas in which the activities of community work occur, and are not the activity itself. In much the same way, it is fallacious to suppose that community work is constituted by any or the sum of its particular objectives. Since these are determined by the issues of a particular time and place, they are liable to change, and thus provide no basis for defining community work.

Radical Fallacy

This fallacy is present when the view is put forward that anything progressive is community work, and further, that community workers must get involved or be associated with anything progressive. The corollary is that non-progressive work is not community work. It is quite fallacious to suggest that an activity is valid as community work only so long as it entails or promotes 'political' (usually with a sectarian meaning) thought and action, and this is also an aspect of the partial-abstraction fallacy.

Much attention is often given in definitions of community work to issues of goals and values, producing phrases such as 'to help people identify their needs, to form a group and work collectively to meet those needs'. This is, of course, a basic statement, but it does little to suggest precisely *how* the worker intervenes to help people identify their needs, and to work collectively on the issues they raise. Community work is known for the strongly held beliefs and values of its practitioners and theorists. Statements about values and political and moral commitments thrive in the community work literature and conferences. Rightly or wrongly community workers are identified with radical and progressive thought, a group committed to some notion of change. Behind the slogans and rhetoric, there is indeed a powerful caring amongst community workers about justice, equity and freedom, a strong identification with and commitment to those who suffer from disadvantage, oppression and powerlessness. Yet there is no one set of beliefs that most workers subscribe to, or which dominates community work thinking and practice. These beliefs are quite heterogeneous – community work is a broad church of radicals and dissenters.

It is possible to doubt whether values and beliefs should appear in a definition. They are contingent factors, and say more about community workers and the occupation than the *intervention* of community work. Whilst they may be useful to describe or explain the intervention, they must be used with caution to define it because:

- the range of beliefs in community work is so diverse; a statement to which everybody could subscribe could doubtless be formulated, but it would be so general and abstract that it would be pointless.
- most individuals change or refine their beliefs, and groups of people holding similar beliefs will also change as the population of community workers change. The values of workers in the 1970s will doubtless appear as inadequate to those of the late 1980s as those of earlier periods now appear to us.
- community work involves more than its community workers. It comprises those who fund, manage and train for the intervention, and the belief statements of its workers are only partial accounts of beliefs and values in community work.

This is not to deny the force of values amongst workers; on the contrary, community workers must retain their caring, commitment and engagement with the powerless and the poor. Community work is fundamentally concerned with politics, government and welfare; but political statements about these and community work that offer a particular analysis define the worker(s) and not the intervention. Adequate definition of the intervention must have some independence of the characteristics of the workers and the occupation, simply because these change and develop over time and with experience. Moreover, there is so much posturing in community work that beliefs and values take on an exaggerated tone; as such they lack reliability and credibility. Beliefs about society are powerful motivating factors for workers, they provide a powerhouse of energy in difficult working circumstances. What they do not provide is a satisfactory basis for the definition of the intervention.

Much the same can be said about role: it too is contingent on particular circumstances so that it cannot provide a secure definitional basis. Roles will vary with the historical circumstances of society and with the particular needs and interests of groups. Likewise, the use of particular tactics and strategies is contingent upon the circumstances of the time and issues.

Community work is a mode of intervention whose purpose is to start and sustain community and administrative activity where this has not happened spontaneously. It is a planned and conscious intervention; the worker's role and function is different, though not necessarily superior, to those of the resident or staff member in whose systems and processes the worker intervenes. The worker may be a complete outsider or a local resident who has taken on the job in a paid or unpaid capacity and has made the transition to a new role and function that is different from those of neighbours who occupy leadership or membership positions in the group. These facts about the difference in role, function (and responsibility for the work of the group) and the planned and conscious nature of the intervention help to explain why community work has developed as a specialist occupation, or public service function, with corresponding provisions for learning the skills and knowledge to do the work.

The definition of this intervention is best based on certain principles which can be applied to the work that people do, and which will determine whether or not it counts as community work or some other kind of intervention. This approach is one that was taken by the Accreditation Working Party of the London Council for Community Work Training. Their 1979 report says:

Applicants will have to satisfy the Unit that their experience has actually been with the use of community work methods. It is recognised that these methods can be found in a variety of work situations such as neighbourhood work, work with special groups, advice/neighbourhood work, liaison work in local authorities, outreach work, community action, etc. Not all an applicant's work experience either paid or unpaid will necessarily have employed community work methods. In order to select what is accreditable the Unit is guided by four sets of questions. The answer to these will determine whether the applicant is a community worker.

This report is helpful, not because the guidelines or principles used were necessarily correct or the only ones, but because its approach helps us to pick out those people doing community work who may not be called, or see themselves as, community workers, as well as those people who say they are community workers, identify with the goals and values of community work, but whose interventions are nothing of the sort.

The principles that are now put forward are done so tentatively, as a basis for discussion and elaboration. As one learns more from research and practice, they will be refined, and some may be discarded, and others added. The first step is to distinguish between *worker* and *group* aspects of the principles that guide community work interventions. The 'worker aspects' concern the characteristics and approach of the person to that work, whilst the 'group aspects' relate to the features of the group of people worked with. These principles are, on the whole, as relevant to defining community work's contribution to, say, social planning and community organisation (where the work might more often be with agency staff) as to neighbourhood work. However, some of the principles (for example, felt needs) may be less useful in understanding work with agency staff than with neighbourhood residents; certainly we need to be aware of some of the constraints upon agency staff that merit caution in applying these principles to our work with them. Community work, then, is direct face-to-face work with groups or agency staff, in line with the following considerations:

Group Aspects

(1) FELT NEEDS

The needs which people (whether resident or agency staff) want to work on are their own felt and expressed needs, both at the start of work and as they develop over time through success and increased confidence and awareness. Not only is the imposition of normative or professional definitions of need anathema to community work, but they are not likely to lead to involved and successful work by participants.

(2) PERSONAL RESPONSIBILITY

The commitment of community work is to people doing things for themselves and taking responsibility for them, and not having things done for them or to them. Participants determine their needs, priorities, goals and strategies, and manage the task and maintenance functions of the group. This includes the autonomy to dispense with the help of a worker, and to reject his/her advice and resources if this is seen as appropriate.

(3)   PERSONAL EXPERIENCE AND NEED

A group is made up of people who have experienced at first hand the problems which have led to the setting up of the group, and who stand to benefit from its work.

(4)   VOLUNTARY

Involvement is voluntary and not the requirement of legal or administrative rules.

(5)   CONSTITUENCY

The work will benefit a wider constituency than those actively involved in a group, and perhaps produce benefits for the wider community. In other words, the members of a group are not the only, or even the principal, beneficiaries of the action, and there is some contribution to the 'public good'.

Worker Aspects

These are mostly principles, some held in common with other occupations, which help to determine work with the kind of groups identified in the above section on 'group aspects'.

(1)   COLLECTIVISATION

A central requisite and skill area in community work is to be able to collectivise the problems that individuals may at the beginning perceive only as their own. To be able to see, and help others to appreciate, 'that not only Mrs Jones has problems with damp on this estate, but so do most tenants' is the obvious first step in forming a group and appreciating the potential of community, as opposed to individual, action on an issue. Community workers will, of course, support individuals in their group membership; community workers may also undertake advice and representation work for individuals, but this cannot count as a community work intervention, any more than can the community worker's administrative and office chores. Of course, work of this kind with individuals may be necessary as an important first step in helping people move into collective action; in helping people make this transition the worker may have to adopt roles and carry out tasks that do not in themselves count as a community work intervention, but which are crucial in establishing the base from which that intervention can be subsequently made.

The other important aspect of collectivisation is the bringing together, where appropriate, of groups with similar aims in order to achieve their common goals. This need not necessarily extend to building alliances and federations but, as the Association of Community Workers has suggested, might first involve creating unity between groups within the locality based on mutual respect around issues of common concern.

(2) PARTICIPATION

The community worker is interested in promoting participative forms of membership and decision-making, and to create a group climate and norms that especially facilitate the involvement of those who have had little opportunity to exercise leadership and responsibility.

(3) PARTNERSHIP

It cannot be denied that the community worker has a position of potential influence and domination in a group. But it is essential in the practice of community work that 'community workers should do all they can to break down hidden or open unequal power relationships between the people with whom they work and themselves' (Association of Community Workers, 1981c). The partnership or collegiate ethos in community work is also conveyed in such phrases as 'working with people and not for them' and 'start where people are at'. The worker does not seek to lead groups, or to use them to pursue his own ends, or to promote dependence by the group on his leadership and skills. The ACW attempt at definition is quite explicit on this point: Workers assist people to work on issues that the people define, they do not impose their own or agencies' agendas or ideologies, they always work to enable people to speak for themselves and generate their own leadership, and 'should not allow themselves to become, or be seen as, spokespeople or leaders for the community' (1981c).

The LCCWT paper defines this key aspect of partnership, not simply as the absence of statutory powers on the part of the worker, but as her ability to help the group reassess and reject her commitment to the group, to be accepting of the group's democratic control of her own activities in the group, and to be loyal to the group, that is, to give primacy of the claims of the group over those of the agency.

Partnership is, first, and foremost, an *attitude* on the part of the worker about how she structures her relations and assists people define and use her contribution to the work of a group. But the worker has to translate this attitude into practice; the ingredients of 'partnership practice' are clearly laid down in descriptions of role that stress facilitating, enabling and non-directiveness. Properly understood these roles are highly participatory; they have been misunderstood and much abused in recent years but they form a fundamental element of community work intervention.

(4)   PROCESS

Community work is an intervention which explicitly seeks to promote the confidence, skills, knowledge and consciousness of individuals who take part in group activities and action. It is an opportunity to learn certain civic and administrative skills, to develop personal confidence and ambitions and to understand better the factors that affect people's life situations. The previously discussed ideas of personal responsibility, self-determination and partnership are not just goals in their own right but means to ensure that group involvement provides opportunities for learning and development.

(5)   TASK

But community work is only concerned with groups of residents or staff who wish to achieve certain goals. As Pat Sills has written, it is necessary to give 'a deliberate emphasis on the pursuit of tasks in order to distinguish community work from group work, a term usually associated with therapeutic work directed at individuals through group processes' (1980). The emphasis on task together with the distribution of benefits to a constituency and wider community means that some work with therapeutic, growth and consciousness-raising groups is not (however valuable) community work; nor is work whose sole objective is to bring together agency staff to liaise and 'swap information'. The task element is concerned with achieving changes in the distribution of resources and/or building up social relationships and networks in a community. It is concerned, too, with establishing the status and influence of community interests in the process of government as described earlier in writing about community work's developmental functions.

(6)   PERSPECTIVE

Implicit in the emphasis on tasks is the characteristic emphasis of community work interventions on those aspects of a problem that 'lie outside the person'. These aspects are, first, the political and administrative arrangements (government and private enterprise) that determine the distribution of resources; and, secondly, the extent and quality of social relations and interventions in a community. Analysing the reasons for problems as external to the people experiencing them can and does produce a wide range of political/ideological positions in community work. These positions and the variants of them are, of course, only personal preferences and it is only what they have in common (that is, a perspective on the reasons for problems being 'outside the person') that is a defining characteristic of community work.

Secondly, it is implicit in the emphasis on 'process' that community work is concerned with the 'exercise, use and control of power' (CCETSW, 1974). It is concerned to help groups (whose members may be quite well off, though they are mostly groups whose members are deprived and disadvantaged in a number of ways) to assert their interests in decisions about resources, and to enter those interests in the process of government. The taking of responsibility for defining one's needs, and the learning of skills and confidence to meet group goals, is a process of empowerment, as is the building up of social relationships within a community and between different groups. Involvement in community activities helps people understand how power is differentially distributed in society, and community work helps those who are feeling powerless to exert some influence. This exercise of power may result in protest and conflict, but a good deal of its exercise is 'relatively undramatic and routine in nature'. Joining in the activities of a community group set on achieving a particular task is potentially a process of empowerment, and intervening in the process of elective and administrative politics is equally an opportunity for influencing the exercise of power.

The separation of process and task has been made only for the purposes of analysis; a central aspect of community work practice and theory is that process and task are interrelated. The development of learning and skills helps to give people a sense of power and achievement; but this also comes from obtaining specific, tangible improvements and in carrying out the tasks they have set themselves. Task and process are locked in a virtuous circle: when people are effective in community action they acquire a sense of their own ability and power, and enhance their understanding and competence. This helps to make them feel more confident, more positive about themselves, more capable. This in turn makes it more likely that they will engage in further community activity and thus improve their lot, and that of others.

The integration of learning and task achievement contains a paradox that is not adequately appreciated. The values of community workers, and the methods of their work, are towards collectivisation; this was discussed earlier and may be restated thus: the values and the instruments of change are essentially those that involve the egalitarianism, fraternity and potency of the collective. The primacy of the collective in community work has three aspects. First, community work is largely concerned with problems in their public or social aspects and is less interested in working with individuals' experience of these problems. It is concerned more with policy than with case, more with collective situations and benefits than with services to particular individuals or families who are in need. Secondly, if the beneficiaries of community action are a larger collective (a street, an estate, a neighbourhood) then, on the whole, benefits are not achieved through individual negotiations, petitioning, or protest. The emphasis in community work is on groups of people, whether residents and/or agency staff, taking action in order to secure benefits for a wider population. These first two points suggest that there is in community work a concern with both moral and methodological collectivism.

Thirdly, community work is concerned with participation and with a spirit and methods of working that 'include people in'. It thus stresses a collective approach to problem-solving and decision-making about needs, goals, priorities and programmes. This inclusive approach is as much apparent in work with agencies as with neighbourhood groups.

The paradox is that whilst collectivism is central both as a moral imperative and as a method, the concern in community work with learning and process necessarily gives an equally central position to the individual. Much attention has been given in British community work theory to the tasks of changing structures and institutions but much of community workers' practice is concerned with helping individuals to change. A good deal of time in practice is spent in working with individuals, extending their knowledge and skills, helping them to understand and work within group processes and supporting them as they experience changes in their self-image, sense of power and capacity to take on new responsibilities. What is important in helping to distinguish community work as an intervention is that these person-centred educational and, indeed, therapeutic, goals are integrated with a collective's goal to achieve specific changes in resources, structures and institutions.

The concern in community work with learning encompasses agency staff as well as local people in community groups. In practice, and in much of the theory, the first group have received little attention or priority. What follows applies as much to agency staff as to local people but it is written primarily about the latter.

Learning occurs primarily in people's capacities for *reflection, vision, planning* and *action*. In practice, learning occurs simultaneously in these areas, and we find they are interlocking and mutually supporting. Reflection, in the sense of an internal process of contemplation and reasoning, is a means through which people and groups become able to understand and articulate what impinges on their social, economic and political lives. Reflection of this kind may produce an understanding of how to intervene to affect these forces, and to predict, control and overcome them.

The community worker will work with people to develop a critical awareness of themselves in their local situation in respect of an issue around which a group is forming. Group members will come to grasp, first, a sense of their own marginality in the community and in society at large, and a linked understanding of the futility of individual efforts to achieve the goals they have in mind. Secondly, reflection produces an understanding of the dynamics of how decisions are made and institutional interests defended, and an appreciation that there are people and agencies who need to be changed in order to achieve something. Thirdly, there develops in reflection an understanding both of the varied potentials of people in a group, and the potential powerfulness of group action. Here, too, the individual begins to conceive of himself as part of a system acting with others for change, and to recognise new roles and responsibilities.

Reflection is part of the process through which local people achieve the changes in identity or self-image that are often fundamental to success in community work. Reflection should help individuals to give up defining themselves as powerless, and their own or neighbourhood situation as a constant, immutable given. There are, in principle, no limits to the objects that may be reflected upon, and eventually the community worker may find an awareness in individuals about wider issues in society.

Reflection enables people to understand the situations that limit them and to attempt to overcome them. *Vision* follows on from reflection – increased consciousness of me-in-this-situation can lead to a vision of me-in-another-situation in the future.

Effective action is contingent upon local people being able to conceive of themselves as 'new' people – a conception of themselves working at tasks, taking on roles and exercising skills and knowledge in ways previously unimaginable to them. The community worker's task is to facilitate people's ability to articulate a desired future state of affairs (such as better housing, a new playground), and then to work with them to realise it. The challenge facing the community worker, however, is that before and at the outset of people becoming organised, group members are often not visionary. They may perceive something is wrong, but often they do not know what they want to do by way of improving the situation, or how to go about it. The community worker's task, then, is to develop in people a capacity for visionary thought, to help them cross 'the frontier which separates being from being more'. The community worker will often be purposively catalytic in galvanising group members to cross the frontier. The worker can do this by using his own vision of a better world to inspire group members. Haggstrom has written beautifully of the mobilising effects of the community worker's vision:

> An organiser must not only perceive how people are, but it is also essential that he be unrealistic in that he perceives people as they can be. Noting what is possible, the organiser projects this possibility and moves people to accept it and to seek to realise it. The organiser helps people to develop and live in an alternative reality in which their image of themselves and their abilities is enhanced . . . People are moved to accept the new world of which they catch a glimpse because it appears to be attainable in practice and intrinsically superior to the world in which they have been living. (1970)

But moving people to accept this new world requires at least three things of the community worker: first, that he works with group members to develop an appropriate organisation and decision-making process; secondly, that he works with the group to transform visionary statements into operational goals; and thirdly, that he helps people to see leadership as located not just in himself but in themselves and other members of the group.

As the vision establishes itself the means to realise it become important concerns to the members, and the community worker seeks to stimulate an awareness in the group about the need for *planning* – the need for conscious, intentional and purposeful decisions and activities that take the group forward to the achievement of its goals. Daniel Schler (1970) has suggested that people need to acquire and improve their skills in:

- rational goal-setting, so that the activities of individual members are more likely to be focused on collectively agreed tasks and targets;
- identifying, acquiring and planning the use of resources in and outside the group so as best to achieve the goals of the group;
- rational processes of dividing up labour, in order, for instance, that no one person becomes overburdened with the group's work;
- administering and co-ordinating the various subgroups and activities within the ambit of the neighbourhood group.

Planning also involves the formulation of strategies and tactics on the part of neighbourhood groups, and here again members need to acquire competence and confidence.

As far as *action* is concerned membership of neighbourhood groups demands of individuals that they learn new skills and knowledge, and extend what they already bring to the group. This is particularly the case with those who take up leadership roles such as chairman, secretary and treasurer. People are called upon to expand their skills in both task performance and group maintenance, both of which require that group members gain *technical* and *interactional* skills and knowledge.

Technical Skills and Knowledge

There are a variety of jobs to be done in a neighbourhood group, and they will vary with the nature of the group's concerns. But in most groups individuals have to develop civic or committee skills to some degree or other – drawing up agendas, writing minutes, implementing decisions, keeping financial accounts, printing and distributing a newsletter, using a telephone and writing letters. The writing of letters is usually one of the first significant explorations of personal skill and confidence by group members, and attention has been drawn both to its importance in the process of personal change and to its limitations as an instrument of negotiation in social change. Members in many groups have also to master techniques involved in, for instance, doing a survey, getting round a petition, arranging a deputation to the town hall, holding a press conference and organising a rent strike or demonstration.

People are also likely to improve their knowledge in matters like personal, work and welfare rights; aspects of social problems and issues; legislation and conventions that impinge on the work of the group (in housing, health, play and planning, for instance); resources in the neighbourhood and wider community; political processes and the workings of private and public bureaucracies; tribunals and public inquiries; and the knowledge and roles of specialists in the community, like the planner, the health inspector, the community worker and the solicitor.

Interactional Skills and Knowledge

These are of two kinds: first, political skills and competence; and secondly, caring and supportive capacities within the neighbourhood group.

Group members need to become adept in political transactions within the group, and between the group and the constituency that it represents. The group also has to develop skills in managing its relationships with, for example, the town hall, service agencies, potential resource people and groups, the press and television, other neighbourhood groups, councillors, MPs, trade unions and private and public industries. Relationships with all these require broad political skills in representing, and negotiating for, the interests of the groups. Political skills also include competence in executing and evaluating chosen strategies and tactics.

People who take leadership roles in neighbourhood groups also need to be caretakers of the emotional life of the group, and to be aware of the effects of people's relationships (within or outside the group) on the group's work, as well as events in their social and economic lives. Caring for the group also involves 'training' members for leadership roles, sharing the burden of the work and attending to the recruitment of new members. The community worker and officers need to understand, and mobilise in the group's interest, the original and changing motivations for membership of the group, and to be sensitive to the effect of behaviour in the group like scapegoating.

People in neighbourhood groups thus develop in the four areas of reflection, vision, planning and action. But what is the effect of this change within and outside the community group? Three levels of application of change are apparent. First, the individual develops in ways that are of application within the context of the skills, knowledge and confidence needed to perform assigned roles and responsibilities within the community group; and between the group and those bodies and agencies outside it.

Secondly, the effects of the changes may be felt in the individual's life outside the community group − at home, in the neighbourhood and at work. It is often hoped that learning acquired within the group will enable individuals to become more aware of, and more effective in, their civic and political (including trade union) responsibilities.

The mere act of involvement in a neighbourhood group can provide relief from, and support in, domestic and work situations. Membership provides opportunities for friendship, support, ventilation, a legitimate outlet for anti-authoritarian/anti-establishment feeling, the use of previously unused talents and energies, a sense of creativity and fulfilment, and the excitement of discussion and controversy.

Women often experience some liberation from traditional and oppressive sex roles as they take up leadership in community groups, and this has an effect on their relationships with their husbands and family.

Participation in neighbourhood groups helps some people to become more ambitious about the direction of their lives, and thus to try, sometimes successfully, to develop more competence in traditional roles like spouse, parent and breadwinner. Local people improve their jobs, 'go straight', acquire mortgages and houses, attend training courses, and aspire to and take on jobs like welfare rights workers and play group leaders.

Thirdly, the acquisition of knowledge and expertise becomes especially clear when local people pass on their new-found competence to others within the group, their families and to people in the wider community. The role of group members as educators becomes apparent when they feel confident enough to participate in activities like advising other neighbourhood groups; attending inter-group meetings in the community; taking community work students on placement; giving lectures and talks to college students; representing constituents at tribunals; getting up petitions; using the press and the television; and producing newsletters.

REVIEW

Direct face-to-face interventions with a group or organisation can be identified as community work if it is in accord with the following principles: (*a*) *that the group's members* join voluntarily; take responsibility for the work and management of the group, including defining their own needs; have personal experience of those needs; and are working to achieve outcomes which will benefit a wider constituency; (*b*) *that the worker* collectivises people's problems and seeks to understand and work on the external reasons for their existence; as such he works with a group to achieve specific tasks and goals which are conceived of as an exercise of power by group members; conceives of his role as one of partnership; seeks to promote participative norms and structures; and tries to help people acquire confidence, skills, knowledge and greater awareness of their life situations.

These principles are meant to be used sensibly; they are not intended to provide hard-and-fast rules. They are presented as a working guide to look at a particular activity within one of the five approaches and to enable us to say that sufficient of the 'principles' are present in the activity to allow us to accept that intervention as community work.

It must be stressed again that these 'salient principles' identify community work as an intervention; there will clearly be groups and individuals who help to organise in communities, that have none of these characteristics. Whilst the work of these groups and agencies may or may not be valuable, it cannot be identified as community work. Rather, they may belong to a wider category of community politics, in which community work is but one intervention. This kind of differentiation may be resisted but it gives funders and employing agencies the tool with which to distinguish community work from other concerns in community politics (this is not to say these should not be funded) and it gives trainers some base from which to conceive of training programmes.

These principles also allow us to bypass a number of perennial discussions in community work. For example, the controversy over 'soft' and 'hard' community work: there are those who argue that activities such as developing neighbourhood care schemes, luncheon clubs, play groups, client action groups and volunteer schemes are not community work; there are also those who criticise involvement with groups such as the unemployed, the homeless and various minority groups on the grounds that it is 'political' activity, and not community work. I suggest it is better to apply the salient principles to the activities in question; we could then see that some neighbourhood care schemes were, and some were not, community work; and that some work with the unemployed or homeless was, and some was not, community work. This is a much more refined and productive way of identifying community work interventions than classifying a whole group of activities as community work or not, as the case may be.

Resource centres and information and advice centres are not inherently community work interventions, even though they may employ a community worker, subscribe to general community work goals and values, or have a particular mode (informal, accountable, non-bureaucratic) of service delivery. Resource centres are agencies or settings from which it is possible to carry out a number of interventions, including community work. As such resource centres are part of the infrastructure of community work interventions and citizen activity, and cannot be counted as the intervention itself.

These salient principles derived from aspects of both the worker and the group provide a way of distinguishing community work interventions from others; they must be used with flexibility and openness and will be modified as we learn more from experience. These principles define community work as an intervention at various levels, such as neighbourhood work and social planning. Some concreteness can be given to the definition by looking at what it is that workers do in their practice. The tasks of workers vary between neighbourhood work and social planning, for example, but these tasks can be usefully displayed as a process of stages or steps. For example, one way to see neighbourhood work (a phrase that refers to most of the interventions of community workers that contribute to the approaches of community action and community development) is through the following process;

(1)   Planning and negotiating entry
(2)   Getting to know the community
(3)   Working out what to do next
(4)   Making contacts and bringing people together
(5)   Forming and building organisations
(6)   Helping to clarify goals and priorities
(7)   Keeping the organisation going
(8)   Dealing with friends and enemies
(9)   Leavings and endings

At each step in the process, the worker needs to draw upon certain skills, knowledge and resources. The skills and knowledge needed for community work have been discussed by ACW (1975) and CCETSW

(1974) and from these accounts it has been suggested that, as far as group organising is concerned, the relevant skills and knowledge areas are:

(1) INTERPERSONAL KNOWLEDGE AND SKILLS

The ability to relate to and 'get on with' people; understanding and empathising with them in their situations; and understanding people and groups within the context both of their class, ethnic and other histories, and contemporary environment.

(2) GROUP WORK KNOWLEDGE AND SKILLS

The ability to work effectively in both small and large groups, and in particular, to help people organise themselves into a group and to work towards their goals. It also includes skill at understanding group processes and dynamics.

(3) INTRA- AND INTER-ORGANISATIONAL KNOWLEDGE AND SKILLS

The capacity to understand, work within and change one's own and other organisations, including the ability to relate to people in different roles and functions in those organisations. The worker will need knowledge about political and policy making structures, and the formal and informal ways in which decisions are made. These skills are sometimes referred to as 'political skills'.

(4) SELF-ORGANISATION AND MANAGEMENT SKILLS

Managing time and other resources, setting priorities, planning work, as well as administrative skills like recording, filing, book-keeping, and so on.

(5) KNOWLEDGE AND SKILLS IN FACT FINDING AND SOCIAL STUDY

The capacity to collect, collate, analyse and present data on a number of subjects, including needs and resources in local communities. It also includes an ability to 'get to know a neighbourhood and the people in it' and to analyse a variety of neighbourhood and organisational situations in which the worker finds himself.

(6) EDUCATION AND TRAINING SKILLS

The ability to share one's knowledge and skills with people in the community, and to help them acquire confidence and abilities in a number of administrative and practical tasks.

Workers also need to comprehend the issues with which residents are concerned – for example, planning, housing, transportation, health and education. Participation in social planning and community organisation will require the worker to be proficient in another set of tasks, some of which I have described elsewhere (1978). The purpose of community work training, to be examined in Chapter 5, should not be confined to ensuring that students have acquired a level of skills and knowledge, but should also help them understand the developmental processes of political responsibility and communal coherence to which community work is one contribution.

The personal characteristics or qualities that are needed to do community work are also important in rounding off an explanation of community work as an intervention, and complement the more formal elements of a definition. Bryan Symons (1981) has written an excellent article on the skills, knowledge and qualities required for most forms of community work, and this chapter finishes by reproducing in full his comments on these matters. He writes that community workers need a broad grounding in the social sciences; knowledge of a wide variety of legislation; a detailed understanding of local government in their particular area; the ability to develop a wide range of contacts and allies among bureaucrats and politicians; experience and knowledge about the working of committees and groups; the judgement to intervene in group meetings in such a way as to help the group work out policies but not to dominate them; and a sufficient understanding of tactics to be able to supply advice on dealing with the authorities.

Certain personal attributes are also necessary for successful community work. A worker requires a practical ideology based on a belief that people are capable of controlling decisions and should be encouraged to control their own lives, and a conviction that this can most effectively be achieved in a co-operative and collective way. A belief therefore that flows from this is that resources should be distributed more equally in society than at present. Without a firm commitment to these ideas it is difficult to see someone making a really effective worker. This is not the same as saying the worker should be a heavy ideologue. Indeed, such people generally make extremely bad workers as too often they are concerned to impose their own views on the community, and not to encourage it to learn for itself.

But 'correct' political attitudes and understanding are not enough. Community work is a long-term process. It is concerned to enable people not just to demand and get things now but to enable people successfully to organise in the future. Community work is partly a way of encouraging people to learn, and the best way of learning is through experience and understanding rather than having ideas imposed by someone such as a highly educated community worker, who is articulate and able to impose his or her views. Similarly, workers who attempt to speak and demand on behalf of a community that they do not represent not only undermine the credibility of community work but provide people with little experience of organising for themselves. Community workers therefore need the ability to help other people develop and grow. This is a slow process – patience and a willingness to do without instant results is a necessity.

One other related quality should perhaps be referred to – the ability to stay in a job for long enough to achieve results. This is actually one of the most difficult tasks! The work is exhausting, often depressing and requires a good deal of evening work. But it takes time to build up trust in a community, time really to get to know how a particular authority works and time to build up contacts. Many of the personal qualities cannot be taught; good training can, however, certainly encourage the development of particular aspects of the personality and can help develop many of the skills necessary. The management, organisational setting and support services can also help encourage good work practice. This last matter is looked at in succeeding chapters that deal with the organisation and infrastructure needed for community work practice.

NOTE

1   I regret that the word 'approach' is rather flabby. I would have preferred to use 'developments' but this would have caused some confusion because the more limited term 'community development' is also used. The five approaches or developments convey the fact that thinking, policy and practice in a number of fields have tended to move incrementally in a certain direction, together with several naturally occurring social processes. The word approach was chosen because it is capable of subsuming both these natural processes that occur within, say, community action and community development, as well as the more strategically pursued goals and policies within, for example, community organisations or service extension. 'Approach' is flexible enough to accommodate the great number of inconsistencies and contradictions that occur between and within each of the five phenomena; it also allows for the fact that people and agencies will have been contributing to certain processes without knowledge, conscious purpose and direction, as well as those that were trying deliberately to influence policy and action in a particular way. Using 'approach' helps, too, to understand that each approach is made up of a mixture of action, policy, theory, ideology and vision.

4 *Practice in the 1980s*

The purpose of this chapter, as well as the three that follow, is to look ahead to the remaining years of this decade in order to see with which problems community workers will be asked to help. It is a hard chapter to write because of the difficulties of forecasting and because the emphasis on the content of practice may highlight the distributive functions of community work, rather than the developmental ones. A further complication is that the content of this chapter will move between three distinct but related topics: first, what developments can be expected within the five approaches of community action, community development, social planning, community organisation and service extension? Secondly, what contributions will community work be making within these five approaches? Thirdly, in what ways will community work develop as an occupation? Most of this and the following chapters will be concerned with the last two topics, because a comprehensive analysis of the first lies outside the remit of this study. Yet it is precisely this first issue that provides us with the opportunity to see how community work contributes within a wider developmental framework.

One of the few people who has consistently taken a strategic view of community work is Hywel Griffiths. In an unpublished paper given in Dublin in 1979, he suggests that community development has become identified with one strategy: the employment of a professional community worker. He argues that this has had an adverse effect on the evolution of a variety of general strategies towards community development, and the employment of paid workers 'is no more than a strategy the utility of which must be measured against other strategies in the circumstances and with the resources available'. Three alternative and complementary strategies for community development that he discusses are the provision of education about and for community development to professionals and local residents; the provision of necessary resources directly to those taking action; and the promotion of organisational development and liaison. These strategies would, of course, require resources and workers.

The idea of community work as one strategy for the development of community was taken further by Griffiths in a paper given to a community work training conference in Southampton in 1981. Looking ahead to the 1980s, he identifies two major issues: the development of communities for social change and the development of agencies for social change. The first is about the evolution of social policies with explicit reference 'to the manner in which the energies, initiatives and participation of the people will contribute to the achievement of goals and even to their definition'. There is likely to be more reliance on self-help and community-based initiatives, and more facilities for information exchange. On this matter, another correspondent to the study wrote:

> Just as video and off-set litho provided some significant new opportunities for some community groups in the seventies, so I would expect that computer facilities and word-processors would do the same for some community groups in the eighties . . . Word-processors could help community groups produce their own written material and help them participate more effectively in planning. In fact, I would see computers playing a major role in resolving the dilemma of how you can have discussion on a small scale that nevertheless leads to major decisions; it could be a way of speeding up and rendering more effective communication between groups on policy formation in detail in the longer run.

The development of agencies for social change will occur as other professional groups and departments incorporate community work ideas and skills. Community work, Griffiths forecasts, will come in out of the cold and develop as a specialist intervention, concentrating on organisational development and inter-agency planning and co-ordination, with the major purpose to mould agencies into instruments of social change. This may be accompanied by the disappearance of the middle-class university-educated community worker, who will be replaced by local people taking on the job. This new breed of worker, Griffiths suggests, will develop much better relationships with elected members, and this will aid the development of agencies in promoting change.

The emergence of social planning, community organisation and service extension as major strategies in the 1980s is, not unexpectedly, taken up by a number of American writers. Harry Specht, for example, summarises the concern in the 1960s with organising the unaffiliated and the development of neighbourhood organisations. The focus was 'upon work with populations that were excluded from the decision-making social institutions – populations that were frequently characterised as alienated, powerless, socially deprived and politically oppressed'. He argues that in the 1970s in America, practice became more concerned with what was happening within established institutions, and he sees this trend continuing into the 1980s, with community workers needing the technical expertise of social planning in order to deal with a more complex set of social and economic issues, affected in large part by the functioning of government institutions. Implicit in his account is the view that neighbourhood organising will be of less importance in the 1980s; the extensive legislative requirement in America for citizen participation in planning and decision-making has removed community groups to the centre of social institutions where, he suggests, they have become bureaucratised and stultified. But whatever the effects, there is now an extensive system of grass-roots participation in government 'and professionals who are committed to serving the poor must understand this system and help their clients to master it' (1978).

Jack Rothman (1979) assumes that the decade ahead will be one of economic constriction and he suggests that professional activities will increase in four general areas of practice: social policy and planning, efficiency and accountability, local initiative and social advocacy. Decreased resources within social services, together with increased demands made upon them, will enhance the importance of allocating resources in a planned and efficient manner; Rothman sees social planning as an activity whose time has arrived in the 1980s.

But Rothman also anticipates that neighbourhood organising will become more important and he predicts that in the face of austerity local communities will 'respond in a determined, self-actualising way, applying indigenous energies to maximise whatever potentials exist in the local situation'. Neighbourhood-based self-help programmes, grass-roots advocacy and social action will be part of the response to the deleterious effect on neighbourhood resources and services of a worsening economic situation; the interest shown in the 1970s in neighbourhood government and neighbourhood self-reliance as alternative approaches to urban reform and to dependence on the state and big business will continue to develop in the 1980s.

Rothman's comments on neighbourhood organising are similar to those of S. M. Miller writing on the 1980s in *The Socialist Register 1980*. Current political life he suggests is occurring around feminist, environmental and neighbourhood issues. He discusses the strengths and weaknesses of neighbourhood organisations, and concludes that 'a major problem of the eighties is to draw the neighbourhood groupings toward a national economic and political agenda without weakening their strength in the neighbourhoods'. He writes:

A great hope of the neighbourhood movement is that it demonstrates the possibilities of local citizens taking charge, of new forms of democratic participation. Decentralisation and 'enpowerment' are the themes . . . [groups] are likely to have continual success in the basic organising of neighbourhoods because of crass business policies that exploit consumers by raising oligopolistic prices and that disrupt communities by closing down plants without consultation with the workers or the community, and because of governmental policies of reducing public spending and services. Successes in such struggles may lead neighbourhood-oriented organisations to become emboldened and to broaden their outlook and construct a national political and economic agenda.

Miller suggests that a key organising question in the 1980s will be to link neighbourhood organisations to each other, 'and to national organisations and issues, especially around economic policies dealing with inflation and employment'.

In their different ways, both Rothman and Specht give most attention in their papers to community activism and institutional functions and reforms, and relate these to the interventions of professional organisers. Galper and Mandros (1980) offer a different kind of analysis, and one that is similar to the approach of this review. They try to assess some features of the occupation of community work. Their particular concern is to explore the relationship between community work and social work. They suggest that the relationship in the past has been ambivalent, and community work's position in social work practice and training has been marginal and insecure. The critical issue, they argue, is not compatibility between each intervention's skill, knowledge and value areas but social work's 'ambivalence about its commitment to social change'. They present a useful analysis of the relationship between the two, and what each can contribute to the other; yet their conclusion is powerful because they stress the potential autonomy of community work that may emerge in the 1980s.

> Community organisation will happen, with or without social work's help. If social work cannot identify organising as part of its conceptual scheme, organising will find a home elsewhere, and once again, another discipline will have claimed something we should have taken for our own . . . What history can teach us is that the support for community organising must come from a wide range of arenas. Sources of support must be explored and analysed carefully. Organising cannot depend on variable political climates, nor can we expect that the funding and the consent to organise will come from those we want to change. We must realise that a commitment to organising is a commitment to create our own climate in which organising can occur.

Community work on the initiative, being active in asserting its independence from host disciplines and its coherence as an occupation, is also a theme taken up in the English context by Pat Sills in a paper given at the Volunteer Centre in 1980. The future possibilities for community work to survive and develop depend on a number of factors about itself that Sills elaborates. These are:

● to develop and demonstrate the awareness and the skills that community work has to offer, but also to be realistic about the

kind of achievements that are possible with limited resources;
● to clarify attainable objectives to do with service and care, the improvement of people's living conditions and the progressive reshaping of community and societal structures;
● to marry the personal and the political and to convince service-providing agencies of the connections between caring and campaigning;
● to use the present period of retrenchment to consolidate and develop 'practice theory' by trainers and practitioners.

Occupational identity has also been given prominence by the editors of a collection of papers about Youth and Community Work in the 1980s (Booton and Dearling, 1980). The editors note that 'for the first time in 30 years youth and community work in this country has come to the end of a decade without an official report on its recent past, or a policy for its immediate future, being available to us'. The absence of such a review, they argue, will add to doubt and pessimism widespread in the youth service, and will sharpen the issue of 'whether it is prudent any longer to leave the development of important elements of education and welfare provision on the fringe of social policy without the thought, coordination and accountability that are applicable elsewhere in the public services'.

The most extended analysis of community work in the 1980s in Britain has been offered by Paul Waddington (his views were also developed in a paper given at the Corrymeela Centre, Northern Ireland. It is published, together with other papers on the 1970s and 1980s, in a volume compiled by Hugh Frazer published in 1981a.) He anticipates that the future task of community workers will be

> to manage the multiplicity of new groups and organisations which will have to be brought into being to engage the long-term structurally unemployed and to provide the new community-based social services. An increasing part of their work will involve the professional supervision of a new tier of para-professional, sub-professional and non-professional volunteer workers. The new community workers will act as the outreach agents, the eyes and ears, of the corporately managed major established institutions in helping them to better monitor their environments and manage feed-back and to handle increasingly complex inter-organisational relationships. The larger existing quasi-statutory and quasi-voluntary organisations, like the Councils of Voluntary Service and Community Relations Councils, which already act as mediating organisations, will be strengthened and new organisations will be created where necessary to fulfil similar functions. In the establishment of this new system, increasing use will be made of staff secondment by statutory to voluntary

organisations as an alternative to the direct funding of new posts by the supplicant bodies. (1979)

As to the role of community workers, Waddington's view is not unlike those of some American writers on the 1980s. He anticipates that community workers will spend more of their time in deskbound activities and will do less direct fieldwork. They will, he argues, be more involved in management, in making policy and in controlling budgets and resources. 'Looked at overall, their work would assume a shape which might better be described as "community organisation and social planning" as it is called in the United States . . .'

Thus Waddington believes that the institutionalisation of community work will continue into the future; coming to terms with the inevitability of this will provide a major challenge to community workers: 'There will continue to be spaces for conscientious and radical community work, but workers who seek them will increasingly need to think and plan much more vigorously and strategically than has tended to be the case in the past in order to be sure of finding and keeping these spaces.'

But alongside this institutionalisation, Waddington believes that 'there will be struggles for control from the periphery and the grassroots'. There will be new and challenging organisations such as 'workers' cooperatives, black and feminist consciousness groups, resource centres and other organisational forms which may grow out of debates within the labour movement'. Here Waddington identifies an emerging split within the occupation. On the one hand, there will be the 'professionalists', those stressing the technical and the social planning aspects of community work and mainly adhering to consensual/pluralist models of society. They, says Waddington, will find many attractive perches within the new system. The other broad camp will comprise the radical dissenters 'who regard community work as essentially part of a broader social movement for change and who see its aims as inextricably linked with the major social and political issues of the day'. This group will need to look for the relatively autonomous spaces in the new system, and

> to seek out the subversible areas, identifying and working on the contradictions. They will find ways of disrupting the progressive routinisation of the system's operation which will tend to be the consequence of increasing institutionalisation, by generating debate and conflict. Towards this end, it will continue to be necessary to create counter-organisations – like, for example, the new Resource Centres – which have the capacity to develop the materials and provide the resources which are needed to support more broadly based campaigns and to foster the development of alliances between different progressive interests. And above all, they will need the strategy and the stamina for a continuing struggle.

The split within the occupation will be reflected in, and reinforced by, community work moving substantially towards further professionalisation. He writes that

> The decision of the Association of Community Workers in 1973 to voluntarily reverse what is regarded as the normal process of professionalisation can be seen in retrospect as a way of temporarily ducking the issues involved rather than of permanently resolving them, given the considerable ambivalence towards professionalisation which is to be found in community work circles. When it was realised that the field had been left open to others and the quasi-statutory Central Council for Education and Training in Social Work began to move into the space, this forced an attempt at a pre-emptive reaction which has led to the creation of the Federation of Community Work Training Groups, another half-way house.

As a related process, Waddington sees social work and community work coming closer together, not least because of changes within social work itself. Waddington suggests that the managerialists will welcome both the professionalisation process and the closer integration with social work. The radical dissenters, he hints, will survive as splinter groups within the profession, and some will 'drift away from community work and cease to recognise the title. The seeds of a possible new grouping lie in recent developments within the broad field of adult education.'

The view of the non-professionalists is nowhere better exemplified than in *Community Action* magazine. Reviewing the past, it states that

> The last ten years has seen a major shift in the kinds of demands made by tenants and action groups and other labour movement organisations. Many of the demands of campaigns in the early 1970's were directed at stopping state financed projects such as motorways and the clearance of older housing areas, as well as office and town centre development schemes during the property boom. Much of this state spending has been slashed over the past five years and the property boom has been attacked with increasing force. Campaign demands are still defensive, but of a different kind because they are not trying to change or stop state spending but are aimed against the cuts and arguing for *more* spending. (1980)

In assessing the impact of working-class struggles in recent years, it suggests that 'the record overall for the past few years has been as depressing as it is now'. The article goes on:

> Despite several successes in some places, in many areas of the country there have been few if any gains, and what was won elsewhere (often

at the expense of weaker groups with less resources) is now threatened if not already cut. Few campaigning groups or federations have kept strong for long. Many people have become worn out, disillusioned and divided, frightened to risk the loss of tenancies or jobs.

People are paying more in rent, rates and charges for less and worse services. No powerful trade union/community alliances have developed with enough strength to fight off attacks on jobs and services. Meanwhile the power of the state forces — the police and the army — is being constantly increased to crush effective organising, demonstrating, picketing, striking and occupations, and the smashing of hospital work-ins by police and management is becoming almost a regular event.

We need to rethink both the strategies we adopt and the way we organise.

The magazine's views of the 1980s is located within its analysis of the real power behind local and national government — private capital. The priorities for the 1980s are seen as:

● taking on the institutions of private capital through direct action, investigative research and alliances with unions;
● building local and national alliances between the various kinds of working-class groups, with major priority being given to building a tenants' movement that is strong locally/nationally;
● exerting more influence over the media;
● creating a positive working-class and socialist culture through such things as community arts, theatre and newspapers;
● creating more opportunities for accessible and democratic educational facilities.

Particular attention is given to new directions for child care campaigns, anti-nuclear campaigns, building a militant tenants' movement, organising unemployed workers' unions, campaigns against closures, increasing public awareness, and helping with individual problems in regard to benefits and rights. The larger framework for these campaigns is provided by the notion of alliances between the community and the workplace, focused around the work of trades councils, joint shop stewards' committees, combine committees and the involvement of unions in action on community issues. Socialist centres opened by, for example, women's groups, unemployed workers' centres, and the trade union and community resource centres already active in some cities are seen as some of the places where worker — community links can be forged.

It is important to disentangle views about community action and activities from those about community work as an occupation. The future of community work as an occupation is dependent on the future thinking, policies and attitudes of local and central government departments; a consequence of this is reflected in the literature and submissions to this study: views about these departments (though they are mostly incorporated within the concept of 'the state') determine predictions about the survival and function of community work. For example, the probability of the various elements of Paul Waddington's predictions is dependent on the realism of the highly managerialist functions of the state that he portrays. There is no doubt that up to 1979 there was a gradual strengthening of the managerialist function as government intervened in so many aspects of economic and social life. But what can we observe today that suggests contrary trends in the 1980s, particularly about the functions of the local state? What do we see that indicates that the relationship of local to central government is changing, as it is to the powerful spheres of national and multinational business?

A difficulty in answering this is the diversity of local government, both across the country and across the departments of a particular authority, and nowhere is this diversity more evident than in policies about community work. This diversity suborns attempts to generalise about local government but the following trends seem important to set against the managerialist nightmare. First, the effects of central government cuts in public expenditure have been particularly severe on local government departments and this, many contributors have suggested, is or will have the effect of creating local alliances of politicians, officers, activists and community workers 'up and against the central state'. Second is the related phenomenon of the 'radicalisation' of politicians in some urban local authorities. Both these points suggest the growing opportunities for transformational rather than managerial community work practice because local councillors will see the value of community work in stimulating local action against the cuts, in facilitating alternative community strategies of self-reliance and as part of their radical approach to their role as elected members. The fate of community work will probably be linked to changes in the composition and attitudes of elected members in the next ten years, with community workers helping to enlarge perceptions of the elected members' role and benefiting in turn from these developments, in some cases, perhaps, as officers seconded to work with councillors.

Thirdly, local government is likely to change in response to the concern from many quarters for greater welfare and economic pluralism. This concern to 'bypass' the state in the matter of welfare and employment, for example, and to create more locally autonomous and responsive services, is reflected as much in the trades councils inquiry *State Intervention in Industry* as it is in a document such as Francis Gladstone's *Voluntary Action in a Changing World*. The socialist and conservative conceptions of creating welfare and wealth at the local level spring, not unnaturally, from quite different analyses, have incompatible goals and would probably be operationalised in different ways. For the socialists, there is, too, the possibility that these local initiatives would lead to the development of alternative forms of political power. The various visions of bypassing the state will sit comfortably with those that talk of the decentralisation of local government into smaller and more locally accountable units, and with those that stress the importance of neighbourhood government and the empowerment of local communities.

The relationship of community work to local government will depend in part upon the occupation's willingness to demonstrate that it has some expertise to offer. This demonstration must contain more clarity about the nature of community work skills, and the ability to explore how these could be applied within the responsibilities of particular departments. Awareness, too, of community work's distributive and developmental goals may produce more interdepartmental initiatives on community work. For example, the concern with process and product goals might be reflected in joint funding by social work and education departments, or by social work and voluntary agencies such as the churches which have persisted with their commitment to process goals. The responsiveness of some departments to their area's long-term economic problems will be another factor, and nowhere is this more clear than in the imaginative response of leisure and recreation departments, as well as adult education, to the issues of long-term unemployment, early retirement and shorter working weeks.

The most puzzling aspect about the development of community work in the 1980s concerns the status and survival of neighbourhood work, by which I refer to most of the work that contributes to community action and community development. There are a number of different influences whose effects are by no means uniform but whose cumulative impact may be to undermine or confuse the contribution of neighbourhood work. There is, first, the influence largely from academia to emphasise social planning and community organisation; there are those such as Harry Specht to whom planning and organisation are the preferred and most relevant forms of intervention, and those such as Paul Waddington for whom a concentration on social planning is logically entailed by their analysis of the nature of the state. People such as Harry Specht see the greatest good for the poor and deprived occurring as a result of creating more humane and responsive service agencies. The service-planning element becomes more dominant, as well as the skills to integrate groups within consultations and participative procedures. I have argued elsewhere for the need for community workers to become more proficient in social planning skills, but to emphasise them to the exclusion of neighbourhood organising is unhelpful, not least because it ignores the developmental goals of community work, which is something more than an intervention to achieve merely distributive goals. Specht's vision is faulty because it construes community work only in terms of welfare achievements, and ignores the longer-term process of education and development to which community work contributes.

Secondly, there is the push to move the campaign and action elements of neighbourhood work away from any occupation such as community work and to ally it with the labour movement or with counter-organisations associated with various social movements. This influence over the development of neighbourhood work is exemplified, for example, in the article by Corkey and Craig who see that 'what is required is for tenants and residents to join in collective action with those in the labour movement active in the class struggle to bring the capitalist system to an end . . . CDP's do not now on the whole see themselves in the business of community work but involved in supporting the political struggles of the working class . . .' (1978). There is little sympathy for, and indeed, considerable criticism of, community work as a public service occupation amongst workers who hold these views; the logic of their interest in trade unions and in union-sponsored projects and resource centres is to take neighbourhood organising away from community work and give it a more overtly political base. Community work would then be left with narrow welfare functions (community care and planning, for example).

Thirdly, there is political pressure to redefine neighbourhood work only as community development with a particular emphasis on self-help and community care.

The effects of these tendencies in the 1980s to trim community work of neighbourhood organising would be enhanced by the reluctance of community work practitioners and trainers to be clear about:

● the knowledge and skills they bring to neighbourhood work, and which provide the basic legitimation for the occupation's involvement; and
● the long-term developmental process to which community work contributes, and which comprises a vital political as well as welfare element.

These trimming effects may be reinforced by the increasing difficulty experienced by workers in organising people around neighbourhood issues. It can also be argued that campaign-based neighbourhood work was essentially a product of the growth economy of the late 1960s and early 1970s, when it made sense to campaign against local authorities who then had the authority and resources to make an appropriate response. Another view is that in the 1980s neighbourhood-based work will be threatened precisely because it is an established form of intervention: 'in the search for new ideas', wrote one contributor to the study, 'and new solutions, neighbourhood work can easily find itself taking a back seat, less attractive to funders, less attractive to community workers themselves, who tend to move, as they become experienced, into specialist and city wide roles'. Community work will need to develop more sophisticated forms of organisation and resourcing without neglecting the neighbourhood base, because without its experience at neighbourhood level, suggests one contributor, 'community work has no basis for credibility at other levels or in other areas'. The pressure to search for new things to attract funding will be all the more intense if community work cannot advance from its present state of ambivalence towards its 'hosts' such as social work.

The consolidation of community work around social planning, community organisation and service extension might be hastened by two other factors. First, issues such as nuclear power, energy conservation and social movements based around racial and sexual issues may distract and attract middle-class organisers away from neighbourhood work. This tendency might be reinforced by a decline in neighbourhood work jobs or by a tighter supervision of such posts by employers who were able to use the 1970s to learn about community work.

Secondly, there is a belief that whilst neighbourhoods will need to organise in the 1980s there will be less and less need for neighbourhood organisers. It may be argued (and it would be convincing argument for those seeking to rationalise their drift into the politics of labour and social movements) that the competence and confidence for organising was laid down in the 1970s and that communities will be able in the future to organise collectively without the aid of professional organisers. There is little evidence to support this argument, which implies a very static picture of community work. As one correspondent suggested:

The idea that the competence has been given to communities who will now be able to organise for themselves is somewhat optimistic. Our resource centre experience suggests not for any number of reasons. There are still plenty of neighbourhoods without experience of any sort of organising. In any community the activists are few and need support if they are to sustain their involvement, even more if they are to take on anything new. We find new initiatives are the first thing to go when a community work team is withdrawn. The resource centres found that unless they were able to go out and work with groups their users tended to be the more sophisticated groups. Also people need the additional *time* a community worker offers. Groups come and go, new issues arise, etc., etc. The kind of resources needed *include* neighbourhood organising skills . . . There is nothing to suggest they will become obsolete . . .

It may be that more local people will become community workers, but this is not to argue that in the future communities will necessarily be able to organise without the aid of community workers and other forms of support such as that provided by resource centres. What seems certain is that neighbourhood work will itself change and develop; intensive neighbourhood work will still be required to build up basic organisational skills and strength but it will be set alongside short-term contractual work and issue-centred work where workers will become specialists in a particular field (housing, jobs, health, and so on) and will service a number of locality-based groups.

THE CONTENT OF PRACTICE IN THE 1980s

This section is not an exercise in gazing into a crystal ball. The main areas of practice are already clear in outline because they are evident in present social and economic trends. It would be unwise to try to be detailed about any area of practice because these will be decided by local circumstances and national factors which are as yet unclear. It is evident that there will be no shortage of issues on which community workers will be asked for their help, but there is little validity in me (or anyone else, for that matter) announcing which of these issues ought to have priority. Priorities will be properly decided by the local participants in collective action, and workers must accordingly respond to these within the constraints set by their agency's mandate, and their own values and abilities. This response to the issues of the 1980s must be informed by what we have learnt in the past; community work, warned one correspondent, ought as a discipline to accept the burden of substituting experience for ideological purity.

I stress this point about the autonomy of participants in settling the priority of issues, not just because it is a cardinal principle in community work, but because the range and urgency of issues in the 1980s may tempt agencies, community workers and others in the field with good intentions and considerable social concern to pursue their own interests without regard to those felt within local communities. The importance to agencies of community care, for example, may lead them to give it priority, even though it is not seen as such within particular communities. Another example is to be found in the relation of community work to the labour movement: particular ideological preferences of some workers to concentrate on building links with trade unions may not be shared by neighbourhood groups. The examples can be taken from every quarter and their point is clear; we might expect in the 1980s a greater degree of tension between, on the one hand, agency and practitioner concerns with social justice; and, on the other, the distinctive responsiveness of community work to the felt needs of individuals and groups which might be pitched at levels of consciousness that are different from the preferences of agencies and workers.

Although it is not a difficult matter to describe the content of practice in the 1980s (unemployment, housing, health, and so on) it is more testing to determine how we *think* about these issues, and think about them in terms of the goals and principles of the occupation. We must try to relate thinking on the expected content of practice to the wider concept of development described in earlier chapters; in particular, to understand those aspects of issues that relate to the promotion of political responsibility and communal coherence. Another value of anticipating the content of practice in the next decade is that it should assist us in decisions about the development of community work as an occupation. It should help us to be more prepared and practical in relation to the issues that present themselves, and in particular to think about what might be the appropriate forms of employment and funding of community work. Perhaps most important of all, our anticipations about practice should be used to inform the content of training in community work so that people are being equipped with some ability to deal with issues that emerge during the decade.

Themes of the 1980s

I want to suggest that there are three major themes in relation to which community workers will be able to contribute their knowledge and skills. They are:

reconstruction
renegotiation of status
realising the community

The themes are separated only for the purposes of analysis; in reality, they are intimately connected and an area of activity classified under one theme will also appear in practice under one or more of the others. I will discuss several different issues within each theme; the advantage of conceptualising areas of work as themes is to emphasise planning and strategy in employing and deploying community workers. It becomes possible to link different community work interventions to one another, and to link them to other kinds of efforts that are made to deal with particular issues.

(1) RECONSTRUCTION

The theme of reconstruction emerges from interviews with, and the written papers of, a variety of sources concerned with community work, reflecting quite different interests, responsibilities and political views. The theme concerns the social and economic reconstruction of communities, and is thus connected to the decline of the British economy since around the mid-1970s, and the particularly serious consequences for local economies of the Conservative government's policies since 1979. The theme embraces not only the reconstruction of economic and welfare systems but also the reconstruction of relationships between people and between groups that have suffered as a consequence of economic decline. There is, too, the need for a reconstruction of British political institutions and practices; the direction of such changes were discussed in an earlier chapter and included the recasting of electoral politics, as well as the continued development of community and industrial politics. Political reconstruction will involve strengthening the political significance and competence of people, as well as continuing attempts to develop the role of elected members and their responsibilities to, and relationships with, local residents and groups.

The theme and urgency of reconstruction are evident in the following passages from staff in different parts of the country. A report from community workers in a London borough, for example, suggests:

there will be a further depression of the national economy and a corresponding increase in unemployment . . . all the indications point towards a general shortage of both council and private accommodation . . . and an increased number of sub-standard dwellings . . . an increase in the numbers evicted either for the non-payment of rent or mortgage . . . there could well be an increase in poverty in real terms and the creation of many more poor people, those unemployed or homeless. This situation could lead to a polarisation of views, greater intolerance towards disadvantaged groups and a hardening of attitudes between, for example, young and old, black and white, employed and unemployed. There would be resentment towards women workers as men are seen as, and often see themselves as, bread-winners . . . all these social factors will put a greater strain on social services departments . . . it is probable that many potential recipients of the state welfare services will be forced to fall back on their own personal, family or neighbourhood resources. This may be desirable for some but will cause great hardship for many others and undoubtedly some will find illegal or socially unacceptable consequences.

This argument was reflected in another paper from a community worker in Wigan. He suggested that since unemployment will continue to be a major factor in the economic structure of the 1980s, there will be more individual frustration and alienation. He continues:

> Whether this will lead to social unrest and change is a matter for speculation. We can safely predict that there will be less productive activity and more leisure time, some within shorter working weeks, some enforced by unemployment . . . Community work along with community education, more enlightened planning, real community health . . . and trade unions may well have the ability to co-ordinate and to involve people in leisure which could well be problem-solving in social work terms. The other alternative might be leaving leisure initiatives to Big Business and their electric space-men at 20p a go and the mass media to keep us more riveted to the television screen, a fairly mindless population becoming even more ready to leave any decision-making to the 'experts' with more and more alcohol and drugs for more and more immediate suppression of unhappiness . . .

The scale of the task facing local authorities and their communities was emphasised in a paper from a director of a northern social services department:

> The present government's policy is to restrict public expenditure, and local government will be severely affected . . . At the same time that resources are becoming more scarce many problems are becoming more severe . . . The pincer-like effect of these two factors will result in increasing strains on public services. There could be significant breaks in service due to increasing trade union militancy, resistance to change, and the ineffective implementation of new methods of working . . . This calls for a radical approach where both government and its staff . . . have to totally reappraise their roles. Instead of regarding the community as a place of work and source of problems we shall have to start realising the potential within a community to solve its own problems. The role of government should not be the first line of defence but a creative factor within an overall network of community resources that are directed to social problems . . . The question is whether people will continue to be mute or will their frustration turn to militancy. Increasing investment in the forces of law and order taking advantage of the new technologies is one possibility, but will the consequent loss of freedom and liberty be a price that is too high?

In the face of these trends community work has to put forward viable and constructive alternatives to the drift into chaos and anarchy. It is not enough to call for the radical restructuring of society, we have to map out a route that is feasible.

These extracts indicate the seriousness of the situation in many parts of this country brought about by unemployment, and the effects of public expenditure cuts on health, education, welfare and housing services. They suggest the social disorganisation, fragmentation and conflict that is a consequence of the deterioration of work opportunities and public sector services. I want now to look more closely at some specific areas where community work interventions are likely to be made. It will be difficult to do this because the forces and institutions involved are so much wider than community work; but it is the remit of this project to examine community work and I shall try to do this in relation to employment, housing, health and education.

(*a*) *Employment*
The issue of work has many aspects – short- and long-term unemployment, as well as restricted employment opportunities, as a result of enforced or voluntary schemes such as shorter working hours, job shares and early retirement. There are those people, too, who are 'declassed' – obliged to take jobs 'below' that for which they have been trained or have the experience. Unemployment hits hardest at the working class, and affects some groups more than others – women, ethnic minorities, school-leavers, the disabled and the handicapped. Its effects are more pronounced in some regions than in others – inner-city areas, and the older industrial parts of South Wales, Scotland, Northern Ireland and the north-east and west of England. Unemployment is the cause and aggravation of many other social and political problems that may become more serious – vandalism and delinquency, alcohol and drug dependency, ill-health of body and mind, family breakdown and community disintegration and an experience of poverty and demoralisation.

The dimensions of the reconstruction that must take place around the issue of work and productive leisure are manifold and complex, but contain the four following basic elements:

- reconstruction of the economic base of communities;
- reconstruction of people's lives who have experienced long-term unemployment;
- reconstruction of communities which have suffered disintegration and demoralisation from widespread unemployment;
- reconstruction of attitudes that always looked to the state and to private enterprise for the creation of both jobs and investment in socially useful services and amenities.

Community work has a significant part to play in this process of reconstruction, not least because one of the basic units of reconstruction will be local communities. It is equally clear, however, that the issues of economic decay and regeneration are structural in character, and we must recognise community work not only as a significant contribution but also as a relatively limited one when compared with the other welfare and political initiatives that need to be taken. Community workers must also be clear about their intentions in working on this issue: they have been exposed to temptations to rush into employment work partly because it has attracted funding and partly because of the moral pressure to follow those who have taken up the issue within the broader labour and trade union movement.

Given that community work has a potentially valuable contribution to make, is it, asked one contributor, in a position to take employment issues on board? She continues:

> The question is not entirely rhetorical, since goodwill alone is not going to be any solution and may do harm. In addition, a wholesale assault on unemployment could mean that other issues suffer, in terms both of time and skills. Work on employment issues will require hard skills, and these might be gained at the expense of maintaining expertise which has been built up in other areas such as housing . . . Community work has always entailed mobilising resources and expertise from appropriate sources both within and outside the community. There is no reason why traditional strategies cannot be applied to unemployment . . .

At the 1978 ACW conference on unemployment, Nick Sharman confirmed that community workers were well placed to take a key role in initiatives around employment:

> This role is likely to have a number of dimensions. Basic research is always an important component. Linking a variety of bodies, particularly community and work place organisations is also essential. It is also, given their different methods of work, often difficult. Another area where community workers have important skills is in mobilising the support and resources of local councils.

I want to describe the kind of contribution to be made by community work that is suggested in both these quotations. There seem to be five major ways in which community workers can help with the issue of work and unemployment – organising; liaison; informal education; advice and information; and research.

Organising The ability to organise and support groups is one of the most important skills in community work: the capacity to bring people together, to identify needs and then work collectively to take action on those needs. This ability to organise will be of critical importance in dealing not just with unemployment but with the much wider process of community reconstruction. The organising skills of community workers will be needed in four major areas.

First, in *local work creation* where the task is to help people come together in various kinds of productive ventures: producer, worker and consumer co-operatives, for example, as well as more ambitious community enterprise schemes that aim to create jobs under local management and where the surplus is ploughed back into the community. These work-creating ventures are small scale, have the support of local people and are there to meet local economic and social needs. Although the jobs created are relatively few, the importance of such schemes is that they provide another way for local people to acquire confidence in their own organising abilities; they provide a model or vision of a different kind of economic order; they are part of a larger process of reducing dependence on the state and private enterprise for jobs; and they provide the opportunity to reintegrate the economic aspects of community life with others such as housing, welfare and recreation. In some cases they bring needed services back to the community, as well as raising morale by getting people to do something themselves, no matter how small, about the community's economic base. We might expect a particular interest in developing the potential of economically disadvantaged groups, such as some ethnic minorities wanting to start up businesses. There is already in existence, for example, the Black Business Development Unit at the Polytechnic of the South Bank, London.

There is much suspicion in community work about organising people to create local work and services; there is a disdain for anything to do with business, management and profit. It is time-consuming, with apparently small rewards, and other community issues may be neglected. It is argued that business is no place for amateurism, and few community workers have the business skills and sense to advise groups in their judgements. Co-operatives and community enterprises, it is argued, and management and the control of capital are not part of working-class experience; urban communities are not co-operative cultures and such enterprises do not allow for the mass involvement of a neighbourhood, as would a housing campaign, for instance.

There are clearly many arguments pro and con on this issue and the involvement of community workers in it must be resolved at the local level, taking into account community views, agency remit and the interests and skills of the worker. It is certain, however, that local work initiatives are best seen not as 'the answer to unemployment' but as part of the longer-term reconstruction process within local communities.

Secondly, in *campaigns* involving community groups and workers, including those suggested by Nick Sharman against

- proposed closures and redundancies, making 'the investment decisions of large corporations more accountable to workforce and community';
- low pay and bad conditions, often in non-economical workplaces;
- the rundown of local public services, which provide not only support but are a source of local jobs; and
- those for socially useful products being produced in local industries and co-operatives.

Thirdly, in *organising the unemployed* around, for example, unemployment centres, unions of the unemployed, or support and 'consciousness-raising' groups. The purpose would be not only to get the unemployed involved in work creation and other community and workplace issues, but also to offer them a source of peer support to prevent demoralisation, to maintain optimism and to raise their expectations of themselves and of what they might expect from public services. Such groups would also be concerned with the self- and public image of the unemployed, and be concerned with dealing with the issues of stigma, self-respect and status in the community, as well as the benefits and facilities available to them. There may be a particular role for community work in helping to get together for mutual support and campaigns those who are especially disadvantaged as far as work is concerned. This would include groups such as the handicapped, the blind, ethnic minorities, single parents and the young.

Fourthly, in *productive leisure,* helping those out of work to find alternatives to employment that are satisfying and interesting to themselves, and possibly make a contribution to the community. Jack Grassby, at the 1978 ACW conference, mentioned the development by the unemployed of arts, sports and community groups such as youth theatres, film societies, tenants' associations and claimants' unions.

Liaison Community work has developed expertise and knowledge in bringing together people and organisations through mechanisms such as alliances, federations, standing conferences and more modest working groups at local level. The specific linking or liaison roles would include:

- bringing together the unemployed and residents with experience in community action so that the latter group can advise the former;
- getting local public services to work together on the immediate and long-term implications of unemployment;
- co-ordinating local work initiatives;
- bringing together local groups and trade unions;
- linking up relevant outside resources to local work institutions, for example, people with law, business and accountancy skills;

- linking up groups and activists regionally and nationally, so that people can learn from and support one another.

Informal education   Jack Grassby also referred to the possibility of attending college whilst unemployed, and as a productive alternative to work. Community workers can help in organising mutual learning groups where work, hobby and social skills are analysed within the group, and where informal education can take place about substantive political, social and economic issues. There is a role, too, in helping educational institutions to adapt to the learning needs of the local unemployed. Informal education, stressing self-help and mutual learning, will help to strengthen networks in a community to replace those threatened by the loss of relationships based on the place of work.

Advice and Information   Neighbourhood advice services are especially needed in areas of unemployment, to deal with problems of welfare benefits, fuel debts, rent, rate and mortgage payments. This involves not only an advice service to individuals but the formation of claimant groups and the training of local people in advice work and representation at tribunals.

Research   Community workers can also play a social planning role in working with groups, unions and local authorities to research the income base and future developments within the community. Research will also be needed on the investment plans of surviving local industries.

These, then, are the five major areas in which community work can be expected to intervene on work and unemployment issues. It is not an exhaustive discussion but one that indicates some of the more obvious and urgent points of intervention. There are a number of conclusions:

First, unemployment is a community issue; it is not to be seen as something that is only to do with the workplace, or involving simply trade unions and the labour movement. The unemployed are in their homes and neighbourhoods; the problems caused or aggravated by unemployment are experienced in the community. The process of working on the issue as suggested above makes the territorial community a basic unit of organising, but without denying the importance of wider alliances in the operation of campaigns.

Secondly, our response to unemployment must be within a strategy that perceives the process of reconstructing communities as the fundamental objective; at the least this must argue against piecemeal and ad hoc initiatives by agencies and community workers, who must rather develop proposals for working on the unemployment issue that are set within a wider strategy of reconstruction. The challenge to community work lies not simply in responding to the needs of the unemployed but in a longer-term attempt to reconstruct the social, political and economic fabric of communities, torn by the effects of unemployment and other problems.

Thirdly, it is evident, then, that community work alone can do very little; not only must it press into action other public services and interventions but it must also be able to understand its contribution as part of a larger effort, and work at the skills and knowledge of inter-organisational approaches.

(b) Housing

Housing will continue to be a priority area for community work in the 1980s. We are facing a serious shortage of accommodation in both the private and public sector, as the number of 'starts' of new housing and improvement of existing stocks decreases. There will be an increase in the number of homeless people, caused not just by the shortage of housing but also through action taken against people in arrears of rent, rate and mortgage payments. Tenants in public housing will continue to experience difficulties with fuel bills, and this is likely to worsen in the 1980s as steps are taken to conserve energy supplies. There will be a decline in the quality of much of the public housing built in the 1960s and 1970s, as the unsuitable, sub-standard materials used in construction begin to deteriorate. Allied to this will be a reduction in the resources available for repairs and maintenance, and an overall inability of local authorities to respond to this housing crisis because of the punitive effect on housing budgets of public expenditure cuts.

The decline in quality of housing stock and in the environment will produce a number of related problems: vandalism and delinquency, scapegoating, tensions between tenants and competition between different categories in housing need – between, for example, those on the waiting-list and those who are homeless; between white and black, young and old, two- and one-parent families. These tensions will be exacerbated by the remoteness of housing officials and the lack of resources of the housing department.

Housing groups such as tenants' associations will be needed to work creatively in this situation, and to respond to a number of other issues – the tenants' charter, management and housing co-operatives, council house sales and individual cases of need. Community workers will have to develop local housing action groups as well as federations that can take up city-wide and national issues. Housing will also continue to provide the focus for much other community activity – play schemes, festivals and health projects are just examples, as well as community care and support schemes.

The reconstructive dimension of the housing issue is as follows: the deterioration in the availability and quality of the housing stock will erode and destroy relationships and networks. These will have to be repaired. When steps are taken to replenish and improve the housing stock, housing groups must be there to provide models and pressure for new forms of ownership, partnership and management, with ideas, too, about the design and facilities of new building. These ideas will be important not just to avoid the mistakes of the last two decades but for determining the kind of design and environment that will facilitate productive social relations and responsibilities. The quality of housing and the environment, and the range of networks and contacts that they support, will become all the more important as changes in work patterns (shorter hours, early retirement) and unemployment increase the importance of the home and the neighbourhood for more members of households.

Intimately connected with unemployment and housing are two issues which are really substantive matters in their own right but whose importance is confirmed by changes in the housing and work aspects of people's lives. These are health and education. Changes in employment patterns imply changes in the function and organisation of formal and informal education. Unemployment and worsening housing conditions will bring further mental and bodily ill-health to working class communities who are already disadvantaged in health and environmental matters. Despite the crucial importance of health and education, and even in the face of evidence of the constant and, in some cases, increasing inequalities in health between social classes, community work has given relatively little attention to these issues in the last decade, though more health projects began to appear at the end of the 1970s in major conurbations.

(c)   Health

The relative lack of interest in health issues amongst community workers (and particularly amongst male workers) has a number of explanations. Rosenthal has suggested:

> the National Health Service has never been open to any forms of democratic control and people's experience of it is personal and private. Ill people are often reluctant to complain about the treatment they receive. Ill people made better are often grateful and eager to forget. Ill health itself is often fatalistically accepted. Thus neither National Health Service nor illness itself has appeared to be open to influence and change by the collective action of people in the community. (1980)

In addition, Murray and Hubley (1980) suggest that the NHS is dominated by 'experts' (and, it might be added, by professional bodies and trade unions) with a clear demarcation between them and 'laymen'; it and ill-health are clouded by a specialised language code; and there is no clearly defined and publicly explicit means of redress. These effects are compounded by the 'traditional deference of working class people to authority and professionalism'. Hubley (1978–9) has also suggested some characteristics of community work that have worked against involvement in health issues:

(1) Community workers subscribe to the view that the ill-health associated with poverty could only be overcome by tackling what they see to be the root causes of poverty: low income, poor housing, high unemployment, poor education and lack of power.
(2) The training of a community worker is typically a social work, community education, or community development professional course and while recognising the importance of health, these workers have not felt competent to deal with health matters.
(3) Community workers are employed by local authorities and involvement in health issues other than environmental health and housing would have entailed crossing the boundary between the local authority and the health service.
(4) The adoption of health issues is precluded by the belief of community workers in the non-directive approach where action is developed based on the perceived felt needs of the community. Housing, pre-school provisions and unemployment may be the felt needs of the community whereas alcoholism, dental care, smoking and exercise are not and a community worker might gain little support by focusing on these unpopular issues.

Many respondents to this study defined health as the important area of work in the 1980s: there is now more awareness that health inequalities (the different rates of health and sickness between social classes) are as noxious as income and wealth inequalities; that the issues of health, poverty, education and housing are intimately connected, as demonstrated, for example in dampness, repairs and environmental campaigns; and that health is as much a collective as an individual issue. The main areas of work on health in the 1980s would include the following:

● defending health services against closure and expenditure cuts, and ensuring that they become more responsive to the needs of their users. One community worker wrote: 'The community health projects in London have found that local residents (at least the women who are the main people who got involved) are too fed up with NHS services just to fight to keep them. They want changes if they are to join the fight to save resources.'

- the greater democratisation of the National Health Service.
- making health care more accessible, particularly in areas where the need is greatest. This involves campaigning against the centralisation of services, maintaining public transport facilities and effecting a better distribution of health care facilities.
- funding of more community health projects. These would be neighbourhood-based projects using community work methods to assist local people to take up health issues and improve their own level of health care and understanding. Women, in particular, experience keenly the strong patronising male influence in many health services. Access to and use of these services by ethnic groups, who are subject to demands for passports and cross-questioning, will also emphasise the significance of organising around health issues in the 1980s.
- when community work on other issues (such as dampness, repairs, drainage, play schemes) creates the appropriate climate for health education and action. This would also involve helping particular groups (for example, women, pensioners) to develop their own agendas for health care and awareness.

It must be stressed again that the development of community work in the health area must not proceed because it is fashionable or money is available but because it is seen within an overall strategy of community development. Councillor Tony Worthington (1980) has made this point in the following way:

> does the enormous amount of self-inflicted ill-health indicate something rather disturbing about the national state of mental health? . . . one, and only one, possible cause may be that we have privatised our lives too much? A question about our personal happiness relies too heavily on questions about the interior health of our families . . . is it reasonable to infer that our expectations of contentment within marriage are unrealistically high and demand too much of our partners and children. One way of avoiding this may be by building up the level and content of community life, enticing people out of their homes and lessening the claustrophobia within them . . . is it not likely to be true that a lively, vigorous, animated community will be a healthier community . . . we have to ask ourselves whether we can afford not to stimulate community self-help . . . a community that is working together will show a gain in health terms.

It would be wrong to suggest that community work alone can rectify health inequalities and other issues of care and education, and I do not want to suggest that the issues community workers choose to work on are the only or the most important health issues. As in other areas, interventions by community workers must be shaped by an understanding of what can be realistically achieved by the intervention, and this will often be much less than is indicated by the causes and extent of social problems. What community work offers is the opportunity to reconstruct at local level different approaches to, and awareness of, health issues and in so doing to add to the layers of networks and relationships that are naturally present and being created through collective action on other issues. The removal of health, and other, inequalities lies outside community work in the realm of political and policy decisions.

(d) Education

Educational inequalities between different social classes are as evident as those of health, wealth and income, as the differential rates of educational services and attainments testify. The persistence of such inequalities vitiates the democratic principles of our political system, and nowhere is this more clear than in the educational field where, for example, those disadvantaged in the educational system are denied the confidence and the knowledge that would contribute to and strengthen democratic practices. Our educational system is, Worthington has argued,

> imprisoned by its past. For historical reasons, our resources have overwhelmingly gone into the perceived needs of the young . . . after school leaving age, the resources for adult education have been given to educational successes. We have justified this by seeing education as dominated by the need to give qualifications to the young for presentation to their future employers. We have an educational system obsessed with the cognitive. The affective domain and the expressive arts have had a raw deal and scant attention. The forms of knowledge imparted are frequently removed from the knowledge needed in the everyday world . . . Adults have enormous learning needs too, but they are unlikely to want to return to a formal authoritarian system. The incongruity between the expert resources we give to our children and the lack of attention to the needs of adults grows all the time . . . the second reason for challenging the dominance of the school sector is that all the signs are that the relationship between schools and work may well have permanently changed. (1980)

For Worthington, community work has shown us that 'we shall never have sufficient people involved in community activities until they can shrug off their perception of their own inadequacy . . . there is nothing more exciting than seeing people discard [through community development] their mistakenly learnt and taught perception of their own inferiority. He argues, too, that we have to redesign the way we consider the relationship between work, leisure and education. This means looking at the local residential areas in which people live as places in which the full range of self-help activities can take place ranging from small workshop activity to service to fellow citizens to the full range of sporting, recreational and artistic activities. If we do not embrace this challenge, then the jobless growth of the future looks frightening.

As with other issues that are determined by larger political and economic factors, we can ask of the education field: what are the points of change and development where community work will be seen as a realistic intervention, often acting in concert with interventions made by workers in other fields, and with initiatives undertaken independently by local residents and members of movements and interest groups? Within the formal education system, there will be the need to defend services against withdrawal and closure, working with unions to fight staff losses and school closures in areas where school rolls are seen, in the short term, to be falling. The democratisation of the educational system will be an issue, involving community groups and parent-teacher associations, to make schools, teachers, resources and educational decisions more accessible to parental and community influence. Changes in employment patterns will mean radical changes in the conception of education provided in infant, primary and secondary schools. There will be more emphasis on how schools can become more community-orientated, particularly providing services to those not at work. Community workers can help residents to take action on these issues. In addition, school curricula will have to give as much emphasis to 'living' skills as to vocational ones: preparing people for a more active and knowing involvement in the political and social life of their communities. Opportunities for second-chance education will be demanded from further education, not just for the unemployed but also for those who were disadvantaged in, or were prematurely withdrawn from, the educational system in their younger days.

There will be pressure for equally radical changes within informal education, and here again there seems to be an important role for community work in such endeavours as community arts, advice and information services, and mutual support and learning groups. There will be a particular need to form city-wide and regional networks for informal educational activities, and priority may be given to enabling the 'elder statespeople' of community action to share their skills with less experienced local activists. There seems, too, a growing commitment in community work to providing more training courses for local activists, and this need will constitute only part of the pressure that will be put on local educational institutions (including community centres, youth clubs and the Workers' Educational Association) to respond to the growing demand from adults for forms of continuing education.

The various services in formal and informal education will, it is hoped, be instrumental in providing the direct services to facilitate the educational process that was outlined in an earlier chapter. These were, in particular, resources to provide:

> role education
> social and political education
> community education
> social leadership education

Community work has an important role in working with groups to bring about the changes in educational structure, philosophy and practices that are necessary for the service to respond to the different educational and community circumstances of the 1980s and beyond.

Employment, housing, health, education and the environment provide the issues around which the reconstruction of local communities must take place in the 1980s. It is a reconstruction not only of the physical and material fabric of communities but also of the attitudes, relationships and networks between individuals and groups. It would be folly to leave this reconstruction to the state or to private enterprise; local initiatives will be important though these will inevitably depend on funds and other resources from government. It must be a bottom-up reconstruction, informed by the inspiration and commitment of communities, with priorities that reflect local social needs and values. Community work will be only one contribution to this process of reconstruction, and there will need to be changes in the way in which public services contribute to community well-being. The departments of the local authority, for example, have much to contribute to the reconstructive process, but their own reform will itself be part of the reconstruction, and it will be part of community work's contribution to help bring about the necessary changes in the philosophies and operating procedures of those departments.

The reconstruction of the public services will involve not just the restoration of services and resources but making them less bureaucratic and centralised, more amenable to community values, ideas and influence and more responsive to community needs. It will be important for community workers to help services adapt to become more accessible, and to make decisions in ways that are open to community scrutiny and participation. The resistance to inter-organisational and social planning tasks in community work must be disregarded: public services have a pervasive influence on the lives of working-class families, and these services must be kept at the point of offering the best possible policies and resources to their users. What is as important is that key public agencies such as social services departments are able to conceive of their operations as a contribution to the reconstructive process, and that as a consequence the efforts of different agencies are linked to each other, and to other interventions such as community work.

(2)   RENEGOTIATION OF STATUS

A number of groups in the 1970s have started the process of renegotiating their status within society, and some have made more progress than others. Women, gays and black people are examples of these groups. The matter of status is, in simple terms, the issue of how people see themselves and are seen by others, and the pattern of power, opportunities and resources that is consequent on these perceptions. People's attitudes to themselves and to others, and the kinds of relationships members of low-status groups have with the rest of society, are caught up in the matter of the distribution of resources, services, facilities and rights, and thus with the distribution of power. Looked at in another way, status is about

● how groups are differently treated as objects of social policy and political decisions; and
● day-to-day relationships and attitudes as manifested in degrees of prejudice, discrimination, misunderstanding, and so on.

Thus to renegotiate status is to improve how one sees oneself, and is seen by others, and to better one's access to resources, services, power and influence.

The renegotiation of status is, of course, inherent in many of the activities involved in the reconstructive process, described above: the enhancement of status is an important outcome of work, for example, on the issues of housing or unemployment, and this is seen vividly in the following account of a South Wales tenants' group, who described their campaign in an issue of *Community Action* (1980):

> In the process we, the tenants, have had our consciousness awakened. It seems that by taking militant action in most cases you are taking control of your life for the first time. By asking one question you question everything about your life and society and the system . . . I've never thought so much or hurt so much. I no longer take the word of the so-called experts, doctors, etc., whereas before I would just accept things as they were and the role I was supposed to play. Is it completely satisfying for a woman just to do housework, look after children, and then grow old and die? That's what I see a lot of women do.

I think perhaps because we're women we felt cowed down all our lives. I think every woman has got that aggression which she'd like to release and maybe what we've done is released that anger about being women and being treated the way women are treated.

A lot of council tenants live in fear that they will be evicted if they speak too much against the council. Some tenants would say we were foolish to do what we were doing. I think that probably they were afraid it would react on them. Before a demonstration I always felt very nervous, but I've learnt fear is something you've got to face and when you've faced it you feel a tremendous amount of achievement.

For years I've listened to politicians and all those well educated articulate people who said they cared about the working class and I couldn't agree with what they were saying. But I thought I'm not a very well educated woman, just a working class woman, I must be wrong. But since I've been going to conferences and meeting an awful lot of people I realise it's not me that's wrong it's them. They've completely lost touch with the working class. They just don't know how we live at all. I think the only way things are going to be changed is for people like us to work together.

This account indicates that through community action it is possible to achieve enhancement of status in a number of roles – in this case, those of woman, parent, tenant, consumer and member of the working class. Involvement in community activities offers opportunities for redefinition of one's self, roles and relationships with other individuals and groups. The tenant's account suggests, too, that the concern with improving political significance and competence is both a means and an outcome of becoming a participant in community activities.

Whilst the renegotiation of status is thus part of community organising, it is for some groups a major goal in its own right, and it is to be expected that in the 1980s community workers will be able to offer their resources and skills to these groups. Black people, women, older people, the young, single parents and the physically and mentally disabled seem likely to be groups who in the next decade will be involved in the renegotiation of their status, and to whom community workers will give some priority. Members of these groups are not only particularly affected by issues of housing and employment, but they are, too, marginal to the political process and discriminated against, ignored, neglected, patronised and exploited. It is hoped that the 1980s will be a decade in which the position for these, and other, groups will radically improve, as well as one in which their rights will be safeguarded and extended.

Many respondents to the study suggested that in the 1980s community work would need to give priority to ethnic groups, young people and the elderly. Work with the first two groups will clearly include some of the issues of employment and education. The issues of racism, ageism against young and old, and sexism will continue to be important items on the community work agenda, not least because of the radical temper in community work and the assertiveness of movements amongst ethnic groups and women. Much work in inner-city areas will revolve around the needs of black British people, and we should expect to make changes in the recruitment and training of community workers to reflect the urgency of this priority. There is likely to be an emphasis not just on protective organising against discrimination, injustice and harassment but on assertive collective action to eliminate the disproportionate disadvantage experienced by black Britishers in, for example, the education, housing and employment markets.

There is less grounds for confidence, however, in relation to so-called 'client groups' such as the elderly and the physically and mentally handicapped. These groups contain some of the most disadvantaged yet they have received relatively little attention from community organisers. The reasons for this are complex, and are to do with the nature of the groups themselves, and with the evolving characteristics of community work. One correspondent suggested:

> The main reason why community workers have not got involved in this field and are unlikely to do so in the future is that they share to a large extent the contempt for work with the elderly and the handicapped that is near universal in the personal social services and derives in the end from the fact that unlike other client groups they are thought unlikely to engage in violent action or to make a significant contribution to material production.

It was easy enough in the early and middle 1970s to identify deprivation and powerlessness in such groups as tenants: the issues were clear, tenants were eager to take action on them, and this accorded well with the anti-establishment ethic in community work that sought to battle with local authorities to wrench away the resources which, at the time, they possessed. Work with the elderly or disabled, however, requires another kind of perspective; although there are important campaigns to be fought for resources and rights, community work with these groups must also concern itself with a process of developing self-awareness about status, and the learning of confidence, skills and knowledge.

The challenge for community work in the 1980s is to broaden the selective radicalism of the 1970s that blinded many practitioners to the existence of disadvantage outside the more obvious categories such as tenants and unemployed workers. The contribution that community work can make is to help groups such as the elderly to

- organise campaigns to do with resources, facilities and welfare and civil rights;
- develop neighbourhood support schemes and other facilities (according to community work principles – see my earlier definition);
- improve the range and quality of the services provided by statutory and voluntary agencies;
- ensure the needs of the elderly are taken into account in the framing of social policies.

Work with all the kinds of groups discussed in this section will be a mix of campaigning, awareness-raising, care provision and change in systems and attitudes. Community workers may also need to do more to involve members of such groups in general community organisations such as tenants' associations, and to be aware themselves of how racism, sexism and ageism are present in, and influence, the work of these community groups.

(3) REALISING THE COMMUNITY

The discussion in this section is developed from the material in Chapter 2 about social development and communal coherence. The theme of realising the community is to do with realising the potential of the affective and material capacities of communities; that is, strengthening networks, on the one hand, and facilitating more reciprocal relations between individuals and between groups; and, on the other, making 'the community' a more significant unit for analysis and action in the sphere of social policy and economic regeneration. The development of the community in this sense may be expected to be a possible outcome of the distributive function of community work; that is, a consequence of helping people work together to achieve the goals they have set themselves in areas such as housing, play, education, health care, and so on. But realising the community is, together with the evolution of political responsibility, part of the developmental function of community work as described in Chapter 2. It is a major goal in its own right, and hence some of the earlier discussion on this matter is restated here to emphasise its key position in any strategic conception of community work.

There are territorial communities and functional ones, those bringing people together, irrespective of territory, in the pursuit of common interests; a claimant's group is an example of a functional group based on affinity of interests. The theme of realising the community refers to both kinds of communities, and indeed much of the content of the last section on renegotiating status was about the development of communities of interest amongst a number of groups in the population.

But I am concerned in this section to discuss the importance of community in terms of territory or common residence. The objective of realising the community in its territorial sense is not to be dismissed as a nostalgia for the idyllic and romantically conceived world of pre-industrial society; indeed, it is features of post-industrial society that suggest the imperative to become less dependent on the state and private enterprise for income and welfare, and the urgency to renew networks in the community that have become fractured in the long postwar boom. The rationale for realising the community is that it is, in the words of a report from the Non-Violence Study Group (1980):

- a unit large enough to be a political force and small enough to account for, and relate to, the individual person;
- an optimal location to develop alternative models of social (and economic) organisation;
- a point of mobilisation of people to effect social change which can be self-organised;
- a unit of people which can command sufficient resources to establish alternative institutional arrangements;
- a unit for analysis which will identify the forces and material conditions determining social relations.

Most of community work that has been concerned with communities of residence has been in neighbourhoods; locally based strategies of community action and community development have been described as neighbourhood work or neighbourhood organising. The word neighbourhood is used to refer to the small geographical area in which people live and with which they may identify; it thus contrasts with the city or part of a city or town. Residence, together with some local facilities like shops, pubs and clubs, is about the centre of a web of relations involving family, friends and neighbours. Thus neighbourhood may be a small housing estate, a part of a larger one, or a pattern of terraced houses or a tall block of flats; what is certain is that the size and characteristics of 'the neighbourhood' will vary.

But why is the neighbourhood important, and likely to be more so in the years ahead? Primarily because that is where people will be: unemployment, early retirement, shorter working hours, other factors such as financial and energy restraints on travel, demographic changes such as the increase in the population of the elderly and social policy initiatives towards community care, will all mean that there will be more people spending more time at the point of residence and neighbourhood (people will *also,* of course, be in other networks to which the neighbourhood may be irrelevant, such as groups based on age, race, religion, recreation, and so on). The significance of the neighbourhood will be enhanced by regeneration of the economic base through local employment initiatives, and the development of consumer and producer co-operatives. Solidarity between people with common interests is influenced by experiences within the neighbourhood; no one can doubt that federations and alliances are important, but their credibility depends on effective neighbourhood representation. Joint campaigns between trade unions and community groups are likewise important, but they cannot succeed unless the groups have been developed at neighbourhood level. It is fallacious to scorn neighbourhood organising in order to emphasise the value of working within the labour and trade union movement, as if that were the only or most effective way of working with working-class people. The majority of the working class in many parts of the country are to be found in their homes and neighbourhoods − at the point of reproduction and not at the point of production − and these include the out-of-work, the very young, the elderly, the handicapped, schoolchildren, women who work at home and workers who work in neighbourhood-based services and facilities.

Neighbourhoods may contain different kinds and intensities of networks that express people's support, care, trust, responsibilities and obligations to one another. Neighbourhoods will vary in the presence or absence of these networks, and their functions will vary in this respect over time and place. These networks comprise the links between friends and neighbours, as well as those present in participation in a range of community activities, and membership of recreational, political, civic and economic associations. These relationships are important where they exist not just because they are the source of services and of satisfaction and fulfilment, but because through them people have the chance to learn to know each other, and to know each other in a number of different roles. There is more to this knowledge than the reciprocal utilities that it can support; it provides the core of identification and commitment between people which in turn nurtures the various networks. These networks, and the knowledge of neighbourhood people and events that they facilitate, not only provide a source of coherence and support but can, of course, be experienced as intrusive.

Community work is, or ought to be, part of a development process that is concerned with these linkages between people (as individuals, and as groups) and between them and systems of government and administration. Fractured social relationships can be presumed to be bad in themselves; hostilities that arise between groups in a neighbourhood (for example, on the basis of race) are to be avoided, as is the oppression by some sections of a community of another (again race, but also sex and age). Strong neighbourhood linkages are to be welcomed for the opportunities they give for various kinds of learning about oneself and other people, and for the development of different kinds of roles to be played within one's work, household and community. These linkages are important, too, for the initiation of action campaigns on particular issues, as well as for the emergence of neighbourhood forms of welfare and economic self-reliance. Such campaigns and community events such as festivals and community arts programmes are facilitated by these linkages but they also provide the opportunity to foster new, and strengthen existing, contacts between people and groups.

The existence and strength of neighbourhood networks is also crucial to the development of political significance and political competence. Helping people to participate more knowledgeably in politics is more than the matter of organising skills and cognitively understanding political issues. An authentic source of political motivation and knowledge may be the strength of the relationships that hold people together, and the sense of common purpose that this can provide. The converse of this statement (rule by division) is more easily accepted than the truth of the statement itself. It is true that in community work we often find references to the power of the collective but this is too often taken to mean simply the leverage that can be exerted by a group to achieve its specific goals. It is a truism that people who are united in their goals and methods have greater chance of success. Community work has been able to understand this truth only in relation to individual issues and organising tasks; it has understood the need for specific solidarity on particular issues but failed to appreciate the need for *systemic solidarity* within a community, the kind of solidarity that was described in Chapter 2 as communal coherence. The groups who have come closest to understanding the process of systemic solidarity in extending individual and collective strengths are perhaps to be found amongst women and some ethnic minorities. Systemic solidarity – the existence of multiple linkages and interactions between people, and the knowledge of self and others that ensues – is as valid a goal in neighbourhoods as it is in the kind of liberational groups associated, for example, with the feminist movement.

Communal coherence or systemic solidarity, and the kinds of campaigns, caring structures and neighbourhood events it will support, as well as the possibilities it creates for more political significance and competence, will not necessarily occur through simply calling for it, by sloganising or merely through the cumulative effect of ad hoc campaigns and specific initiatives. Community workers must learn in the next decade that communal coherence is established in a diverse number of ways: the emphasis is both on on-going and contractual linkages, and thus sports clubs, leisure groups and parent–teacher associations are as important as tenants' groups and action campaigns. It is folly to dismiss some forms of linkage because they are not 'radical' or because they do not appear to be overtly connected to political issues. On the contrary, political significance and competence may depend in part on the existence of communal coherence and this is fostered by programmes that 'work on different issues and with different groups in order to build and to draw strength from the links between them' (*Community Links Report,* 1980).

Thus the theme of realising the community confronts us with the indivisibility of neighbourhood issues and needs, and the indivisibility of community concern and strategies to meet needs. Communal coherence is something to be worked on by enabling a wide range of initiatives to occur in a neighbourhood; it demands an integrated approach from workers, and this requires staff with different kinds of expertise so that all the aspects of a community's needs are addressed. This integrated approach will take up issues to do with housing, work, play and other action campaigns but will also be involved, as the Community Links Project is, with children and youth work, community arts and education, legal and welfare rights and advice, adult group work, community care schemes, and a host of other activities.

Realising the community will also involve specific programmes that will both reflect, and contribute to, the growing importance of the neighbourhood. Examples are the decentralisation of agency structures and services, the emergence of mediating (or intermediate) agencies, the development of neighbourhood care and support schemes, and the evolution of neighbourhood councils and government. The neighbourhood will come to be more important for economic reasons too; the success of many local initiatives towards reconstruction will depend in part upon the development of communal coherence in neighbourhoods. For example, the emergence of community enterprises and other economic ventures based on co-operatives within the United Kingdom seem to have taken place mostly in Celtic regions. There is a suggestion here that such endeavours are dependent on existing bonds of identification and commitment that facilitate working together for a common good, and which support individual hard work and sacrifices. Relationships similar to those based on common ethnicity may be needed in neighbourhoods to support a wide range of local developments.

Giving more emphasis to communal coherence would represent an important extension within the assumptive world of community work, which has in the past largely been concerned with the values of egalitarianism and emancipation. An interest in fostering more and better linkages within a neighbourhood may suggest a concern with the value of fraternity. This is a difficult issue to deal with in community work not least because the word is sexist. Fraternity and the matter of networks and linkages have been brought into disrepute partly because they were dealt with in such a starry-eyed fashion in the early days of community work ('fostering community spirit') and partly because they were associated with consensuality and the inability to see the differences of interest within and between communities and between them and departments of government. The idea of fraternity – of relationships of caring, respect, support and mutual aid – was probably also devalued by its association with the hippy and flower power people of the late 1960s. The urgency to do something about inner-city issues in the 1970s, and thus to take action against resource-holders, served to emphasise the value of egalitarianism and the interactions between neighbourhoods and resource-holders, rather than interactions within neighbourhoods.

The spirit of collective action was competitiveness and the assertion of self-interest as neighbourhood groups struggled against each other to win resources. One response to this has been the formation of federations and alliances which are a recognition of the importance of fraternity and altruism. This recognition must be extended to include the centrality of fraternal relationships within neighbourhoods, and not just between representatives of groups at the city-wide or regional level.

This point about fraternity may be put more generally: the pursuit of fraternity and altruism entails mutual acts of responsibility, and these may be broadly classified as *personal* or *public*. The former comprise the range of interests, responsibilities and deeds of help that individuals and groups take on themselves in relation to helping others – 'being a good neighbour' is an obvious example, but personal responsibility goes further than this and includes responsibility for the community's processes of, for example, social control and socialisation. The public expressions and acts are to be found in the sanction we have given to the development of state welfare systems: these systems show how our responsibilities for each other are being expressed impersonally through third-party agencies and their staff. It is no surprise to see how the increase in the range of public acts has corresponded with a decline in the importance and efficacy of personal acts. The relative material prosperity of the long postwar boom not only made possible the financing of state welfare systems but produced at least three major effects that were to influence personal acts adversely. First, the expansion of work opportunities and the search to maximise income left little in the way of time and energy for personal acts of fraternity. Secondly, this time and energy was further eroded by a wider range of leisure activities that became possible with material prosperity. Thirdly, household living became more privatised and remote from events in the community; the home became a place for consuming personal leisure products, and for recuperation after a hard day's work. The diminution in personal acts was worsened by the break-up of established communities in clearance schemes, and their dispersion to new estates and tower blocks where the design and scale of the housing, the environment of which it was a part, and the absence of social and community facilities, did little to establish linkages between people and groups.

The message is clear for the 1980s: state welfare services are necessary but not sufficient. Public acts of responsibility must be accompanied by personal ones centred within the household and neighbourhood. The challenge of the 1980s is to defend the resources of the welfare state, and to develop them in a way that is supportive of personal acts of responsibility and intervention. The values of fraternity are to be realised in the combination of the welfare state with welfare neighbourhoods, in the development of public and personal acts of responsibility; welfare neighbourhoods suggest people taking more interest in the well-being of others, in mutual aid, and functions of social participation and socialisation. Putting welfare back into the neighbourhood will require appropriate resources, as well as the development of the services of the welfare state in a way that is compatible with neighbourhood-based responsibilities. This process must be congruent with the reconstruction of neighbourhoods discussed earlier, as well as with the goals of renegotiation of status of groups. It is evident, for example, that welfare neighbourhoods should not be achieved by restricting the opportunities of any particular group, for example, women. It also needs to be said again that community work will be only one contribution to the processes of reconstruction, renegotiation of status and realising the community. The realignment of resources, attitudes and relations that is required is so much bigger than community work, yet its contribution can be important and will depend in large part on its ability to move away from a residual conception of its function. This and other matters are discussed in the following section.

SOME CONCLUDING THOUGHTS

The task for community work in the 1980s is twofold: to contribute effectively within the kinds of political and social programmes discussed already in this chapter; and, secondly, to develop thinking about its contribution that will make its chances of being effective all the better. What community workers will be doing will naturally be of much import to themselves, local people and agency staff, but how they *think* about what they are doing will influence how effective they will likely be. The way in which we conceptualise practice will, for instance, shape our ideas about strategy, funding, auspices and training, and I want to look at these matters in later chapters.

The themes of reconstruction, renegotiation and realising the community are ways of thinking about practice that suggest how workers and their agencies can develop an overall strategy in which community work will be a contribution; it suggests, too, the order of numbers of workers that will be needed, how they might be organised and supported, and what pre- and on-the-job training will be appropriate. These themes point to the role of community work within a much broader social and economic development plan working in harness not just with local groups but with statutory agencies, institutions such as schools, other professionals, social movements, trade unions and voluntary organisations. Whilst the three themes will be dominant, we must remember that community workers will continue to work on a number of issues which are not encompassed within the themes, as described in this chapter; for example, play provision.

Three key elements of a strategy to work on these themes are:

(1) Community workers will become effective in the tasks and roles of community organisation and social planning, as well as in community action and community development.
(2) The neighbourhood will continue to be a key focus for organising, even though work at other geographic and policy-making levels will be essential.
(3) Community work will be more consciously aware of its developmental as well as its distributive tasks.

This suggests that community work will develop an idea of itself that moves away from residual definitions of its functions. There are two elements in the meaning of 'residual'. First, how community work is seen by others – politicians, professionals, policy-makers, public at large – and how they define its goals and activities. This is the 'view from outside'. Secondly, how community workers themselves (and their trainers) define community work – the 'view from inside'.

Viewed from the outside as a residual, community work is seen as a last resort safety net that enables disadvantaged groups to make known their needs and take action on them; as a residual function, it is seen as something that makes good failures within local and central government departments, within communities and within the economic and political operations of capitalist society itself. Where people locate these failures and inadequacies will indicate something about their values, but wherever the failures are located, the common element is that community work is seen as a residual, reparative mechanism. This residual conception of community work is given expression in a number of different ways: for example, in the common feature of the 1970s of funding the single community worker based in a large team of social workers covering a hopelessly large geographic area; or in the continuing drive to adapt community work to deal with 'new' problems as they are revealed in communities, or in the operation of services, and where there are no established services or procedures able to respond to them. The inadequate arrangements for funding community work, for in-service training and for personal development and promotion, are other organisational expressions of its residual function.

When we view from the inside, we see that we ourselves are much to blame for this state of affairs; as an occupation, we have shown a singular lack of vision and complexity in the way we conceptualise our work and its functions, and have tended to offer definitions of community work which confirm its residual nature. This is most evident when we define community work only as oppositional campaigns against the local state; or when we define it as advice- and information-giving in neighbourhood centres; or when we emphasise the role of resource centres in providing 'technical' advice and facilities. I am not saying that campaigns, advice and resource centres are not important − on the contrary, they are, or can be, essential elements of the community work task; but they are only residual activities − the bare minimum of intervention that provides a safety net. My suggestion is that during the 1970s we did much to confirm the residual view of community work held 'outside' by defining community work in terms of narrow operations and goals, and by producing explanations of our work that ignored the complexity of the issues with which we worked. The community work task became partialised and often fragmentary (and this reinforced residual conceptions) as different interests seized on community work in order to achieve their particular goals. This state of affairs was not adequately balanced by the development of complex or holistic conceptions of community work which offered a measure of conceptual fit between different approaches working together in a state of changing integration and conflict.

The task of the 1980s is for community work to achieve an 'institutional' view of itself (as well, of course, as emphasising its residual activities where these are under attack or not even developed in some areas). This word 'institutional' is a difficult one in community work, because it has other meanings that are often pejorative. Again, it has two elements. Viewed from the outside, community work becomes recognised as a normal and integral function, carried on as an established activity within and outside services such as social work and education. It is seen as a basic part of social and political institutions, and not just as something that becomes necessary when these institutions appear inadequate. Part of the task for the 1980s is for community work to become credible as an institutional activity, and to do this without jeopardising its autonomy as an intervention. To become an institutional function without falling prey to the worst perils of institutionalisation is the prize of the 1980s.

Whether this prize can be grasped will depend in part on the second element of being an institutional function − how community work sees itself, the 'inside view'. As an occupation we must move away from definitions of our functions that serve only to reinforce a residual view of community work. We must try to articulate (and express in practice) a broader view of our contribution, and I hope this view is evident from the discussion in this chapter. It is one that recognises we must work on issues of care and self-help as well as on campaigns, and that these must be integrated with influencing social policies, plans and agency services, linking up in a coherent strategy with other occupations and movements. I have also suggested that an institutional view of community work must include its developmental function to promote political responsibility and communal coherence. This point can be put another way: the definition of community work in terms only of product and process goals is an incomplete formula and suggests only the two elements of a residual conception; the institutional and more complete idea is to add a third concern to product and process goals and that is the promotion of linkage goals. These are to be seen as important in their own right and as means to achieve product and process goals. There are already examples of linkage goals becoming more important in community work (federations and links between community groups and trade unions) but the time has come to acknowledge the need to strengthen and diversify linkages within neighbourhoods. Put another way, our skill will be to understand why the neighbourhood is an important unit, even though many of the variables which influence the well-being of neighbourhood residents lie outside it.

There are two other factors that will affect the emergence of an institutional view of community work. First, as an occupation we must make clearer what our claims to competence are based upon and to do so without turning community work into a closed, professionalised occupation. Recognition of the bases of our competence must enhance our case for more resources to train, support and advise community workers.

Secondly, we must recognise that community work has both a *specific* and a *synoptic* contribution to make to community action, community development, community organisation, social planning and service extension. As with other occupations and movements who contribute to these five approaches, community work has a specific contribution; workers do what they do in a particular way that defines community work as distinctive from other interventions, and I discussed in an earlier chapter what the distinguishing features of community work were. What is special about community work, however, is that it has also a synoptic contribution; it seeks to bring together and to understand all the other interventions in community action, development, and so forth. Community work has the opportunity to be an integrating and cohering power in the organisation of groups, the development of services and the determination of policies.

5 Training for Community Work

Do not go gentle into that good night.
Rage, rage against the dying of the light.
Dylan Thomas

Community work is more than its field-based practices, that is, what workers do in their interventions with local people and agencies. Attempts to narrow down community work to mean only its practice are at the heart of difficulties in the relationship between its practice and its training, research, literature and theories. To define community work only as its practice is immediately to place these other activities outside the boundaries of community work, and this will produce a different attitude to those activities from that which is possible when we see practice and training as all falling (even though they are different activities) within the boundaries of an occupation. My assumption, then, in discussing community work practice and these other matters is that they provide the constituent elements of an occupation. Community work is thus

- its practice
- its training facilities
- its research facilities and their yield
- its literature
- its continually evolving set of values, theories and concepts
- its organisational forms, for example, Association of Community Workers, Federation of Community Work Training Groups[1]
- its managers, funders, sponsors and the kinds of administrative arrangements made for the delivery of community work

Abstracting practice from these other constituent parts of community work not only does violence to the concept of practice itself (equating it with a kind of 'mindless activism') but also prevents the development of a unity of approach between practice and the other elements. Thinking of community work only as its practice has produced an imbalanced occupation, one that is attempting to work with the gravest kinds of problems but is handicapped by the absence of political will and resources to develop an infrastructure that will help that practice to be effective.

In this and the next two chapters, I will look at some of the major features of the infrastructure of the practice of community work; that is, the ideas, institutions and resources that support the doing of community work. The contribution of the infrastructure is to ensure that community work is practised as competently as possible. I shall examine the following parts of the infrastructure: training; research; knowledge and theory development; information services; in-service provision; and peer group support. There ought to be a dynamic interaction between the practice of community work and its infrastructure, and I hope it will become clear that the development of community work in the last decade in Britain has not been accompanied by a commensurate resourcing of infrastructure to guide that practice.

This chapter will be concerned with various forms of training; in Chapter 6 I shall look at the recruitment, auspices and funding of community workers. Chapter 7 will explore certain issues to do with the development of literature, theory and research, and conclude with an examination of the need for, and the functions of, a national community work organisation.

TRAINING

I use 'training' in the broadest sense to mean preparation and continuing updating to do a job of work; training thus links with entry to an occupation, the successful application for employment, career paths and financial rewards. I shall use training to encompass three methods of preparation:

(1)   training through formal courses in further and higher education bodies that lead to certification;
(2)   training through apprenticeship schemes that may or may not lead to certification;
(3)   learning through experience that may or may not be subsequently recognised and accredited.

The first is often referred to as college-based training and the other two as field-based, though much college-based training has a substantial field component (and, in this respect, the development of community work student units was a significant factor in enhancing the quality of field training). The purpose of training is to ensure that people who are given paid employment in community work have appropriate expertise for the job, and this in turn is to ensure that the recipients of community work interventions receive the best possible service. Training through the three methods indicated above is to do with competence, and thus an examination of training in and for community work must look at the following issues:

- In what do trainees have to be competent?
- What forms of training and learning are most effective?
- What are the most appropriate ways of assessing competence?
- What are the ways of signalling a successful assessment to the outside world – in particular to employers and users of community workers? This is the issue of certification, accreditation and a more public and specific statement of the contents of training experiences.

There is a greater concern today with the question of competence in community work than in the early part of the 1970s. This is partly to do with the higher expectations of employers and community groups, and partly with the greater complexity of the issues facing communities. This was well put by one writer to the study:

> As we move towards a much harder economic climate so the pressure for greater accountability and for expertise to produce results will increase. Certainly present day youth work is much more complex and more demanding in terms of the range of knowledge and skills than it was fifteen to twenty years ago. I think the same can be said of community work as the workers find themselves coping with the extremely complex problems of inner city areas and urban management. Community workers need a sound personal and professional kit if they are going to survive themselves and be able to help constituents in neighbourhoods and communities work out actions which can positively confront and tackle the problems and issues in such areas. It seems to me the scene is a very tough one and the going is likely to get harder so that there are not going to be many soft options open to cover up lack of knowledge, skill and competence.

It is competence that should be the key factor in making appointments and negotiating salary grades. This competence should be seen as relevant to the needs and issues at hand, and the person concerned judged to be appropriate (personality, values, life-style, attitudes) within the demands of the situation. It is quite wrong to elevate qualifications as the only or most important indicator of competence, and as wrong to elevate experience. Both can seriously mislead as to a person's competence, and neither is per se a more reliable indicator of competence than the other. What is more important is the *content* both of qualifying training and of previous experience, and the use the individual has made of them, and schemes to accredit courses and individuals have the potential of making clear this content.

There are two other values of concern in community work training besides competence; they are *diversity* and *access*.

There is a general agreement in community work about the need to diversify the kinds of learning opportunities available both to community workers and voluntary activists. But people come at diversification by different routes; some arrive there from a critique of college-based education, whilst others accept the value of the college but see diversified opportunities as

- an acceptance that different formats are needed; not everyone will learn best at a college, and a variety of financial and family reasons will prevent many from attending a formal course;
- a way of preparing for the unpredictable events of the future.

The overall mood in community work is for the reformation and development of existing college-based training, together with diversification of other forms that are more directly linked to field and agency. The reformation of college training includes not only continuing work on the curriculum and the balance between class work and placement but also clarification of goals (are we training people to be 'community-minded' social workers or community workers?) and the consolidation of what one correspondent called 'a limited number of full-time, exacting and rigorous courses in community organising, for paid community workers'.

The value of diversity suggests we must continue to evaluate field- and college-based opportunities against one another, as we learn more about what learning opportunities are right for what kinds of people. This critical comparison of one against the other must avoid both the romanticisation of the field and the doctrinaire dismissal of colleges. It will be important in the 1980s to avoid polarisation of college- and field-based training, move away from stereotyping their strengths and limitations and, whilst diversifying field-based facilities, work for the improvement of college-based courses, which are still in their infancy and have much to do to develop further.

The value of *access* suggests that training opportunities be as open as possible, not just to voluntary activists but to people leaving other occupations, and to graduates with degrees in other fields. Diversification is only one means to ensure better access; there may be a continuing need for affirmative action towards certain groups in student selection procedures, as well as the running of community work classes in the evening and lunchtimes. Such affirmative action should not, of course, disregard an individual's general capacity to undertake the role which will be required, or the fact that the role of community worker is not necessarily the most appropriate role for voluntary activists. This raises a point to be discussed below that training voluntary activists need not be confined to training them to be community workers.

The other issue about access is whether community work is to be an open or closed occupation; there are few people who argue that it should be closed. On the contrary, there seems support for the views put forward by Ian Smith (1980) that a closed occupation would end the richness, vitality and variety that have been community work's hallmark. An open occupation is also essential to ensure that the most suitable people come forward to take up community work jobs; open access is therefore necessary to optimise the value of competence, so long as there are adequate procedures to indicate to employers and groups that this competence in training (in the broadest sense used in this chapter) has been achieved. I do not agree with Ian Smith that some form of national or regional qualification or accreditation will necessarily lead to, or implies, a closed occupation; on the contrary, our success in keeping community work open will depend on the confidence of funders, employers and community groups in the competence of those people entering the occupation. This confidence can be sustained by having a national qualification that applies to all field- and college-based training opportunities. There is also the point raised by a correspondent who said 'that unless we have a national qualification under our own control, the large state agencies which still employ the majority of community workers will look to other paper qualifications which are less relevant'.

There is ambivalence in community work about the idea of expertise. The training group of the Association of Community Workers (which itself recommended in 1976 the setting up of a community work training body) published a paper (*Community Work on CQSW Courses*) about what should be taught on these courses and, in a supreme contradiction, suggests that 'the notion of "the expert" is contrary to the spirit of community work'. The trained and paid community worker is or ought to have expertise in her work; without such expertise there is no justification for the training and salary such people receive, and no justification for the trust and responsibility given them by employers and groups. The fact that part of the worker's expertise is to pass on his skills and knowledge, and to do so participatively, is not to deny that worker's expertise; rather it indicates the need for expertise, not just in community organising but in the role of the informal adult educator.

The ambivalence about competence conceals a fear and a vision; there is a fear that community work staff will continue to be middle-class graduates and a vision that they should be replaced by working-class people. Sometimes this vision excludes a rational appraisal of what the future may need; the strengths and limitations of the paid 'outside' organiser are not adequately assessed, and there is equally little consideration of the strengths and limitations of the indigenous organiser.

There can be no alternative to the development of appropriate skills and knowledge in community work, even though the earlier 'generation' of community workers who entered the field in the 1970s without training were successful in their organising efforts. But, as we noted earlier, this success occurred despite their lack of preparation and was due to the relative ease of organising people in that period in campaigns against local authorities. It was also due to a very high level of energy and commitment in which sheer enthusiasm triumphed over many mistakes. Appropriate skills and knowledge, however, are no substitute for, and will remain mechanical in their application without, a strong sense of purpose on the part of the practitioner. Indeed, it is a basic task (and skill area) for the worker to define his goals and be open about the political and moral values that influence them. This sense of conviction, which will necessarily entail beliefs about the causes of deprivation in society, is essential to sustain the worker through the physical and mental demands of community work, and the pressures he will be subject to from community groups, his peers and his employers. There must be some balance in the development of skills and a committed conviction or vision; a worker with skills and no vision, and a worker with vision and no skills are, in their different ways, equally a source of harm to themselves and community groups.

College-Based Training

An analysis of college-based training constitutes a major inquiry in its own right; I have been able as part of this wider study to give only limited attention to the matter. What I have done is to scan the content and structures of community work courses, and to organise two rounds of discussion papers and a two-day workshop with a number of trainers from social work, youth work and adult education courses that offer community work training. I have not been able to carry out the more detailed analysis that was a feature, for example, of the first two Gulbenkian reports, but it is with these reports that I wish to start this section.

Community Work and Social Change was a report in 1968 of a fifteen-person study group set up by the Calouste Gulbenkian Foundation. Its terms of reference were to recommend the content, forms and methods of training for community work, in light of an analysis of its present and future roles, objectives and settings. It found very little provision for training community workers; there were some university degree courses, for example, social studies or sociology, which gave a series of ten or so lectures on community work; community work on professional social work courses was almost wholly confined to lectures or discussions, and observational visits, about the 'community implications of a caseworker's job'; and there was some community work teaching in training for other roles such as community centre warden, teacher and youth worker.

Its main recommendations were:

● an expansion in in-service training for existing full-time community workers, and for others who were becoming aware of the community work element in their work;

● the initiation of 'a few carefully planned full-time courses of training for community work within existing patterns of training and leading to one of the severally recognised university or other qualifying awards';

● that these courses should have sufficient staff to supervise students, and 'to give extra help to inexperienced field teachers to collect and edit case records and other teaching materials and meet regularly for consultation about the content of the courses and Student assessment';

● one-year 'cadetships' near a course centre to enable newly qualified community workers to consolidate their skill under supervision: this would help, too, in producing better qualified community work teachers and supervisors;

● an independent committee or council set up by the government to promote training for community work, including the co-ordination and validation of standards.

The second report, published in 1973 as *Current Issues in Community Work,* looked only briefly at training as part of wider terms of reference. It noted that the promotion of community work training was a specific responsibility of the new Central Council for Education and Training in Social Work; and that there had been a marked increase in the number of courses in youth work, social work and adult education teaching community work, as well as the emergence of a few specialised courses. It concluded that

The considerable increase in the number of courses teaching about community work, with or without fieldwork, is, as we have said, the reverse of what the Study Group thought desirable for a 'strategy of training'. Perhaps inevitably in an uncontrolled situation with much pressure on institutions to introduce community work teaching, its plea for a few 'centres of excellence' in advance of general expansion has been ignored. The pressure for community work courses has come from staff and students themselves, from the larger number of social services or social work departments and education services, and from changing perceptions of the nature of social work. There has been a shift from concentration on casework to a new concept of social work, based on ability to assess a social situation and intervene in whatever seems to be the most effective way, whether primarily with the individual, family, group or community or with other social systems; this had led to the conclusion that even social workers who will practise primarily as caseworkers must have some abilities in and intelligent understanding of community work. Thus the trend to include community work in social work and youth work courses arises from the nature of changes in the situation since 1968. These trends are likely to continue.

The trends certainly did continue throughout most of the 1970s; the expansion in community work training on social work courses was further stimulated by the adoption of unitary approaches to social work training and practice. This expansion was, however, extremely uneven and combined a variety of goals and educational formats.

The expansion since 1968 was not accompanied by an appropriate deployment of staff and other resources; those given responsibility for community work teaching were soon overloaded with class and placement responsibilities. The 1973 study group concluded that

> it seems as though many teachers of the subject are overburdened, with too little time for study, for regular meetings with each other, for close contact with practice and for the demanding activities entailed in 'creating' field teachers in community work . . . To a large extent community work teachers and supervisors too are working in isolation with little chance to discuss their teaching, their problems, their successes and their burdens with each other.

This study group's summary of the training situation was equally terse and pointed, and suggests how little had been done to temper the piecemeal, ad hoc expansion of community work training with the requirements of a more strategic approach. The study group reported:

> There is a real danger, in training, of divorce between teaching and practice, since methodical field studies are lacking; teachers have little time for contact with practitioners or projects; fieldwork supervision is inadequate; and there is no systematic study of the actual task in community work. Those concerned should be brought together to consult urgently on how to remedy this situation; and the remedies should be applied without delay.
>
> There is a need for continuing study groups on curriculum content and planning, fieldwork and in-service training; also on the ethics of community intervention and on the application of the social sciences in training and practice . . .
>
> A few full-time qualifying courses in community work should become 'centres of excellence' so as to promote effective advance

in theory, practice, research and evaluation. Training is needed for the inter-agency and planning levels of community work as well as for fieldwork . . .

It is to be hoped that the separation of social work courses and youth and community work courses will be reviewed. Adult education should make an increasing contribution to community work training in social work courses and social work to training in adult education courses.

The difficulties about the teaching of community work were understated by the Gulbenkian report. Teaching staff are an integral part of community work's infrastructure not only through their contribution to student training but also as consultants to local workers and projects, and, in a wider sense, opening up the facilities and students of a college as a training resource to local neighbourhood groups. teaching staff are well placed to encourage the concept of learning in community work as an area-based partnership, as exemplified, for example, in the Southampton area. Trainers have, too, a responsibility to develop the research, literature and theoretical aspects of community work's infrastructure. But they are usually the only person's with responsibility for teaching community work as a specialism, and as an introduction as part of social work or youth work. Because of an interest in such matters, it is common to find the single community work teacher drawn into the teaching of group work, and into foundation studies such as social policy. they have to work at the same time in preparing placements in community work and this can be a time-consuming business, often involving much travel away from the college. Their non-contact hours will not necessarily be available for research and writing; most community work teachers will have to devote considerable time informally and at staff meetings to promote the case for community work in the course. They will be concerned, too, to do some community work themselves in a local community, partly to inform their teaching, to make the resources of the college more widely available and to earn credibility in the eyes of their students. Time will be spent in developing community work outside the college in organisations such as the Association of Community Workers. The community work teacher will also feel obliged to offer consultancy to local workers and agencies. Many teachers will also have to give time to enhancing their own skills and confidence as teachers. All these responsibilities will seriously diminish the time and energies available for activities such as research and writing and, more importantly, indicate the extent of the burden carried by the community work teacher.

The trap for the community work teacher is evident but difficult to avoid: the more he or she expands the time available for teaching community work on a course, the less time there will be for his or her own fieldwork, writing, consultancy and some of the other activities listed above. These difficulties must be seen within the context of the course environment in which the community work teacher operates, and Goetschius has written a helpful piece in understanding these issues within a social work course; my discussions suggest that the picture he described in 1975 persists to the present day (though with considerable variation, as we shall see later), and is as helpful in looking at community work in youth work courses as in social work. Two areas of concern stand out from amongst Goetschius's long list of problems:

First, the community work teacher has often to face the indifference of other staff (and sometimes students) to community work, and also their different ideas about social work. The ideology and methods of casework remain paramount, with an emphasis on working with the individual, who is seen as responsible for the problems he or she suffers. The hegemony of casework not only prevents teachers with this orientation from accepting community work as a legitimate intervention but ensures that:

- support studies such as social policy and human growth and development are taught in a way to buttress casework; and
- community work often does not acquire a proportion of the timetable that gives it parity with other interventions.

A further aspect of this hegemony is the difficulty of accepting that 'the learning process of the community work students is based not on the personality of the participants but on the efficiency and effectiveness of their task performance'; social work tutors, too, are resistant or indifferent to the concern of community work students with concepts of social and political action, group and community processes, and of participation, autonomy and power.

Secondly, the students who take community work options on a course are often more vocal and questioning, and keen to change both the course and the placement agencies. They will be associated with a radical critique of social work, and it is easy for the tutor to be 'held responsible' for the students' attitudes, and to be resented for his own challenging of the ideas of his fellow social work tutors. It is easy in this situation for 'students, staff and supervisors sometimes [to] project on to community work the social change function that belongs to the whole [social work] profession'. Within social work, traditional approaches based around clinical models of individual pathology were also being challenged by unitary conceptions of social work, and, in particular, by the critiques of casework that came both from research studies and radical ideologists in the profession. Traditional forms of understanding and training that had developed within separate child care and mental health courses were also undermined by the introduction of the more generic CQSW courses, and the elevation of the generic worker in the Seebohm report. Little wonder, then, that community work would be resisted; it was easy to label it as being 'responsible' for the threats to established ideas in training, but the resistance was not merely defensive. There was justified cynicism in social and youth work courses about community work's credibility; it failed to articulate its skills and knowledge, was publicly derided as an intervention by some of its practitioners, was critical of social work and its relationship to it, and failed to clarify just how it could help with the responsibilities of social work.

The failure of belief in community work that was most evident in the mid-1970s amongst community workers had its counterpart within its supporters in the social work and youth work professions. Community work was advocated and supported primarily as a means in the reform of social work – it represented the completion of an incomplete profession, and a useful ally in weaning social work from its overly-clinical approaches. But as an instrument of reform it necessarily had a subordinate status to that which was being reformed, and this was evident in the meagre resources allocated to it in practice and in training. There was more interest in what was being reformed than in the strategic development of a different form of intervention or occupation. The result was a half-hearted and half-baked reformation in social work in particular; community work was added to casework and group work but the parity of resources implied by generic assumptions was rarely achieved; George Goetschius saw the operation of the 'generic contradictions' within his own course at the London School of Economics, which was a particularly hostile environment in which to develop a community work option:

> The generic approach claims that all modes of social work intervention have a common knowledge, understanding and value base, and that even the basic skills are common to the various methods. If this is so (or believed to be so), why is casework still seen as the fundamental discipline, since in generic theory it is simply one expression of the same helping process? If you can learn all you need to know about theory and practice in two casework placements, why not two group, residential care, or community work placements? The answer is not that we do not know enough yet about the other methods, but is that (*a*) the psycho-social is still interpreted as psychological and (*b*) the ideas of 'the individual' still permeate social work thinking. (1975)

It is evident from the material gathered in the study that these difficulties that originate in the traditions and ethos of host courses are compounded by attitudes towards training within community work. There is what one teacher called the 'draining, exhausting ambivalence' of community workers to training, to the notions of expertise and competence, and to the idea of passing and failing people and the award of paper qualifications. College-based training was under attack on two grounds in the 1970s: that it excluded certain categories of people and biased community work as a job towards middle-class graduates; and that it did not adequately prepare people for the job of community worker. There was also the hostile attitude of some community workers to social work, and resentment that community work was apparently so dependent on social work for its training opportunities. The community work teacher stands in an exposed position on the boundary of social work and community work, where it is easy to feel, with much justification, that one's contribution is undervalued both by the host discipline and the body of practitioners in the field. The boundary position tends to a crisis of identity in another sense: the community work teacher is caught between the world of academia and that of the field for the criteria of respect, progress and advancement in academia and the field are different. The strain of this position is deepened by fears about how secure one's job is; the demise of community work that might occur through public expenditure cuts or the ascendency of narrower visions of social work and youth work imperil the future of someone in community work teaching. It has become apparent to some trainers and student supervisors that in the last part of the 1970s students have been moving away from community work, choosing 'safer' specialisms and placements that they believed would be more likely to gain them a job in the social services departments of local authorities.

The need for community work teachers to meet together to achieve support in these circumstances (that was seen as a priority by both Gulbenkian reports) was not met during the 1970s. Teachers continued to work in isolation of one another and opportunities to meet nationally and regionally were extremely infrequent. Little has been achieved to end the compartmentalisation of teachers according to their host disciplines of social work, youth work and adult education. Neither the ACW nor the Joint Universities Council community work group were always effective in providing an adequate forum for teachers, who often found it difficult to find the money and the time to attend meetings with each other.

I want now to move on to outline where community work training is available in colleges, and then to discuss the consequences of the variation in the length and content of community work courses.

There are only four full-time community work courses which lead to a Certificate of Qualification in Social Work:

● University College, Swansea: Diploma in Applied Social Studies (one-year postgraduate)

- Goldsmiths College, London: Certificate in Community and Youth Work (two years)
- Westhill College, Birmingham: Certificate in Community and Youth Work (two years)
- Birmingham Polytechnic: BA(Hons) Sociology (four years/ends 1982/3)

There are, in addition, a number of post-qualifying courses such as those at Bradford University (MA in Social and Community Work Studies) and the National Institute for Social Work which are approved by the Central Council for Training and Education in Social Work (CCETSW).

There are a number of full-time courses in youth and community work that lead to the Certificate in Community and Youth Work and approved by the Joint Negotiating Committee for Youth Workers and Community Centre Wardens (JNC). The number of these courses that prepare community workers is difficult to estimate, because the importance and balance of the emphasis on community work varies considerably.

Finally, there are courses or options within departments of adult education, such as that at the University of Manchester, which lead to a diploma in community development, with the possibility of advanced work towards a higher degree.

The small number of these full-time community work courses is in line with the recommendation of the first Gulbenkian report for a limited expansion in full-time training opportunities. I want to say very little about these courses, partly because the most problematic aspects of community work training are not to do with full-time courses. On the contrary, the courses at Swansea, Goldsmiths and Westhill, for instance, are commendable as examples of the evolution of training that tries to give a thorough grounding in the basic skills and knowledge of community work. What is interesting about these full-time courses is that so many are within the field of the education service (youth work and adult education). This fact must be considered within the account given in a previous chapter about the respective interests of social work and education in the development of community work in the 1960s. It is clear that whilst community work was to expand within the personal social services in the 1970s there was not a comparable provision of basic qualifying training under the aegis of social work. The influence of education over training is even more apparent when we note that much of the provision of community work training in Scotland took place within courses of community education, most of whom emphasised youth work, often in traditional settings.

No central body is responsible for all forms of community work training; the CCETSW is responsible for community work training within the personal social services, and the JNC for training within the youth service. CCETSW has had a particular influence on the development of community work training and practice; this has extended beyond its acceptance of community work 'as a legitimate element in CQSW courses' and its recognition of the four courses mentioned above that specifically train community workers. Its contribution has also included its publication on *The Teaching of Community Work* (1974) and its financial support for short courses, conferences and the write-up of projects such as the Harlesden Community Project. It has also given professional support to student units in community work, and through the interest of individual officers, been involved throughout the 1970s in various developments in community work, including field-based opportunities.

The most problematic aspects of community work training occur when it is taught as part of a social work or youth work course. Here community work will, typically, be taught as part of an introduction to social work methods in the first year and as an option or specialism in the second year of the course. The difficulties facing community work staff on these courses have already been discussed above, and here I want to examine this aspect of community work training to see whether it can be said adequately to prepare persons for the practice of community work.

I shall concentrate in this section on social work courses but much of what is said holds true for the teaching of community work as an element on youth work courses. There are some fifty CQSW courses which, according to the CCETSW report on training for community work (1979), claim to provide an emphasis on community work training. The CCETSW report concluded that

The community element in the general range of CQSW courses is very varied and in many cases could not be regarded as more than an infusion of a community context to social work or an orientation to what community workers do. In other cases it appears that some courses which teach the unitary approach see this as giving a community dimension to the practice of social work.

There are, too, those general CQSW courses which, because of time, staff and resources devoted to community work, claim or may be seen as preparing people for the practice of community work.

There is no body which adequately helps prospective students and employers to distinguish these courses which offer an introduction or orientation to community work from those who say that they prepare people for its practice. In respect of the latter, it is not laid down by CCETSW or any other body what proportion of a course the community work option must be, legitimately to claim to prepare people for community work practice, or what the core elements of training on such an option ought to be. My analysis of two-year CQSW courses in universities and polytechnics revealed the extent of the variation in the time allocated in the course for community work teaching: introductory sessions in the first year ranged from two hours to thirty-six. In the second, the time for community work as an option or specialisation ranged from thirteen hours to thirty-nine. There was variation, too, in the length of community work placements beyond the minimum laid down by CCETSW. Colleges differed, too, in the number, if any, of placement-related seminars, and in the provision of foundation studies relevant to community work.

The variation in content is as pronounced as that in the time allocated to community work, and there is clearly a relationship between the two. The choice of content is not just a function of the limited timetable sessions given to community work but also of the interests and values of those responsible for teaching community work. Many community work sessions, for example, are actually courses in radical social policy, or critiques of local government and of established social services. No matter how important or relevant these may be, they do not amount to the adequate preparation of people for the practice of community work. Some of the most desultory options in community work offer no more than a potage of outside speakers, films, a quick trip around a local neighbourhood and a couple of sessions on community work in different settings. Such courses are inadequate as an introduction to community work, and as a way of training people to practice community work. As one correspondent put it:

> We have had some fairly bad experiences of placements from these kinds of courses – where the students have little or no preparation for the placements or understanding of what community work is – and projects end up doing the tuition themselves with inadequate liaison from the college . . . Placements should not be seen as alternatives to teaching.

Even when these dangers are avoided, and where community work is given a substantial part of the curriculum, teachers are faced with a difficult choice: either to concentrate on building up knowledge on the substantive issues of community work – housing, employment, planning, racism, sexism, and so on – or to concentrate on the methods, principles and techniques of the intervention. Skill-building and knowledge development are both needed to do community work, and often the choice is to go for the substantive issues. This may be because of the lecturer's own interests and background but also because teachers may feel they do not have the time to deal with skill development or believe it ought to be left to the placement. The evidence from course materials submitted to the study is that only a handful of trainers work on skill development through class-based techniques such as role play, simulation games and the use of television for feedback and improvement of performance. Practice or application classes are equally rare. Where skills are specifically addressed, they will often be rather practical ones such as silk-screen printing or using an offset litho, with less attention to enhancing more complex interactional and technical skills. All these difficulties are exacerbated within one-year courses. The fundamental issue is that even when community work has achieved parity of time and resources in a course this may still be insufficient to prepare people for practice, particularly where the community work content is more to do with policy, value and knowledge development than with the identification and practice of basic methods and skills.

The variation in time and content of community work teaching means that there is no comparability between courses. Students are leaving social work and youth work courses with different levels of skills and knowledge in community work, and presenting themselves for jobs as community workers on the basis of quite inadequate training. Both prospective employers and users of community workers have no way of knowing what the community work training of, for example, a former CQSW student amounts to. Community work teachers in evidence to this study confirmed that (and this includes those whose community work had received parity of timetable) the students they were turning out were not, on the whole, fit to do the community work job they were taking up. A particular anxiety was that not only were they inadequately prepared to do neighbourhood work but they had received little, if any, training in the tasks of community organisation and social planning. Teachers confirmed that they could offer only a 'threshold experience' in community work, and it was a matter of luck and personal ability to survive as to whether the student could build on that threshold experience in their work without doing too much damage to himself or to community groups. Students often found it necessary to return to their former tutors for in-service training and consultancy, though this was possible only if the student took up work near his former college and where the employer had available funds.

It is clear from this review of length and content, and from the difficulties experienced by community work teachers on 'host' courses described earlier in the chapter, that the teaching of community work, where it is not a full-time study in its own right, is in a highly unsatisfactory state. It would be too easy to cast aside college-based courses because of these difficulties and to extol the virtues of field-based schemes, which, in any case, are equally, though differently, problematic as we shall see later. The challenge for the 1980s is to bring some order, clarity and comparability to community work teaching as it takes place within host courses in social work and youth work. This must involve both a rethinking of these courses to accept or reject community work as a legitimate form of intervention, and the setting down of some guidelines about time and content by bodies such as CCETSW and the JNC. A starting-point would be to separate three areas of 'community work' content to be taught on social and youth work courses. These are: a community orientation for the social/youth worker; an introduction to community work methods and principles; and threshold training for doing community work.

A COMMUNITY ORIENTATION FOR THE SOCIAL/YOUTH WORKER

This is the category used in the ACW discussion paper on *Community Work on CQSW Courses* (1981). Whilst it may be taught by community work staff, it is not really to be seen as a community work method or intervention. The justification for this orientation course is, argues ACW, as follows:

(1)   To assist social workers (and other professions) to establish an attitude, an expectation and a grounding about what in practice to look for in the community setting in which they work, why and how, in order to be of use to it and within it.
(2)   To assist social workers to deal with people's personal problems. Social workers require knowledge and experience of the situations in which their clients live. Without it they cannot successfully perform their traditional role even of providing individual casework or groupwork.
(3)   To help develop some of the prime roles of the social worker in, for example, prevention, promotion, advocacy, criticism, management and facilitation.
(4)   To help social workers to work with community workers and to have some understanding of their work. A community orientation course thus includes reference to community work from the point of view of the social worker.
(5)   To provide a middle-level bridge between social work practice and between psychology and sociology as taught on social work courses.

This kind of orientation course is likely to become more important in the training of social and youth workers with the growing emphasis on patch work, self-help and the use of community, as against institutional resources as discussed in the Barclay report. The importance of being able to help the individual and the family within an understanding of the communities of which they are a part is likely to make the orientation element a compulsory element of basic training. The range of content of such an orientation element is discussed in the ACW paper. It must be stressed that social work is used only as an example of the contribution that this kind of orientation course can make to the training of a member of other occupations.

AN INTRODUCTION TO COMMUNITY WORK METHODS AND PRINCIPLES

This title is deliberately specific about methods and principles; this element of social or youth work training would serve to give trainees a grasp of community work as an intervention. This element would be 'knowledge-about community work', rather than count as an opportunity to acquire a range of skills, though some of these may be acquired as part of a placement. The purpose of this introduction element would be to ensure that, within a generic framework, the trainees have an understanding of the relevant interventions of their chosen occupation, and are able in practice to use the specialist skills of community workers. There is need for both CCETSW and JNC to monitor the content of these introduction elements to ensure a focus on methods and principles.

THRESHOLD TRAINING FOR DOING COMMUNITY WORK

The purpose of threshold training would be to prepare the student for practice in community work; the concept of threshold training recognises the limitations of time, staff and resources inherent in being part of a social or youth work course (or, for that matter, any pre-employment training) and so threshold training seeks to provide a minimum grounding in (*a*) basic skills, methods and principles of community work; (*b*) knowledge on specific issues with which workers might be involved, for example, housing, employment, play; and (*c*) the development of awareness and insight into political and economic issues that affect local communities and service agencies. Considerable emphasis would be given to skill development through placements and class-based methods of skill-learning such as role plays and simulation games. The amount of time to be made available in a course so that the community work teaching could be counted as threshold training is something to be decided upon in discussions following this study. The ACW paper on training recommends a minimum time allotted of twenty sessions of one and a half hours, plus a full-time three-month placement or its equivalent. This is certainly too little; a respondent to the study suggested at least a year of a two-year course. This is an important issue for further discussion, and my own views are that threshold training must be accompanied by a period of supervised practice after the course. It would be equally important for CCETSW and JNC to monitor the content of threshold training and to ensure a reasonable emphasis on building up skills. The proposed community work option in the ACW paper would, on this count, not be regarded as threshold training, as only one of its ten sessions is explicitly given up to skill development.

In summary, then, there are two needs: the first to establish teaching that offers a community-orientation or an introduction to community work, and the purpose would be to ensure more competent and rounded social workers, youth workers, or whatever. Such training would not prepare people to practise as community workers, and this fact should be made clear to prospective students, employers and users of community work. Secondly, that threshold training would be consolidated in some courses to prepare people to practise as community workers. The CCETSW and JNC would be expected to indicate the time and content required for an element of a course to be considered as threshold training, and to make known to prospective students, employers and users those courses recognised as providing threshold training in community work.

The need for this toughening up and rethinking of community work training is evident from:

(1) the view amongst community work teachers themselves in social and youth work courses (including even those with some parity of time and resources) that their graduates are not sufficiently skilled and knowledgeable to do the community work jobs they take up;

(2) the extreme variations in community work training in time and content, and the need to remove or improve the highly unsatisfactory sessions on community work that currently take place within many social work and youth work courses;

(3) recognition that sessions on a community orientation to social work (or whatever) should not continue to be seen as, or confused with, training for the practice of community work; but that such sessions are invaluable in their own right as part of the training of other occupations such as social work;

(4) the need to have more skilled community workers to undertake the range and complexity of work identified in a previous chapter on the content of practice in the 1980s. That chapter indicated the importance of a range of neighbourhood-based activities, for which committed and skilled workers will be required. The need for workers with some skills in social planning and community organisation was also evident, and it may be helpful if both post-qualifying and basic full-time courses in community work gave more emphasis to these aspects of practice.

The recognition by CCETSW, JNC and other relevant bodies of threshold courses is necessary to help employers and users have confidence in the kind of training in community work that has been undertaken by prospective employees; and to give a measure of recognition and support to community work teaching staff working within host courses, and whose difficulties have been described earlier in the chapter. Recognition provides a means of validating the position of threshold training and thus to give an element of 'independence' to the community work programme within host courses.

The proposals about threshold training and a year of supervised practice, and the concern with the regulation of length and content, are not intended to turn community work into an academic discipline; quite the contrary is intended. The urgency is to make community work training more focused on practice skills, and it may be expected that part of the resistance to this will come from university departments who fear that even at the moment social work and youth work courses, and their staff, are not sufficiently academically minded and research-orientated. I would ask readers to look at these proposals in the light of my previous conclusion to maintain community work practice and training as open, non-exclusive activities, and for diversity in the means by which people are trained. The proposals so far put forward are designed to produce more *competent* practitioners from diverse training opportunities for an open occupation. The danger is that unless there are reforms in community work training, the position of community work as a specialism on host courses will be jeopardised, as it falls into disrepute amongst employers and social and youth work teachers, and as community work teachers themselves become so disillusioned with what they are able to do that they themselves give up the ghost. The immensity of the task that faces community work and related jobs in the 1980s requires that we express concern with the *quality* and *effectiveness* of community work training, and move away from the kind of considerations of quantity and extent of provision that has dominated previous discussions, such as, for example, the last CCETSW policy document on community work within the personal social services (1979). It is time that we acknowledged that college-based community work training is in a highly unsatisfactory state (with some notable exceptions) and that we must proceed with its reformation.

Field-Based Training

Ideas for field-based schemes emerged in the latter half of the 1970s. These were a response to the perceived limitations of college-based forms of community work training and a reaction against the poor quality of teaching on many social work and youth work courses. In an occupation such as community work when training develops at the same time as practice there is inevitably a limited body of knowledge from which to teach. Many community work teachers in the 1970s had little personal experience with which to supplement this knowledge; students often found that they had more experience than their lecturers. These facts played a part in the scorn in which college training was held in the 1970s.

Field-based schemes were also seen as opportunities for local working-class people to be trained as community workers. The issue of training for this group of people (whom I shall refer to as voluntary activists) is much wider than the issue of field-based training.

The training needs of voluntary activists seem to be fourfold:

(i)   to help them train to become, or be accredited as, community workers, if that is what they want, and they have the general ability to do the job;

(ii) to help them be more effective in their roles in their communities as activists. Such training would enhance their civic, committee and administrative skills, as well as process skills such as group work, facilitating, and so on. It would also include substantive knowledge about the issues with which activists were concerned;

(i) and (ii) above are different training needs because the role and tasks of the voluntary activist are different from those of the paid community worker.

(iii) to provide broader-based adult education opportunities for residents about the issues affecting their communities;

(iv) to help local residents acquire the skills to pass on their own learning; that is, to acquire the confidence and abilities to be the 'teachers' in their own communities.

Items (ii) (iii) and (iv) may be called *in-action training;* its characteristic is to help local people become more effective in voluntary activist roles. Such training is geared to local needs and issues, and comprises events that will usually be part-time, sometimes be residential and may have, at their best, some form of supervised study. Some local groups of the FCWTG have put on in-action training for local people, usually with community workers as the teachers, and the FCWTG estimates that nearly a thousand people attend the training events of its regional groups throughout the year. Some of the federated groups are developing interesting programmes of training and related publications, and in this respect the work of the Southern, North Eastern, Northern Ireland and Strathclyde groups are particularly informative.

The developing scheme between workers and residents in Sheffield with Northern College is another example of in-action training of local residents. This scheme provides a practical and educational experience in community work for those without formal qualifications, but who already have experience of working with people. The workers are paid a salary, and work (for a period of twelve months in the first place) under the supervision of a full-time community worker in a relevant statutory or voluntary agency. Fieldwork is integrated with the adult education service in Sheffield and with residential periods at Northern College.

In-action training (which I repeat is *not* about the task of training local people to be community workers) is an essential aspect of a wider process of the development of community. It is part of the means of achieving the educational goals described in Chapters 2 and 3; in-action training is part of the strategy to promote:

role education
social and political education
community education
social leadership

As such, in-action training must be considered alongside more formal adult education provision, and be seen as supporting the indirect educational gains ('process goals') that are possible when people organise together to take action on a particular issue. The process of social and franchisal development is incomplete when it has to rely for the achievement of its educational goals on the learning that occurs when individuals take part in community activities and groups. The provision of direct educational services through, for example, various forms of in-action training must therefore be seen as a major opportunity to achieve educational goals. The reinvigoration of political significance and competence is closely connected to the provision of in-action and other forms of adult education about political and social matters.

The development of in-action training in the 1980s must be of some priority; must be set within other developments in formal and informal adult education; and must be understood within the opportunities presented for such education by the numbers of unemployed people in communities.

It would be wrong for the concern with in-action training for voluntary activists to overshadow the need for similar opportunities for learning for groups such as councillors and staff of voluntary and statutory agencies. Continuing training for these groups about community issues is of considerable importance where it is recognised that the local authority has a crucial role to play in the reconstruction work identified in the chapter on the content of practice in the 1980s.

I want now to look at the opportunities to train for the job of community worker in a non-college setting. These are generally referred to as field-based opportunities, and there are two kinds though only the first is strictly a training process:

apprenticeship schemes
accreditation schemes

Apprenticeship schemes vary in their purposes and methods of work, but they have some characteristics in common. They are a chance primarily for local working-class people to train as community workers and, with some schemes, to obtain a qualification at the successful conclusion of the apprenticeship. These schemes are based in a local agency or project, and the emphasis is on 'learning through doing', on the acquisition of skills through practice. College, resources and tutors are used to service the 'academic' part of the apprenticeship – usually one or two days attending seminars, reading, writing, and so on. The college is local and accessible, and the content and style of the events are appropriate to the relevant and immediate needs of the participants. The setting is likely to be informal and participative with the structure geared to the backgrounds and particular learning profiles of the local people attending. The apprentices are not students – they are paid a wage and are in supervised employment. It is their previous work or voluntary experience in community work which determines their suitability to join a scheme, and not any formal academic qualifications. Actual or proposed schemes envisage an apprenticeship of two to three years, after which the successful participants may be awarded a qualification; for example, the apprenticeship scheme in South London called Turning Point awards a qualification from Goldsmiths College. Turning Point takes ten paid apprentices who work in an agency three days a week, and spend two days in study.[2]

It would be wrong to see apprenticeship-type schemes as a substitute for college-based training; they are an alternative, representing the wish to diversify the opportunities through which people can be trained, and are thus a means to ensure that community work remains an open and heterogeneous occupation. Field-based schemes can also be a preparation for college-based courses: New Directions, another scheme in South London, prepares trainees for social work, community work and youth work courses.

The development of field-based schemes must proceed in the 1980s with the reformation of college-based courses, and represent an important innovation not just in community work training but in the broader field of adult education. Field-based schemes are in their early days of thinking and practice; they experience particular difficulties of resources and acceptance by local employers, and they are only as good as the agency (and its staff supervisors) and the college who service them. They do not see themselves as being exempt from the general concern with monitoring and improving standards of community work training, to ensure that, as with college graduates, the people who leave them are as competent as possible to practise community work.

Some of the difficulties of apprentice schemes and their variants is that they might too easily become a routine learning of skills, allied to a knowledge of particular local issues. The participants can become captured within the local context of training and not easily be able to transfer their learning to other contexts and to other issues. Such a narrow instrumentalism might be confirmed by a lack of adequate back-up knowledge from the social and political sciences, and by limited opportunities for reassessment of oneself as a person and worker. The opportunities for reading and reflection are greater on college courses which may also have more potential for helping students achieve a more radical review of ideas and values. One contributor to the study said that he was 'inherently suspicious of apprenticeship schemes where workers gain experience largely within one location or one agency perspective. It conjures up images of "company man" and commitment to a particular school of thought because it is the only one to which he has been exposed.'

Apprenticeship schemes are presently open to the criticism that they are too 'conservative' in that they emphasise the acquisition of basic skills, with insufficient opportunity for participants to place these skills and the interventions to which they contribute in a broader intellectual context. College-based schemes, on the other hand, seem to give more time to academic and philosophic study, and not enough to the development of skills, techniques and methods. The separate development of field-based schemes and college-based courses should only be a temporary phase. In the long run, it is to be expected that a more effective field and college partnership will be developed.

Accreditation schemes are not concerned with training, but set out to determine whether a person has been doing community work, using community work principles and methods, and using them with competence. Accreditation schemes are thus important for those who moved into community work without previous training, and these will include not just local people but graduates and non-graduates from other disciplines. For example, the report in 1980 of the Working Party on Qualification and Training for Community Work set up within Sheffield's Family and Community Services Department recommended 'that people without formal qualifications considered eligible for appointment as community workers would broadly come from one of two categories . . .

● people with substantial experience of community work but without an academic or professional qualification, and
● people with some experience of community work who have some form of academic qualification.'

The working party suggested, on an interim basis, that to be recognised as qualified, workers without formal qualifications should fulfil both of the following conditions:

● a two-year period of full-time (or part-time equivalent) experience in or related to community work;
● a combination of wider knowledge and skill in community work, to be assessed by a panel consisting of departmental staff and an independent assessor.

The proposed accreditation scheme of the London Council for Community Work Training, which has already undertaken some pilot accreditations of workers to gain experience and show the value of the scheme, has a clear set of procedures for the accreditation. Assessment for accreditation consists of:

● Submission of detailed information by the applicant of her community work experience.
● Interviews by three assessors, two of which are selected by the applicant, of her community work colleagues and employers, members of community groups she has worked with, and so on.
● Interviews with the applicant include an indepth interview designed to assess her understanding of, and contribution to the community work processes in which she has been involved.
● Observation by one of the assessors of the candidate at work in a community group setting.
● A detailed analysis of a piece of work undertaken with one of the groups.
● One or more meetings of the assessors to collate results and prepare recommendations for the recommendations sub-committee.
● A final interview with the candidate.
● A meeting of the recommendation sub-committee which considers all the information so far available.
● A decision is made by the Unit on the basis of the recommendations and information obtained in the course of the assessment. The decision is open to challenge by the applicant.

The purpose of accreditation is to decide on the criteria for practice, to inspect and maintain standards, and to make those standards public. As such, it is as much concerned with competence as with the issues of the diversity and openness of an occupation. It is important to note that 'accreditation' began as a shorthand for 'accreditation of the experience of local people without academic training but with experience'. The debate in community work is now widening to consider not only the needs of these people but also the accreditation of people from apprenticeship training schemes, or from colleges, particularly since having a CQSW, for example, may not mean very much in terms of its community work content.

An important issue in examining apprenticeship and accreditation schemes is that of *comparability*. As they develop in the 1980s, we must ensure comparability within and between schemes, and between them and college-based courses in community work. Comparability does not mean the standardisation of schemes or the restriction of types of entrants to them. I am using it to mean that apprenticeship schemes around the country are working to more or less the same standards of competence, and that these will be similar to those used in accreditation schemes and in college-based training. Comparability within and between field and college opportunities is essential for the sake of their participants; if there is no or little comparability, then a caste system of community workers will emerge with, for example, those graduating from colleges having the advantage over those from other methods of training. Comparability, too, will ensure that workers will be able to change jobs and work in different parts of the country: an apprenticeship scheme run in South Wales, for example, will be accepted by employers in the north-west. Without such comparability participants in apprenticeship and accreditation schemes may become trapped within a particular agency or region. In this respect, it is interesting to note that the ACW training group is currently exploring the idea of a regionally organised and validated accreditation scheme in association with a nationally agreed award. I want to discuss comparability further in the next section which contains a number of recommendations for field and college-based training.

SUMMARY AND RECOMMENDATIONS

I want to pull together some of the main suggestions about training that have emerged so far in this chapter. I shall refer to the need for

● a programme of development of training facilities;
● a plan of curriculum development.

A Programme of Development

I have indicated the need for a more strategic development of training facilities in community work, and for an end to the piecemeal and ad hoc way in which such opportunities emerged in the 1970s. This means a rethinking of the status, length and content of some college-based courses, the need to develop a limited number of accreditation and apprenticeship schemes, and the achievement of comparability *within and between* each of the three routes to qualification, that is to say college courses, apprenticeships and by recognition of experience. Much of the value of providing equal training opportunities will be vitiated if there is little comparability between them.

(I) FULL-TIME COURSES

Full-time basic qualifying courses must be continued, as these will inevitably prepare people for the practice of neighbourhood work. It was suggested that further post-qualifying courses need to be developed with a particular focus on social planning and community organisation.

(II) PART-TIME COURSES

I support the recommendation in the Blackmore (1981) report for more provision to be made for part-time and day-release qualifying courses in community work. These would be particularly advantageous to those whose fieldwork and/or family commitments do not allow them to attend a full-time course, or whose employer is unable to second. The Blackmore report noted how few in-post community workers were attending full-time training courses. The part-time 'distance learning course', run by the YMCA National College, leading to the Certificate in Youth and Community Work, is an interesting example. The recognition of part-time youth work courses seems of relevance to developing models of part-time training in community work.

(III) NICHE COURSES

These are those elements of community work training that are part of − or occupy a niche in − basic qualifying courses in social work and youth work. The variety in status, length and content of these elements was noted; they are inadequate for the preparation of people to practise community work, and confusion is caused for prospective students, employers and users of community workers. There is a need for a clearer separation of goals and contents for:

- 'community orientation' training for social workers and others;
- introduction to and about community work;
- threshold training that, because of sufficient time and resources within a host course, enables students to be brought to a certain point of preparation for practice.

It is assumed that the first two elements will continue to be of importance within social work and youth work training. Relevant bodies such as CCETSW and the JNC must indicate that these two elements do not constitute preparation to practise community work, and, further, to indicate those host courses that do in fact provide threshold training.

A more rigorous stipulation and monitoring of the content of these three elements is required, with the primary aim of ensuring that sufficient attention is given to the methods, principles and skills of community work practice. It would be useful for a public statement to be available which describes the content of threshold courses; this would be something that prospective employers and users of community workers could ask to see. Threshold courses would not be counted as an adequate preparation for doing community work without a period of supervised practice.

(IV) APPRENTICESHIP AND ACCREDITATION SCHEMES

These schemes are needed to optimise the values of diversity and access; they must, however, also be evaluated on the basis of competence. They should not be treated as 'inferior' to the more orthodox college route to competence and qualification. The organisers of these schemes must pay more attention than in the past to the credibility of trainers and assessors fairly to assess competence in the scheme's participants. There is, naturally enough, a strong emotional and ideological predisposition in community work to make such schemes appear workable, and to pass their participants. Such schemes are congruent with important values in community work, and are attractive in the light of inadequacies in college-based teaching of community work. It is in this predisposition and value congruence that we find the scheme's greatest threats: unless the organisers of apprenticeship and accreditation schemes address the issue of competence as forcefully as they deal with those of diversity and access, then they will not be acceptable to people such as employers, and, ultimately, not acceptable to the community users of the 'graduates' of such schemes. It is for this reason that I believe that schemes must be associated with an existing recognised qualification or with a new nationally accepted qualification that applies to all kinds of training opportunities for the practice of community work.

(V) IN-ACTION TRAINING

The provision of in-action training needs to be extended, to provide further opportunities to those who wish to become more effective in their roles as voluntary activists. The existing work done, for example, by members of local groups of the FCWTG or of ACW, should be linked with other initiatives in this area, such as that of the WEA, and set within the context of the development of informal adult education as a response to the needs of those not in full employment. In-action training includes not just the provision of courses and workshops but the strengthening of networks to provide information and advice between activists within regions and across different parts of the country. In-action training must become a recognised part of community work's concern with educational processes and achievements.

(VI) QUALIFICATIONS

The ostensible purpose of the award of a qualification is to signal to the outside world that a person has reached a required level of competence. With the exception of the few full-time basic qualifying courses in community work, I have indicated that the award of the CQSW and the Certificate in Youth and Community Work can be seriously misleading of a person's proficiency in the practice of community work. There is, too, little justification that people who have considerable experience and/or have trained through an apprenticeship scheme should be discriminated against by employers who might prefer nationally recognised qualifications such as the CQSW which can be of dubious value in indicating a person's competence.

There seem to be two important principles to guide the development of community work training programmes:

- that whatever the training route chosen, participants end up with the same, or comparable, qualifications at each level of training (for example, at basic or post-qualifying levels. There is room in community work for different levels of training that complement each other, as the roles to be performed in practice complement each other);
- that, subject to normal variations between courses and schemes, whatever the route chosen, each route is capable of producing participants to more or less the same levels of required competence in community work.

Both principles are included in the notion of comparability within and between various training/qualification routes. I want to suggest that there are three means to enhance competence and comparability. They are:

- closer regulation and recognition as suggested above, by relevant bodies such as CCETSW and JNC of threshold training courses in community work;
- a period of supervised practice or study following a training course;
- a qualification in community work that is achieved no matter which training route is chosen.

The last two proposals are demonstrated in the Table 5.1. The final award of Diploma in Community Work is given whatever the training

Table 5.1   *Training and Awards: an Illustration*

Previous Work/ Study Experience	Training Route:	Award	Supervised Learning:	Award
	2 years full-time community work course	CQSW CYCW	6 months practice	
	1 year full-time community work course	CQSW CYCW	1 year practice	Diploma in Community Work
	2 years threshold training	CQSW CYCW	1 year practice	
	2 year apprenticeship	Pass	6 months study	
	Accreditation	Pass	6 months study	

CQSW = Certificate of Qualification in Social Work
CYCW = Certificate in Community and Youth Work

route taken; these might not be the right words or designation for the award, and it is used here only as an example. The period of supervised learning varies according to the length and type of training route; field-based training routes follow with a period of supervised *study,* and college-based routes with supervised *practice* – an idea, referred to as 'cadetship', that was put forward in 1968 in the first Gulbenkian report. The period of supervised learning is designed to strengthen that aspect of the initial training route which is given least emphasis during the training period. The period of supervised study would be akin to individual consultancy with a local trainer or experienced worker; it would vary in its arrangement from locality to locality, and according to the needs and previous study experience of the individual participants.

The period of supervised practice as part of one's full-time employment is of especial importance in making threshold training a viable preparation for practice, together with the stipulation of the minimum time devoted to community work training as part of a host course for it to count as 'threshold'. Much work will need to be done with employers to ensure adequate opportunities for supervised practice, but there are now sufficient experienced community workers available to make 'cadetship' a feasible proposition.

The category of 'Previous Work/Study Experience' is placed in the table to indicate that it is very much a relevant factor in leading to the Diploma in Community Work, and must be taken into account so that the procedure is sensitive to individual situations. There are at least two considerations. First, accreditation schemes must stipulate the minimum length of experience needed before a person can offer himself or herself for accreditation. Secondly, it might be desirable to waive the period of supervised learning for those persons with substantial previous work or study experience. The periods given of one year and six months are presented here only to illustrate the process. The precise details of supervised learning need further exploration, and it is hoped this will be possible in discussions following this report.

It may not be necessary to set up a new organisation or national community work body to oversee these arrangements. Existing organisations such as CCETSW and the JNC are available to monitor the arrangements for supervised learning and to sanction the giving of the community work award, so long as there is comparability between these organisations in their criteria and standards. Thus a student on CQSW course would go through CCETSW for the award, a student on a youth work or community education course would go through the JNC or other relevant body in that field. Likewise, the organisers of apprenticeship and accreditation schemes can choose to link up with award-giving institutions in the field of their choice, and according to the availability of local courses.

It will require much effort and will to implement such changes in the training of community work; this energy will be at a premium amongst fieldworkers, who will also be concerned with setting up accreditation and apprenticeship schemes, and with providing in-action training. Some initiatives must be taken by trainers and those policy-makers concerned with community work education and practice to start consideration of the reforms outlined so far in this chapter. The time has come for community work organisations such as ACW or the FCWTG and bodies such as CCETSW and JNC, together with staff and members from local and central government, to make up their minds about community work, and, specifically, to come to some decision about its status and contribution. The decision must be made either to set community work aside or to take it seriously as an important form of intervention and to strengthen the resources available for its practice, training and support structure. This presents the issues in the crudest possible terms, but, as far as training is concerned, the present unsatisfactory arrangements should not be allowed to continue.

Much the same can be said for community work organisations such as ACW and the FCWTG. They have pressed ahead in initiating, or supporting, field-based training schemes as necessary and important provisions. But they are also limited developments, in that however valuable they might be, the bulk of resources will continue to be given to college-based training routes. There is a role for both ACW, the Federation and the local training groups to press for reforms in college-based community work education. They might, as one respondent suggests, insist on

> getting involved at a consultation level with full time training courses and secondly trying to find ways of releasing the undoubted resources tied up in these institutions in terms of data banks, documentation and libraries. I think they could begin to discuss how joint appointments could be made which could help link the training agencies with the field and so facilitate a much greater interchange and flexibility of resources. I see the way forward with the regional training groups taking on the responsibility of acting as Forums for community work training, of coordinating and helping create working relationships between employers, training agencies, and regional training groups (representing particularly the interests of field workers).
>
> I feel that in terms of producing some results this could be more effective than the debate on validation, recognition, accreditation, qualification which to an outsider must at times seem to be only a sterile/semantic hit and run affair where the contestants are not sure which word to use to hit which target. Is accreditation really any different from qualification? Both of them are in the game of assessing competence. What is important is that they should know what it is they wish to assess, how the knowledge and skills can be acquired. The first is about developing a clear idea of what community work practice encompasses and the second is about developing appropriate forms of learning (i.e. curriculum).

There have been a number of meetings in the past between CCETSW and other bodies such as JNC, ACW and FCWTG to look at issues in community work training. The amount of work that needs to be done to refashion courses and the context of curricula in community work that has been indicated in this section suggests the need for these meetings to continue, and for them to develop as more substantial instruments of reform.

A Plan of Curriculum Development

I have so far summarised some comments about the overall development of training opportunities. Here, I want briefly to discuss changes that seem necessary within the curriculum of college-based courses, though some of this will be relevant to those arranging apprenticeship schemes. The notion of a 'plan' for curriculum development suggests that courses in community work develop according to some basic principles or even common assumptions; and where these are explicit and discussed between staff of different courses this might lead to some comparability between courses in their learning goals and methods.

Many respondents to this study have argued 'that community work does need to become more "professional" if by that we mean becoming an occupational group who have some specific hard knowledge and skills they can offer as community organisers'. I have already suggested that one response to the difficulties outlined is better monitoring of community work courses, in terms of their content and length, and the differentiation between threshold training and 'introduction to community work'. The proposal of a year of supervised learning will also help to equip workers with enough knowledge and skills for competent practice. But as far as the curriculum is concerned, there should be more explicit emphasis on the identification of skills, and a closer integration between field placements and class work, with more of the latter given up to skills training and practice application workshops. The idea for a plan of curriculum development that emphasises skill acquisition should not lead to standardisation between courses; on the contrary, there is a need to maintain the variation of content and approach in order to reflect, for example, regional differences in issues and communities. The emphasis on 'how-to-do-it' methods and principles within the curriculum must be tempered with the need to avoid too instrumental an approach; we do not need practitioners who are narrow or over-technical in their approach, and who do not understand the application of their skills within the social and political context of the issues that are being worked on. The developmental goals of community work discussed in earlier chapters indicate how closely community work is involved with ethical and political issues, and consideration of these issues cannot and should not be avoided either in training or in practice. I endorse the views of one trainer who wrote:

Practice based training runs the risk therefore that it can be extremely conservative since it may only involve the mechanical acquisition of skills which are not themselves subjected to critical theoretical analysis. In other words the involvement in and practice of these skills may become too 'subjective'. Some distancing (objectification) is necessary if this is to be avoided — this basically involves being able to impose an outside theoretical perspective. For the community worker this means at a personal level handling the difficult balance between being both an insider (as practitioner) and outsider (as theoretician and interpreter) at the same time with all the problems of ideology, political position and commitment that this involves. It does mean the starting point for any worker is that he must recognise the importance of needing to have a personal philosophy covering both political and moral issues which is always subject to evaluation, scrutiny and modification in the light of experience. The position is anti-dogmatic since it recognises the uncertain and problematic nature of much of the knowledge with which we operate.

The application of method in community work must be a creative and not a mechanical process in which worker and local participant are distanced from each other. Community arts workers have helped to draw attention to the place of feeling, imagination and creativity in community work skills training. Wim van Rees has suggested that

Thought in action is a key concept in my interpretation of the community work method. The term 'method' is not used to mean a fixed, rigid method to be applied come hell or high water and always producing an outcome but, on the contrary, it denotes a creative problem-solving process which is developed in the course of action, which is polymorphic and which develops new solutions to what are often old problems.

Skills and knowledge must be applied reflectively in relation to the problem at hand, and the community and circumstances in which it arises. Part of the understanding of the problem is

how working class people experience their social conditions and what meanings they ascribe to their experience. How they understand this reality, how they experience it and how these perceptions affect their ability to become politically active are crucial questions . . . the worker's legitimation rests on her ability to work with the subjective experiences of the working class. The meaning that experience has for people is what she must engage with and be guided by if she is to help them to become politically active. (Pringle, 1981)

Neither should an emphasis on skills be achieved at the expense of adequate understanding of theory from a number of disciplines and studies. The ability to use theory to understand what is happening in practice, and to aid the application of skills, is important. The objective in curriculum development ought, in the words of one respondent, to be to turn out alert-minded, imaginative, creative and energetic general practitioners in community work: people with sound comprehension of social, economic and political realities, able to adapt and apply their basic and general skills and knowledge. The expertise required is that of relating theoretical knowledge and practical skills in solving problems in day-to-day practice. There is now enough field experience, as well as the content of the CCETSW and ACW publications, for us to proceed with some confidence about the skills to be mastered for community work practice. (Substantial material on neighbourhood work skills are to be found in most of the Community Project Foundation's publications, and in the books by Butcher *et al.* 1980, Henderson and Thomas, 1980 and Twelvetrees, 1982.)

The emphasis on the skills element of the community work curriculum will be most effective as a preparation for practice where teachers and students are able to draw on ideas about community work from a number of sources. For example, the teaching of community work under a social work aegis must use relevant material from other fields such as youth work and adult education; there would be little value for community work training to be trapped within the cognitive and practical world of the host courses and institutions of which it is a part. A difficulty of confining the accreditation of training routes to existing bodies such as CCETSW and JNC is that it might result in a narrow, uni-disciplinary way of looking at community work skills and knowledge; an advantage of a new community work accreditation body to work alongside, or instead of, existing bodies would be that it could ensure a multi-disciplinary focus or at least create a climate in which courses would have to rethink what to do to meet new standards in curriculum provision.

The notion of expertise provides a focus on practice competence and an emphasis in training on the acquisition of a range of skills. These skills are both interactional (for example, in relation to individuals and groups) and technical (for example, needs assessment). But curriculum formation and development will also be influenced by the definitions of community work that are held by students and trainers, and, secondly, by an anticipation of the demands that will be made of students once they begin to practice. Trainers should be able to specify the tasks a worker will need to carry out. From these tasks, we should then be able to suggest what roles, knowledge, skills and resources the worker or student will need to acquire or have access to. We can then ask: how will our students best learn these skills, and the answer to this question will determine the role of lectures, seminars, placements, skills workshops and the contribution of other disciplines. The methods of learning should also be determined by the make-up of the student group, its size, available resources, and so on. The trainer's approach to learning in community work should embody the values and attitudes he or she would like their students to have in their practice, and we would thus expect community work courses to be participative in the form of learning and in the organisation of the course.

Curriculum development on a particular course may be seen as a process of learning or sharing — between trainers, students, fieldwork supervisors, workers and local groups. Within community work as a whole, it should be seen as a process that brings trainers and others together for mutual support, and the exchange of ideas and teaching materials. This process of exchange has not occurred to any noticeable extent in the last decade, but ought to be given some priority in the years ahead, and might be initiated to explore further some of the suggestions put forward in this chapter. This process of learning can only take place where there is a reasonable degree of open-mindedness about community work, and an atmosphere of interest and toleration. One of the lessons of the 1970s is that community workers (practitioners and trainers) have been less than successful in managing their relationships with each other. We created a culture in the 1970s that was often unsuitable for dialogue, honesty, mutual learning and support. It was an intellectual culture of little curiosity, where prefabricated concepts dominated and where relatively closed systems of ideas prevented the development of thought and practice through interpersonal creativity. It was a culture that let flourish the most banal and crude generalisations ('community work doesn't work in a statutory agency') and one in which myth and folk tales (Batley, Sefton, and so on) took the place of research, theory and adequate documentation. We often found it difficult to handle complexity, as problems and issues were reduced to simplistic formulae and analysis. Those who felt uncertain, tentative, unclear and who were aware of inconsistencies in what they thought and did felt unable to express themselves adequately, if at all. For example, one correspondent wrote:

> I find my views are subject to constant fluctuation, uncertainty and inconsistency, and don't seem to accord with the apparently dominant view as expressed by the more practised absolutist writers on the subject.

The real blocks to more effective curriculum development are not simply the conservatism or professionalism of colleges but also the narrowness of those who will confine community work and its application to a particular interpretation. The wish of the non-directive school to define a pure concept of community work in the late 1950s and 1960s has been replicated by a selective radicalism on the left in the 1970s that wishes to confine thought and practice within boundaries that are prescribed by certain political analyses and relationships. I am aware that the corresponding narrowness of the 1980s might be 'instrumentalism', and those like myself who see the need for a stronger emphasis on skills in practice must acknowledge the need in the curriculum and in the field to foster a dialectic between instrumentality, theory and ideology in community work training. The people community workers work with are, on the whole, working-class people; this class, particularly in the cities and amongst ethnic groups, is one that faces systematic discrimination, and one that experiences gross inequities in matters such as income, wealth, housing, health and education. But this fact, and the complexity of issues in urban communities, also indicates the extent to which skills and basic competence must become a stronger aspect of community work training. Community work requires a commitment to work with the deprived and the least powerful; this commitment, if it is to be worth anything, must include the capacity to offer expertise to as high a level of proficiency as possible. Raymond Pringle is right to say that community work requires training 'because the knowledge, skills and experience required in such work are not common currency. This ability cannot be guaranteed to emerge simply from, and is far too important to be left to the hit-and-miss practices of self-selected individuals' (1981).

IN-SERVICE DEVELOPMENT

This section deals with the provision and use of on-the-job support and development. These include supervision and consultancy provided within or by the employer; peer group support; and in-service training programmes and courses. The latter range from one-day workshops and weekly residential courses to programmes arranged over six months, such as those described in section five of the Blackmore report on community work training.

This heterogeneous range of activities have some common purposes, which might be summarised thus: to consolidate and extend workers' skills and knowledge, both about methods of intervention and substantive issues in the community; to clarify particular work issues or problems; to exchange ideas and keep in touch with new developments; to provide support, not just in relation to the demands of the job but as a member of a network of workers engaged in a common enterprise; and to provide a means of accountability to one's employers.

The first Gulbenkian report that appeared in 1968 saw in-service training as the most crucial means of raising standards and providing support, and keeping workers alert to changing needs and structures. But the second report that appeared in 1973 concluded that progress had been uneven. They saw

a serious gap in provision since those in this field need constantly to bring their experiences up to date and to dispute controversial issues with colleagues who have different work experiences or backgrounds. A coordinated assault on this largely unoccupied territory is called for: we suggest that the CCETSW should meet with representatives of university extra-mural and adult education departments, colleges of education and others in the education field and with the principal statutory and voluntary employers, with the best means of devising a continuous and coordinated programme of in-service training for community work; an integrated programme is required for all staff concerned with the community (not only for those called community workers) in both voluntary and statutory services. The programme should be related to varying types of experience and should make the most economical use of scarce training resources.

Maria Blackmore's report in 1981 suggests that little has been achieved since 1973 to change the picture drawn by the second Gulbenkian report. There have been a few isolated initiatives which Blackmore describes as well as some provision within agencies who have employed substantial numbers of community workers. The inadequacy of in-service facilities in community work is evident when they are compared with what has been achieved in the youth service for youth and community workers through the development of the In-Service Training and Education Panel (INSTEP).

Programmatic community workers appear to have been better served with in-service opportunities. They were more effective, for example, in working together in colleague groups (within CDP, for example, and in the network of resource centre workers), and in agencies such as the Community Projects Foundation there was a training and development programme provided within the agency. Those with the poorest in-service training facilities were workers in the departmental and project streams. The inadequate provision of in-service facilities in social services departments was revealed by the report in 1975 by Thomas and Warburton, an analysis subsequently confirmed by Davies and Crousaz in 1982 for social services and other local authority departments. Supervision and consultancy arrangements were particularly ineffective in these departments: the supervisors of community work were typically area social work managers or senior administrators, with little or no experience of community work, and preoccupied with their own managerial responsibilities. Project workers were even more disadvantaged; they usually worked alone, without management or colleague support, and it was usual for there to be no training element in a project's budget. Money for training was often the first casualty when budgets had to be pruned or when potential funders were thought likely to baulk at the size of a project's grant application. Of all the streams, the project workers were the least well off in respect of having available an infrastructure to support their practice. In terms of their demanding work situation, and often their lack of previous experience and relevant training, this was the stream most in need of in-service facilities, but the group least likely to have the money, time and energy available to make use of them.

The amount of peer group support for departmental and project workers was invariably limited, though there were areas where workers were more successful in developing their own support networks.

The effectiveness of community worker groups in providing training was constrained by a number of factors, as indicated in the report by Thomas and Warburton. The emergence of the FCWTG brought more energy and focus to the issues, though here again the picture was one of uneven development across the regions. The fragmented relations described in an earlier chapter that existed within and between the three streams of workers worked against effective peer group support.

Community work was an innovation or an experiment; how much more important it was, then, to ensure that this innovation did not fail because of the lack of in-service support. The evaluation of community work has been hampered because many of the difficulties that have been experienced may have been the result of the failure to provide an adequate infrastructure for its practice, and the paucity of in-service facilities may have been particularly important in undermining the effect of many community work interventions.

The very marginality of community work within most established departments and agencies, and the lack of strategy in the employment of community workers, was necessarily accompanied by the insufficiency of in-service provision. The conclusions of the studies by Thomas and Warburton and Davies and Crousaz of departmental community work indicate that community workers were provided with insufficient money and other resources to carry out the tasks they had been employed to do. As for programmatic and project work, Blackmore is equally clear in pointing to the lack of responsibility amongst central government funders and trusts: it was exceptional for them to ask applicants for evidence of an appropriate training programme for staff, and rarer to insist on a training element being part of a project's budget. The short-term nature of projects, and the turnover amongst departmental community workers, also worked against the provision and use of in-service facilities; there could be little time or energy within a three-year project, for instance, to attend training programmes and many workers found it difficult even to sustain attendance at monthly peer group meetings. There was, and still is, an ambivalence in community work to training, and, as we have discussed above, to the notion of expertise. Blackmore has perceptively commented that where there was an interest in training it was for knowledge about 'issues' rather than for personal development, and the extension of the worker's own capacities:

My impression of community workers' training needs is that they are not particularly concerned with personal development, and do not make demands for this kind of training; in contrast to Youth Workers who regard it as the most important element in in-service training provision. Community workers have to cover a much wider range of issues in their work than many centre-based Youth Workers and because many community development projects have short term funding or are considered 'experimental', workers are under pressure to show results. They are therefore extremely concerned about issues and on being better informed about national issues and policies which have direct influence on what they are able to achieve in their local areas. Courses advertised to reflect this; for example, community work and the health service, unemployment issues, multi-racial community work and so on. There is therefore a lack of training opportunities which develop the ability to diagnose and assess local needs and resources, clarify objectives, choose priorities and evaluate projects.

It is possible that employers and funders would have given more attention to in-service facilities had community workers themselves in the 1970s felt the matter was important enough to seek improvements in the range and quality of provision. Virtually nothing has been done by organisations like ACW and the FCWTG systematically to negotiate with employers and funders about the value of in-service facilities, or to develop these facilities themselves. Until the late 1970s ACW in particular showed no interest in a training role, and failed to use the skills of its members to organise local and regional training programmes. Several contributors have suggested that the greater interest amongst community workers in training dates from about 1975, and manifested itself in apprenticeship and accreditation schemes, and the gradual evolution of the Federation of Community Work Training Groups. The concern with training was with the development of alternative provisions, as one person suggested:

Community workers have not been willing to put forward proposals which would amount to a sell out of community work principles. Therefore they have not been able to accept ready made models of college based training which benefit an academic middle class. They have also not wanted to set up a pattern of training which would be controlled by a few powerful national figures. Community work has been evolving its own broadly based structure and its own concepts of the nature of training (including field based training, training designed for working class people, and members of racial minorities, and the accreditation of experiences). So far a broadly based structure is well on its way and there are a growing number of schemes which have taken off. Much more is likely to result from these developments in the next five years. One must not underestimate the significance of the fact that 1975 (when the interest in training seriously began to get under way) was also the year when cuts in public spending started to get serious. You must not underestimate what a struggle it has been to get resources for any new developments.

The real difficulty in all this goes beyond matters of staff time and energy 'to do something about in-service facilities', although it is quite evident that bodies like ACW and FCWTG were severely handicapped by having no paid development staff for most of the 1970s. Providing an in-service provision as extensive, for example, as INSTEP requires a commitment to the idea of a more professional (small 'p') occupation; this has been absent in community work, and even the sense of affiliation to, and coherence of, an occupation has remained low during the 1970s. The second difficulty is that a commitment by workers to in-service provision requires that they recognise the legitimacy of employers, funders and trainers within the whole community work enterprise, and not as necessary evils to be tolerated on the boundaries of the 'real' world of practice. More fundamentally, perhaps, we have to accept that the community work role is a legitimate one, and one that is legitimised not just by personal beliefs or commitment to the deprived but by expertise. To accept as legitimate a role and intervention based on certain kinds of skills and knowledge is the necessary step to developing a stronger occupational identity, and from that to making the improvements in the infrastructure that are needed for more effective practice. The persistence in the 1970s of unsatisfactory arrangements for community work training and for in-service opportunities, together with the unchallenged hegemony of 'host' occupations over training, is a testament to how poorly community workers have valued themselves and their efforts. It is also, one contributor to the study suggested, 'an indication of the lack of managerial support and commitment; it is further evidence of the need for a systematic approach to community work intervention'.

I want to look now at what might be done to enhance in-service provision in the 1980s, though it is clear from the above discussion that a precondition for the development of an adequate infrastructure is a radical change in the ways in which community workers see themselves, and their identity as an occupational group with its legitimacy deriving from the expertise of its members.

I shall describe very briefly the extent of the community work infrastructure in the Netherlands, because such a comparison will confirm the inadequacy of arrangements in this country and be suggestive of possible changes to be made in the future. Community workers in the Netherlands are mostly employed in local projects, funded by central government (there is a community work department in the Ministry of Cultural Affairs, Recreation and Social Welfare) via local government. There are hardly any community workers employed directly in local authority departments. The provision for in-service development is as follows: there is, first, a National Institute for Community Work Studies based in Den Bosch; it provides studies, does research, arranges seminars and examines new developments in practice.

Its staff are mainly concerned in carrying out and disseminating research or development work, and in influencing social welfare policies at local and central government levels. Secondly, there are four regional work-development centres for community work. Their task is to help workers and resident groups with the development of skills and methods. Thirdly, there is a network of 'consultancy agencies' funded by national government to provide a consultancy service to community work projects. There are twelve consultancy agencies organised on a provincial level, and each belongs to GAMMA, a national agency with a responsibility for training in community work (and related areas in adult education and youth work) with its own training staff. Consultants employed in each provincial consultancy agency will work to about twelve community work projects each, and will provide consultancy to the local management groups as well as to the community workers. The work of one such consultancy agency is briefly described in section 7 of Maria Blackmore's report. Finally, community work trainers from the universities and the schools of social work are involved as consultants, researchers and trainers with local and regional projects.

The degree of change that is necessary in the provision of in-service opportunities, and hence the amount of resources to be given to them, is partly determined by how far community work will be established as an important method of intervention in the 1980s, and as one that will also influence methods of work in related occupations such as social work. It would be irresponsible and counter-productive to go forward with the agenda for community work indicated in Chapter 4 without ensuring adequate in-service facilities. The numbers of community workers, and the complexity and range of work they might carry out, that were implied in that chapter suggest the need for major changes in the resources made available to support community work practice. The nature of these changes is illustrated in the brief outline of facilities in the Netherlands. Serious consideration must now be given to setting up a network of *development centres* to provide training, consultancy and support for community work and those in related occupations with a 'community dimension'. These centres would be regionally based, with large cities having access to their own centre. The development centres would be funded jointly by national government and a mix of local authority departmental contributions. Since most of the work centres would operate on a regional basis local funding could come from a consortium of local authorities employing community workers in their various departments. They would not themselves carry out community work, or service it directly as do the present kind of resource centres; rather they would provide training and consultancy to community workers, local groups and management committees, with a particular emphasis on improving skills and developing understanding about issues with which workers and groups are engaged. They would be used by projects and departments employing community workers, and also service those in, for example, social work, health and education, working in innovative ways within a community setting.

It might be possible and desirable for these regional centres to be a development of existing services; for example, student units in community work, or some councils of voluntary service, might be expanded (in terms of staff and resources) to become development centres, working in the ways outlined above, as well as providing student supervision. Indeed, the transformation of a student unit into a development centre would enhance the opportunities for student learning and supervision.

In addition to this major change, there seems to be a number of smaller initiatives that can be taken to improve in-service support and development. Clearly, employers of community workers, particularly those in local authority departments, must attend to their in-service needs within their training programmes, or, perhaps, contribute financially to the setting up of regional development centres. Funders of community work projects must insist on an element of training within the budget of a project. The development of a directory of consultants, on a regional basis, composed of trainers and experienced workers would be a valuable resource. Organisations like ACW and FCWTG might initiate a network of local trainers willing to take responsibility for organising some regional training events for workers and for voluntary activists, as some regional training groups have already started doing. Indeed, there is a strong case for ACW and FCWTG to appoint regional training officers both to organise training events and to create a network of trainers and workers who could do the same, and who could put college resources at the disposal of local training initiatives; there is a role, too, for both these organisations to put more pressure on employers to improve in-service facilities, and, in particular, to arrange training programmes for community workers that bring together workers from the different departments of a local authority. There seems to be considerable scope for neighbouring local authorities to pool resources in the provision of in-service facilities, and to bring together their workers in training events.

There are several recommendations to improve in-service facilities made in the Blackmore report. Some tend to emphasise national initiatives, and they refer in particular to the role of the National Council for Voluntary Organisations for whom the report was written. I suggest that there must be an equal emphasis on local and regional innovations in community work's infrastructure, though the existence of a unit located within an existing national body, or the creation of a new national body, might be useful in stimulating progress in local and regional initiatives. I want to return to the matter of a national organisation at the end of Chapter 7.

NOTES

1   Perhaps this is an appropriate point to note that the Federation of Community Work Training Groups was set up in 1979; it was launched with a grant from the Gulbenkian Foundation and is committed to the provision of community work training for paid and unpaid workers; its basic principle is 'about sharing skills and knowledge amongst community workers, the communities they work in and the wider society'. It is funded by the Voluntary Services Unit, and employs a full-time development officer. Three of its federated groups have also obtained funding to provide regional training opportunities.
2   See also the work of the Centre for Neighbourhood Development in Belfast, described by Huber and McCartney (1980). For a fuller account of various schemes see Stiles (1982).

6 *Employing and Funding Community Workers*

This part of the study is about the organisation and implementation of community work practice. It will deal with three matters: the *recruitment, auspices* and *funding* of community workers. As such, this part of the study is about how the definitions and goals for community work (identified in preceding chapters) may be realised. I can only suggest some of the issues of implementation that seem broadly to follow from the goals of practice; but in the local situation decisions about implementation of a project should closely follow on specification of what is to be achieved. Our experience of the 1970s, however, shows that in community work the implementation of an idea was as much influenced by fashion, values, vested interests and administrative convenience as by rational considerations as to what was the most appropriate form of, for example, funding. We have learnt from the past decade that implementation − putting an idea for community work into practice − is fraught with difficulties and that often arrangements for recruitment, funding and auspices are not always conducive to achieving the declared goals of the proposal. This has been as obvious in the implementation of programmatic community work such as the CDPs as in departmental community work such as area social work teams.

But there is now amongst some employers and many more workers greater clarity and confidence about what community workers will be doing in a local area, and this makes successful implementation more likely; during the last decade there was a good deal of woolliness and confusion about why community workers were being employed. We also have the experience of the 1970s to help us be more clear about the kinds of auspices, funding, and so on, that are most appropriate for particular kinds of community work initiatives. People simply did not know enough at the beginning of the last decade about what were likely to be the most effective ways of recruiting and deploying community workers.

RECRUITMENT

The recruitment of community workers is not just about finding the right person for a particular job; it is a process whose individual outcomes have a cumulative effect on the character of an occupation. The cumulative effect of decisions by employers around the country to employ, for example, more working-class people, or to discriminate in favour of ethnic workers, will be on the development of an occupation. We can be sure that in the past the effect of recruitment policies on an occupation was hardly, if at all, in employers' minds; people were sized up in relation to the job. It may be impossible to have these wider considerations in mind but we should still recognise that what happens locally will affect the occupation.

The most fundamental principle of recruitment must be competence – the ability to do the job in question. We must expect tighter assessments of competence in the 1980s; the issues and environment within which community workers will be working will be more demanding and complex than in the last decade. Both employers and local residents will have had experience of community workers and have higher expectations of them (combined with more realism about what they might be able to achieve). For these and, doubtless, other reasons, higher standards of practice will be sought.

There is one essential requirement needed to safeguard the principle of competence in recruitment, and that is to ensure that community work develops as an open occupation. This means that employers (and training institutions) must assess people on their ability, and that the indicators or evidence for this ability must include not just paper qualifications (often of dubious reliability – see the previous chapter) but a person's characteristics, personality and previous experience. If community work became a closed, semi-profession with restrictive entry requirements this would exclude those who on the basis of experience may have the most competence for particular jobs. The strongest argument for encouraging the employment of indigenous working-class people is that an employer may find amongst such applicants the best person to fill a particular community work post.

The values of competence and openness are thus not incompatible in theory; the latter is a way of ensuring the former. Yet in practice there is tension between them; there is pressure within community work to discriminate in favour of applicants on the basis of class, race and sex regardless of whether an applicant is, on the basis of ability, the best person for the job. There is a feeling in community work that it is a 'good thing' to employ indigenous workers, and there is anxiety about parachuting middle-class people into neighbourhoods as community workers. The employment of indigenous workers is compatible with a number of important values in community work. While there is a case for constructive, positive discrimination, the argument for employing indigenous workers has suffered from being based on often inexplicit normative justifications. Such norms within the occupation must be supported by empirical or operational justifications, amongst the most important of which is the fact that openness is a way to ensure that competence remains an essential principle in recruitment. Other empirical justifications for employing indigenous workers include:

- it is a way to create a few employment opportunities;
- it may be important that the worker has personal experience of the problems facing the groups with whom he/she is expected to work;
- a community is known to be 'closed' and unreceptive to the intervention of 'outsiders'.

The employment of indigenous workers is a difficult business, fraught with potential problems for all concerned – this, at least, is evident from the limited use of indigenous workers in the last decade. What is urgently required is a review of experiences in this field, and it would be particularly helpful to make available what has been learnt from the American experience of using para-professionals during that country's various poverty and community development programmes. Finally, we must remain aware of the danger referred to by Paul Waddington of community workers being used as the 'personnel officers' for the greater number of para-professionals that may be used in the welfare services.

The reality of the next few years is likely to be that most full-time community workers will continue to be trained and certificated middle-class people; the greater use of local people is likely to happen where they are employed as community work assistants (as in Strathclyde), as part-time workers with quite specific responsibilities, or as participants in experimental schemes based on the notion of apprenticeship. All these possibilities for the employment of local people (qualified on the basis of experience rather than training and credentials) must be accompanied by adequate in-service support and training; another key variable in making apprenticeship and assistantship schemes work is good supervision from the community worker responsible for the apprentice or assistant, and resources must be available to enhance the supervisory and teaching skills of these community workers.

The use of indigenous workers, even on a limited scale, is not just part of an intervention strategy to deal with local problems; it also represents an innovative employment strategy which will require a different approach from employers (whether agencies or groups) and a commitment to developing the job skills and future career prospects of their indigenous workers. It would be highly irresponsible for community work (and social work for that matter) to employ indigenous workers on the basis of an experiment, or as something that is an opportune way of saving resources. There can be no justification for throwing local people back on the scrapheap of unemployment at the end of a three- or five-year project; and no justification for not preparing in advance ideas for the long-term career paths of indigenous workers.

Indeed, the notion of an employment strategy is relevant to the use of all kinds of workers, and it is something that, in the 1980s, employers and organisations such as ACW will need to consider. The need for an employment strategy comes from the simple proposition (though not widely acknowledged, and even less so in deed) that community work is not just an intervention but also an occupation – it has become a means to earn a living. Those who take up this arduous job do so not usually for money or advancement but from a strong sense of commitment – community work has many of the features of a vocation. This commitment does not diminish the responsibilities of community work employers, or of associations such as ACW, to consider such matters as job security and career progress. If we do not provide a career structure in community work, and especially one that rewards people for staying in the field, then we must accept that people who do community work will do so only for relatively short periods, before entering or returning to some other occupation. The absence of a career structure implies that community work practice and training will remain part of 'host' occupations such as social work and youth work to which practitioners are able to return after their stint in community work.

In forming the essential elements of an employment strategy for community work, we must recognise that it is no longer something that can be treated as an experiment. Enough is now known of its potential contribution within neighbourhoods and to the work of a number of departments and agencies. Seeing it as a long-term process of intervention, that sits as a legitimate part of an agency's responsibilities, suggests a concern for workers' employment conditions that is quite different from that which attends seeing community work as a short-term experiment, marginal to the work of the agency. Not only must there be adequate support and supervision but opportunities for personal development, and upward and lateral mobility. People who are recruited locally and who are accepted on the basis of apprenticeship and accreditation schemes must also feel secure about their ability to move between employers.

The recruitment implications of the work for the 1980s described in Chapter 4 are quite complex. Work in the three areas of *reconstruction, renegotiation of status* and *realising the community* implies, by the nature of the complexity and scale of the task, a shift of resources to more and not less community work. The intertwining of complex problems requires teams of workers in an area that include specialists besides community workers (advice workers, for example) and staff from other occupations or disciplines. Community workers who are expert in neighbourhood organising or specialists in fields like housing and employment will need to be combined with those whose abilities lie in social planning and community organisation. When one understands community work as only one contribution to the five approaches of community action, community development, social planning, community organisation and service extension, then a viable recruitment strategy must accept that

- the process of development of community will require other workers besides community workers (care organisers, volunteer organisers, and so on); and
- recruited community workers must be able to work within this broader strategy and accept the multi-disciplinary nature of the interventions of which they are only a part.

It must be stressed that if community work is to contribute in the ways suggested in Chapter 4, then this can be achieved successfully only if employers make a commitment to providing adequate numbers of community workers, and proper support and supervision for them. It may be far better for community work to die out as an occupation, than for it to continue as a misused and exploited intervention in the 1980s − misused and exploited because employers and funders do not give to it the resources and legitimation that are necessary if it is to be effective in the process of reconstruction that lies ahead.

AUSPICES

I want to say something in this section about where community workers might be employed, and how they might best be organised. My assumption is that in the 1980s programmatic community work will continue to become less important than that carried out in departments and agencies, and that done through projects funded through, for example, urban aid. This will occur not only because of the lack of resources for programmatic development but also because of the institutionalisation of community work (in the sense used in the end of Chapter 4) as part of the main-stream response of agencies to social and political issues. I anticipate, too, that the learning that has gone on in such agencies in the last decade about structure and organisation will be reflected in the evolution of different approaches to where community workers are most effectively located, and best organised. For example, the situation so prevalent in the early 1970s of the single community worker based in a large area social work team will, it is hoped, continue to be much less common; enough is now known from experience and research that such arrangements are often quite inappropriate, unless, of course, the worker is an integrated member of a community-oriented team and engaged in activities central to the responsibilities of the team.

I assume, too, that it is both desirable and feasible for community work to continue to be an intervention within both the statutory and voluntary sectors. The statutory sector will develop in two ways: as an employer of community workers and as a funder or seconder of them. Not only will local authorities employ workers but they will provide more funding for voluntary agencies and local groups to employ them. It will be desirable that such funding will not be through special programmes because there is the need to avoid short-term funding of community work. Rather, it is to be expected that local authorities will see the value in particular circumstances of providing on-going funds to agencies and groups. This will be further explored in the next section.

The direct employment of community workers by local authority departments is also likely to grow in importance; departmental auspices are appropriate to implement a concern with social planning, community organisation and the influence of local social policy. It is in departments such as social services that community work can continue to influence the other aspects of the department's work; and as departments such as social services move towards more community-orientated policies there will be a greater need for the specialist work of community workers. Neighbourhood work may become more valued the more social services develop innovatory attitudes to practice. To the extent that they will be concerned with self-help and community resources and networks, for example, then neighbourhood work will continue to be a significant specialism. Likewise, where social services become more interested in advice- and information-giving roles, working from family and neighbourhood centres, then one would expect continued appreciation of the contribution of community work.

These three factors will be of particular importance for neighbourhood work; social planning and inter-organisational work might be expected to grow in importance where social services become more locally participatory and accountable; more involved in major economic changes in communities; and more pluralist in the number and type of agencies administering services.

Departments of social services are responsible for a variety of services and not only those associated with narrow conceptions of social work; community work is an important intervention within the personal social services, and its role and legitimacy within departments of social services follows from this fact and not from the outcome of a discussion as to whether community work is part of social work or not. Social workers are only one (and usually the smallest) element of departments of social services. Such departments comprise a (growing) number of services and specialisms in addition to social workers; the place of community work as one of these specialisms within these departments is operationally and logically quite separate from any consideration of its relationship to social work. It would be naive, however, not to recognise that, at the present time, it is social work and various views about social work that determine the direction and operations of these departments. The development of the personal social services, and the place of community work within them, will thus be affected by the survival of an institutional conception of social welfare which is, at the moment, jeopardised both by public expenditure cuts and by 'slim-line' conservative theories that will, in the words of one correspondent, restore residual conceptions of social welfare and reduce social work 'to the functions of bureaucratic and "therapeutic" social control of the deserving poor'.

At the heart of the contribution of community work to the personal social services is how far social workers can resolve their ambivalence about community work's developmental functions and its practitioners' commitment to social change. Community workers themselves must also deal with their own ambivalence towards social workers' roles and tasks. In the 1970s, wrote one contributor to the study,

> Only a very few community workers recognised the potentialities of a radicalised social work profession. Most community workers chose to assert their independence from social work and ignored, or denied, the key factor of the political context of the Welfare State. Unable to define clearly what they *are,* community workers sought to identify themselves by declaring what they *were not.* We are not social workers, they said, with the implicit, and quite often explicit, assumption that this denial conferred upon them the status of being better, more effective, more radical, more 'with it' than social workers.

Will this continue to be the attitude in the eighties? I doubt it, not least because community work has become more sophisticated in its analyses of politics and the welfare state, and the messianic fervour of the early 1970s has been recognised as flawed: there is more recognition of community work as a public service occupation, with a discernible set of skills and knowledge. There is, too, the fact that social workers themselves are learning more about community work and, spurred on by the report of the Barclay inquiry, one would expect in the decade coming a more sympathetic understanding of the contribution of community work in the personal social services.

One of the interesting features of community work is that its distributive functions suggest its position within, for example, the personal social services or in planning departments, but its developmental functions indicate that the educational services would also be an appropriate location. These are as much preoccupied with statutory responsibilities, and affected by traditional conceptions, as some parts of the personal social services. It may be that adult education services may become more involved with community work in the future, not least because it will see community work as one method of realising some broader based strategies; see, for example, the growing interest in adult education in 'learning for participation' in civic and political affairs. The discussion paper *Adult Education and Participation* presented in 1982 to the Universities' Council for Adult and Continuing Education stresses that 'public participation is capable of producing better citizens and a better polity. We also believe that increased citizen participation will enrich, not subvert, our system of representative democracy. From this basis, therefore, we have sought to explore the ways in which adult education can in turn contribute to the development of a participatory democracy.' To the extent that adult education will address itself to such major issues as participation then we might expect that community work will be seen as a relevant method.

For similar reasons, chief executives' departments are also a suitable place for locating community workers. If we are to take seriously the contribution of community work to developing democratic mechanisms, and the capacities of people to use them, then community workers might be employed as part of the electoral services teams of chief executives' departments.

The most problematic aspect of the employment and siting of community workers has always been in relation to neighbourhood work. It is extremely difficult to do neighbourhood work if you are not in a neighbourhood base, and it is to be expected that there will be more acceptance in the 1980s of the use of neighbourhood bases for neighbourhood workers. It is to be hoped that this physical decentralisation will imply more recognition by employers of the need to work in small localities and that there will be an end to situations where workers are expected to cover large geographical areas. This is not to ignore the need, however, for specialist workers on issues like housing who can advise existing groups across as large an area as a city. It may be that community centres will become more important as places in which neighbourhood work might be based. They provide a focus for a number of the activities mentioned in Chapter 4 – for leisure, care and campaign activities, informal education and advice and information services.

Neighbourhood advice centres are a valuable resource, particularly in inner-city areas and those afflicted by unemployment where there is increasing demand for advice that relates to household income and expenditure, and the rights of welfare claimants. These advice and information centres provide a local base for community work, where neighbourhood workers can be part of a team that includes the other kinds of workers needed at an advice centre. The concept of a neighbourhood centre with a range of advisory and support functions is one to be taken seriously by social services departments, not simply because it is consonant with a more community-orientated approach but because it is an effective way to pass on advice and information which take up a good part of a social worker's time with clients.

The second important principle for neighbourhood organising must be team work, and the development of teams of community workers in some local authority departments such as Nottinghamshire is to be welcomed. Teams are important for a number of reasons, not least because they are needed to tackle the scale of problems in some neighbourhoods. They offer peer support and guidance to their members, and enable degrees of specialisation and continuity to be built upon in response to the work thrown up in an area. They also follow on as the necessary instrument of service from the work of reconstruction, renegotiation and realising the community outlined in Chapter 4, and the logic of multi-disciplinary teams has already been discussed. Community work teams are better placed to develop a strategic, planned and long-term response to an areas' needs, and thus provide a structure that both enables and constrains the work of individual members. The existence of a policy and membership of a team sets directions and discipline to individual pieces of neighbourhood work, as well as providing support and guidance. It was put this way by one correspondent:

The development of a tight team was a reaction to cowboys in the previous structure here. The team helps to provide a policy and not just an emotional response to issues, and marks the end of the autonomous maverick. We have snuffed out the student politics element of community work and replaced the radical chic of community work with a radical strategy. There is no room for complacent radicalism – our radicalism is more pragmatic. Being in a team is more intellectually stretching, and your work and decisions are up for scrutiny. We are building up knowledge and experience accumulatively, and hope to have city-wide clout at policy level, as well as be involved in our neighbourhoods.

The degree of self-management that team work makes possible creates the opportunity for community work to mature as an occupation. This maturity will be evident in a number of ways; for example, in the evolution of different approaches to composing a team and allocating responsibilities between neighbourhood organising and advice work, for instance, or between long-term work, short-term 'contract' work, and issue-focused work across a city. Another aspect of maturity is that the combined and comparative experience of team members will, as it is discussed within the team, lead to more clarity about the tasks, skills and roles of community work.

It is clear that as structures have evolved through a process of trial and error, so, too, has the level of debate moved on. The unhelpful dichotomies of earlier years (for example, between neighbourhood teams and central units) have been replaced in many areas by a realisation that what matters are the differences between the various ways of organising neighbourhood teams or central units; and that the particular form of organisation chosen in the neighbourhood or central unit must be determined by local circumstances and the work to be done. Once chosen, a particular structure of, say, a neighbourhood team must be allowed to adapt to changing circumstances and may, for instance, change with the phases of a project or piece of work.

The on-going funding of local management groups, or the secondment of workers under their direction, is an important element of the employment strategy for community work in the 1980s. It is associated with certain values in community work, and can be seen as part of extending the educational opportunities that neighbourhood action offers local people. It is, too, part of the process of locating neighbourhood organisers in a way that makes them relevant and accessible to local interests. The use of local management groups, and of local consultative committees, is fraught with difficulties and these have been concisely reviewed by Marilyn Taylor in an issue of ACW's *Talking Points* (1979). She writes that whilst local control is closest to the principles of self-determination that underlie much community work,

> it is not always easy to put into practice. Local control is of little value if it is just tokenism. Many of the local people best equipped to manage already have a lot of commitments, it is difficult to involve people in something as abstract as management. It is difficult to ensure that a group is representative and that there is a flow of information so that management is truly open. Traditional committee structures are often felt to be exclusive, and there is not much training available to equip people with management skills.

She also refers to the point (often expressed by workers who favour local control but opt for some other model) that it may be unfair to expect local people to struggle with the problems of management when they are fully stretched already in working for the aims of their particular action group.

There can be no doubt about the difficulties of involving local people in the employment and management of community workers, but they are difficulties to be worked on than to be avoided. The commitment in community work to more participative forms of service must be manifest in the way it is organised as an occupation. The goals of enhancing political significance and competence, of extending participative and accountable forms of government, must be tackled and made evident in a number of small ways, such as the management of community work staff and resources. At the same time, the problems of time and energy, and of skills and experiences, that are encountered by local people in the management of staff must be recognised; it is to be hoped that in the 1980s there will be developments that will provide support and advice to management committees − a form of consultancy that is already provided for in Holland, for example.

In all this there is a need for caution: there is the danger of much harm being caused by the doctrinaire insistence on local management; although the normative case for such arrangements is a strong one in community work, it must be tempered by consideration of whether the particular local circumstances are appropriate to implement local management. There is, too, the point that the assumption of management responsibilities by local people may be the outcome of a long-term process of community work rather than its starting-point.

The temptation to use definitions of community work to prescribe rigidly the auspices for its practices must be resisted. In principle, community work is compatible on a definitional basis with the operations of a number of different departments and agencies − social services, housing, education, and so on. The concern with welfare goals emphasises the particular appropriateness of community work within, or funded by social services; the conception of community work as an educational intervention, on the other hand, underlies the links with the education service. But, however neatly definitions and the remits of particular departments seem to fit in principle, it seems more realistic to make decisions about auspices that are based on situational factors: that is, the goals of the community work endeavour and the policies, people, resources, and so on, of the particular departments or funders in the area. The very advantage of the fact that community work is tied definitionally to a number of departments is that we can choose amongst them to find the best site for a particular community work initiative. A further advantage is that the kind of multi-agency support that is needed for the interventions indicated in Chapter 4 ought, in principle, to be easier to achieve.

FUNDING

Up to the present, community work has been financed by local authority departments and by departments at central government level. The Department of the Environment, the Home Office (including the

Voluntary Services Unit) and the Department of Education and Science are examples of government departments that have funded programmatic community work (CDP is an example) and project community work through the urban aid programme and the inner cities and partnership programmes. The Manpower Services Commission has also been an important source for funding project community work. Besides these main funders, there has been a variety of less substantial funding by bodies such as community relations committees and councils of voluntary service, as well as contributions from industry and organisations such as the Arts Council, and Development Boards in rural areas.

Local and national trusts have also helped substantially in funding community work, and here the emphasis has been on specific projects entirely within the voluntary sector. I want to look at two aspects of the funding of community work. There are *the policies* which the funding of projects, workers, and so on, are expected to realise; and *the distribution* of funding. It is difficult to generalise in each of these areas because of the many different ways in which community work has been resourced by such a diverse group of central and local, statutory and voluntary funders. But it may be possible to highlight some broad, but important, issues, some of which have already been discussed elsewhere (Mayo, 1982; ACW, 1981*b*).

Policies

It is a truism that funding is the means through which policy-makers give practical expression (in the form of services, projects, and so on) to their policies. Within the assumptions of a rational model of planning, the identification of needs is followed by determination of specific goals to meet those needs; these goals are transformed into concrete programmes and services, for which funding is then sought for their implementation.

Coherence between policies, funding and implementation is, of course, less easy to achieve in the real world outside the assumptions of planning models, and much that has happened in the development of community work is a particularly good case study of incoherence in the above relationship. What is striking is the inadequate development of policies about community work. Community workers and projects were brought into the work of, for example, social services departments with either quite unreal expectations of what could be achieved, or no expectations at all — in many cases, community work was funded as a matter of fad or fashion, or in order to conform with prescriptions about community work that were evident, first, in the Seebohm report and later in the adoption of unitary conceptions of social work practice. Whilst both Seebohm and the unitary theorists offered a policy or framework within which community work was placed, we should be sceptical about how far policy-makers and managers were able to translate these ideas into practice. What Seebohm and the unitary models implied was not just the addition of community work to an existing range of social work services, but a reconceptualisation and transformation of those services. With few exceptions, community workers and projects were simply added to services with little, if any, philosophy about a 'new social work' and little, if any, local policy about social issues and the interventions that were needed to deal with them.

There were many reasons (not least that many community workers resisted the idea that they were there to implement the policies of their agencies) why policy-guided community work was such a rare phenomenon in the 1970s, but amongst the most important must be the absence within community work itself of a policy or strategic view of community work. First, there was no widely acceptable view of development, a theory of development which might have provided a strategic understanding of the contribution of the myriad of individual community work projects and initiatives. The theory of development associated with, for example, Batten or Murray Ross (often referred to as 'the community development approach') was influential in informing some projects in the 1960s but it became discredited in the 1970s, partly because workers and agencies were preoccupied with community work's distributive functions. The idea that a community – its individuals, groups, networks, relations, and so on – is an object whose development can be consciously and purposively pursued as a matter of social and economic policy was not apprehended by councillors and professional staff.

In the 1970s, strategic understandings of community work (such as that provided by a theory of development) were overshadowed by more limited meanings of community work that were provided by the issues with which community groups were engaged and by the purposes and tasks of funding agencies. Thus community work became seen as being about housing problems, or about neighbourhood care schemes, about doing something about urban deprivation, or about making a response to the urban riots. Community work, as I have suggested in another chapter, became very task-centred, and focused on the remit and particular goals of sponsoring departments. There were a number of important consequences for funding and other matters. In the first place, the duration and character of a community work innovation in a neighbourhood would be determined as much by the availability and category of departmental funds as by community needs and by the presence of a strategy that located the innovation within a much wider framework. There were two common consequences of this. The first was the one-off community work project working with few resources in a demanding neighbourhood; it would work on a few selected issues, and it was usual for such a project to close down after a three- or five-year period, *having satisfied the particular goals of the funding agency.* The second was to find a community that had a number of community workers operating in it from different agencies. They would work with minimal reference to each other, within the perimeters set by their own agency's remit, rather than within those set by a common analysis of community needs, or by a shared understanding of how each of the individual projects could be part of a much longer-term, integrated attempt at development of the community.

Another difficulty is that community work initiatives have been resource-led – they followed closely the availability of funds in departments earmarked for issues that were seen to be particularly pressing. One of the problems of this is that equally important issues can be neglected, as one contributor observes:

> Funding in community work has always had its fashions, especially in central government funding. On the positive side this has made it possible for creative new ideas to be floated, but it can also deny money to equally deserving cases elsewhere, or force agencies and groups to squeeze natural developments into new clothes in order to survive. Many areas outside the partnership and programme areas, for example, felt that the inner cities programme demonstrated a failure to recognise that they too had needs. A swing away from community issues other than employment now raises similar problems and could have similar effects. Housing is an example, where current policies will exacerbate the chronic state of crisis in this field. Such a swing would also affect generalist community work and thus strike at the ability to continue to generate and support neighbourhood organisations. It may in particular turn the clock back several years as far as women in the community are concerned, since male unemployment is often the most visible and therefore most likely to attract attention and action. Resources must go into action on unemployment, but not at the expense of other work.

The second consequence I want to discuss falls within the second heading – the distribution of funding – and this is the short-term nature of much funding for community work.

The Distribution of Funding

The assumptions on which funds are distributed will affect the way in which projects and services develop; two assumptions in particular have led to what the William Temple Foundation Group refer to as the 'tyranny of the short-term'. The first assumption that still continues even after some twenty years of experience is that community work is an experimental, innovative intervention (the assumption is 'validated', of course, by the fact that community work continues to be outside the main-stream of most sponsors' activities). The second is really a non-assumption: the absence of ideas about the developmental nature of community work has resulted in a plethora of one-off, short-duration projects and initiatives. The assumption that community work is *only* about dealing with a particular problem has ensured a pattern of short-term funding.

The belief that community work is an innovation leads, as Kingsley has written in another context, 'directly to the justification of funding on an experimental basis'; the twin assumption of innovation and experiment leads to short-term funding for community work, usually of three years, more rarely five. Kingsley suggests that short-term funding

> has a major influence both on the type of services which organisations attempt to promote, and on the development of the organisation itself. Organisations dependent on limited term experimental funding are reactive and insecure, and are thus less able to formulate truly innovative approaches to problems.
>
> There is a high premium placed on innovation for its own sake – what is new is assumed to be always better than what went before. This is reflected in the criteria for the availability of grant aid. Both government and charitable trusts are often more receptive to funding applications if it can be claimed that the application provides a previously untried solution to an old problem. It is important to note the 'problem-orientation' of the criteria. This encourages agencies seeking funding to respond to existing identified and accepted needs. There is little place for programmes which question the description of need, or which attempt to initiate programmes of prevention where 'need' is not yet apparent. Thus agencies are forced into a reactive stance which stunts their subsequent development. (1981)

The issue of short-term funding of community work as an experiment reveals further difficulties. Kingsley suggests that 'funding for experimental programmes implies that the programme itself will be tested in some way'. Little, if any, such evaluation has been carried out on community work, and the con trick is thus revealed: 'programmes are funded as experimental not because there is a real uncertainty about the outcome, but because there is an unwillingness to commit resources on a larger scale. Community groups are increasingly aware of this dilemma, as their "experimental" pro-grammes are withdrawn at the end of the initial period.'

The other justification for short-term finance is that all that is needed to launch a community work initiative is some pump-priming: if a project or idea proves successful, it is argued, then statutory authorities will continue to fund it after its initial period. This assumption has become less and less credible, particularly in times of recession when local authorities find it more difficult 'to pick up the bill'. The criteria of success are also equivocal and controversial: the success of a project in helping groups meet their identified needs may bring those groups into disagreement with departments which are also expected to provide long-term funding for the community work. A good deal of the arguments for pump-priming also depend on assumptions about the abilities of communities to sustain their involvement in community activities after the withdrawal of community work resources; this assumption, like that which expects local authorities to foot the bills of the short-term project, is much less credible in areas and periods of recession and hardship. The amount of work that is required to win further funding after a three-year period, together with the time it takes to get going in the first year of a project, ensures that the time and energy for actual fieldwork is even further reduced. It is also virtually impossible in such a short cycle to evaluate the work done, and to write up and disseminate any interesting aspects of the work. The short-funding cycle imposed by funders is thus partly responsible for the dearth of practice-generated ideas and literature in British community work.

It is, of course, project and programme community work (especially that funded under urban aid) which has suffered from short-term funding. But even departmental community work has suffered in a similar way in that the lack of support resources for community work, and the failure to provide the numbers of workers required to do more than token work, has contributed to the turnover of community workers in departments and agencies.

The short-term funding cycle has also contributed to holding back the emergence of a strategic approach to community work intervention, such as that based on a theory of development. Community workers have often become service-givers, rather than development or education workers; tangible ways of working (such as concentrating on advice and information services) evolve because that is all that is possible in a short period, and it provides the kind of specific and concrete results that can be most persuasive in arguing for a project's extension. There are, as one contributor suggested, 'many areas of community work where intervention is not short-term in nature, and where withdrawal is irresponsible. It is especially difficult for projects in particularly disadvantaged areas, and this includes most multi-racial areas, to work on a short-term basis to overturn the alienation of years . . . it is demoralising to see developments cut short by a frantic and ill-fated search for money to survive . . . A balance needs to be found which continues to encourage new ideas but also guarantees that promising starts already made can be built upon.'

Achieving this balance seems to be one of the critical issues of the 1980s for community work. Short-term projects will often be justified, but they must be seen as 'part of an intervention package', as part of a longer-term strategy of intervention in a neighbourhood that appreciates the developmental nature of the work, and which recognises that the difficulties facing many communities cannot be resolved simply by parachuting in a couple of community workers for three years. Short-term contract work in helping residents with a particular issue or difficulty will also be needed but it must be part of a purposeful strategy of continuing work in and with a community. The kinds of expertise needed over a longer period of time will inevitably go wider than community workers; part of a strategic approach is to recognise when the work of community workers has been completed, or needs to be complemented with other staff and facilities.

I want to end this chapter with discussion of some matters that might bear upon the question of funding in the 1980s. This is a difficult task because the tension between what is necessary and what is feasible is very pronounced. I will tend to stress what seems desirable even though some aspects may be difficult to realise in the present economic situation; it is important to emphasise what is necessary so that those agencies and other funders who are unable or unwilling to provide the adequate resources are fully aware of the consequences for community work and the development of communities. I shall concentrate on the funding of full- and part-time workers and will assume that central government funding through urban aid and other programmes will continue to be important; however, I shall largely be concerned with the local arrangements of funding community work, and in particular with the role of local authorities. The involvement of local authorities in funding community work seems to be quite central, for the reason that they are more likely to have the resources and the political capability of maintaining a long-term strategic implementation of community work, along the lines developed in the various chapters of this book. As we shall see, the role of community groups and voluntary agencies is important within this strategy.

There is, first, a need to set up within each local authority a community development committee or panel; the status and power of such a committee may vary from authority to authority, and may be differently composed of councillors, professional staff from different departments and representatives from community groups and the voluntary sector. The committee would be concerned with the deployment of community work staff across departments and within the voluntary sector. Examples of such committees are already to be found in areas such as Strathclyde and Haringey, authorities employing sizeable numbers of community workers, and where the development of community work has taken place within a broader strategic framework. The location, remit, composition and authority of these committees will vary according to local needs and circumstances, and is likely to evolve through the decade as we learn about their difficulties and opportunities.

A corporate approach of this kind is essential to the development of a local or regional community development strategy; such a committee would be the instrument of that strategy and its ability to direct funds would be its means to ensure implementation of the strategy, and the diminution of ad hoc, piecemeal initiatives in community work. The work of such a committee would be to suggest policy on community work, to influence the employment of community workers in local authority departments and to direct funds to community groups and the voluntary sector in a way which brings them within the broad aims of the policy.

It is consistent with the analysis in preceding chapters to expect local authorities to fund community work *directly* and *indirectly*. By direct funding I mean the employment of community workers (and other staff relevant to the development process) by particular departments. The concern with inter-organisational work and with social planning ensures a place for community workers within departments; the need to help departments such as social services to gain a stronger community base and community orientation likewise determines a place for community work within departments. Decentralised forms of social service delivery around patch systems will also provide a local base for neighbourhood work. The nature of the task facing community work in the 1980s outlined in Chapter 4 also implies a multi-disciplinary or inter-departmental approach. It is to be expected that community work will be jointly funded, and we would look for joint funding arrangements between, say, social services and the health and education services. There might, too, be joint funding between local authority departments (particularly social services and education) and voluntary agencies such as the churches, and the larger councils of voluntary service. It would be difficult to say how there could be coherence in joint funding and projects without the establishment of the kind of community development committee referred to above.

There is an equally strong case for the evolution of *indirect* forms of funding, and by this I mean the giving of funds or the secondment of workers to community groups/management committees and to voluntary agencies. Indirect funding is consistent with current thinking about pluralist forms of welfare services, and clearly consistent both with values in community work about participation and with goals about extending the opportunities for learning to be given to local people. The 'laundering' of local authority money through voluntary agencies and community groups directly to employ community workers is a means of ensuring that community work does not become a monopoly of the 'town hall', and a means of resolving the difficulties that often occur in community work when the local authority employing a community worker is the object of a community group's campaign. Indirect funding helps to ensure, too, the responsiveness of community work resources to local needs, and the accessibility and accountability of those resources to those who make use of them. The arguments for indirect funding must be pragmatic and operational rather than normative; that is, indirect funding arrangements are to be developed because in the local circumstances they seem to be the most appropriate way to organise community work services. Indirect funding to local groups is strongly supported within community work on ideological grounds, but values and norms are considerably strengthened when there are sound operational grounds for indirect funding. Such funding to local groups is feasible only when those groups wish to take on the responsibility of management and have the skills, interests and energy to do so. Indirect funding seems especially appropriate for the funding of particular projects or services; for example, for the funding, management and operation of information and advice centres, where the management committee receives funds from the local authority, and is autonomous in its responsibility for the employment of staff and the work of the centre. Needless to say, the development of particular services and projects should take place within an overall development strategy.

The elements of a funding policy for community work must include not only the ability to fund on a longer-term basis and to fund across departments and the voluntary sector but also the capability to be flexible. The needs of neighbourhoods and groups can change quickly; unforeseen circumstances arise in which funds are urgently needed to start or sustain the activities of a group. The local authority in Sheffield has used the urban aid programme to set aside a contingency fund that can be used in the kind of circumstances described above.

The setting up of a special fund or bank for community work is not a recent idea. The second Gulbenkian report considered the need for a National Fund, and similar proposals have been made by different organisations during the decade. The National Council for Voluntary Youth Services suggested a Voluntary Youth Service Trust Fund; the Royal Institute of British Architects have proposed a Community Aid Fund to enable community groups to use the services of people like architects and planners; Richard Wheeler of the British Council of Churches has argued the case for a Community Initiative Bank to provide money and technical expertise to community organisations; and the National Council for Voluntary Organisations has proposed a Community Buildings Trust to channel to local education authorities money made available by the DES for community buildings.

Most of these funds are seen as attracting finance from central and local government, foundations and industry. They are seen as national funds but this is one of their problems: a national fund would find it difficult to be sensitive to local needs, and to respond quickly and flexibly to community organisations. Far better, in my view, would be a number of regional community work funds, and there is already one of its kind in existence that provides a precedent and some experience. This is the Northern Ireland Voluntary Trust, set up in response to the need 'for a flexible and imaginative source of funding to support new initiatives by local groups because statutory agencies often lack the freedom and flexibility to respond to their needs in the early stages of a project'. It has established priority areas, and initiatives in these areas are supported by the income raised on investing the initial capital of £500,000 given to the Trust by the Department of Health and Social Services.

It is to be hoped that organisations will take the initiative to secure support for similar trusts established on a regional basis in the rest of the United Kingdom. It is always difficult to find the time and energy to begin such a process, and it may be appropriate for government or a foundation to fund the appointment of two or three Regional Trust Development Officers, whose job would be to stimulate support for a regional trust fund in a number of pilot regions. Such an initiative need not preclude the larger local authorities developing their own community work support fund as an addition to the resources committed through departmental budgets and grants to the voluntary sector. One contribution to the study suggests that local authorities should establish 'Community Aid Funds' equivalent to a one penny rate and managed jointly by a local councillor, a local trade union official, a local government officer, a community worker and two representatives from local community groups.

There would clearly have to be close co-operation between such regional and city-wide funds, on the one hand, and on the other, the community development committees of local authorities. The allocation of funds through a regional trust would need to take account of the strategic long-term community work policies developed for particular areas; but, additionally, such a trust fund would also be able to fund ideas and schemes that were not to be given priority within an authority's community development policy, but which nonetheless remained important in meeting local needs.

The proposals in this chapter for community development committees and regional trusts need to be given careful consideration, and, as with many of the ideas and proposals in this book, they are put forward in the hope that further discussion will take place.

This section has dealt with the emergence of local and regional policies about funding. These are to remove the scourge of short-term 'experimental' funding from community work, and to make local authorities either withdraw completely from community work or to accept it as a valid and proven intervention, and then to give it adequate resources. The use of funds is not simply to meet local needs but to do so within a long-term development strategy which can be implemented through the allocation of funds within the statutory and voluntary sectors. Funding becomes, too, a way of developing the occupation of community work − to give its practitioners a sense of security and value; a funding policy will also help to develop the occupation's confidence in its tasks and roles. Funding policy needs to be more concerned with how well people who receive funds do their job, to insist on adequate recording and evaluation, and to provide funds for the in-service training of community work practitioners. Regional funding policies in particular need to look at the infrastructure of community work practice − at the support that is given to workers in the work they carry out.

7 Communication, Research and the Role of a National Body

The literature, theory and research of an occupation should be important elements of its infrastructure. Its literature ought to make available its theories, and those theories will have been developed and refined through research and other means. I want to discuss each of these three elements in turn, though they are intimately connected as aspects of community work's infrastructure. The part that literature plays is in the transmission of ideas; it offers the means to reach a wide audience to discuss issues and concepts. The publication of ideas ought to be a source of guidance to practitioners, keeping them in touch with developments, as well as a corner-stone of the training of students and local activists. The literature of an occupation plays a role in keeping the whole field together, a point of communication and information between workers, students, trainers, employers, funders, researchers, and so on. Whether one likes it or not, an occupation's literature is regarded as a useful indicator of the status, maturity and likely effectiveness of the occupation; for example, the confidence of funders and policy-makers in community work will be influenced by what they read about it, and what estimate they make of its literature, particularly whether that literature suggests that practitioners have the ideas, skills and resources to carry out their own goals, and the programmes of their employers.

LITERATURE

Community work's literature comprises not only books and articles published in academic journals and popular weeklies but also material 'in very ephemeral physical form − in duplicated or otherwise cheaply produced booklets lacking commercial publishers'. Peter Baldock felt even in 1979 that 'whereas you could produce a fairly decent bibliography for most professions that mentioned nothing other than commercially published books or academic journals, it would still be nonsense to try to do that in community work' (1979*a*). He also points out that community work in the United Kingdom still does not have its own journal; it has been forced, like training, to seek refuge in journals and magazines of other occupations such as social work and adult education, or to give the *Community Development Journal* more of a British emphasis than was originally intended. The use of host journals and magazines has helped the dissemination of community work ideas in these other occupations, but it has made more difficult the dissemination of ideas to community workers in all the various fields in which they are to be found.

I have used the bibliography of British community work prepared by Adrian Lanning (Henderson and Thomas, 1981) for an analysis of the literature by counting the number of entries in each of its sections and in each year for the period 1960–79. This analysis is necessarily limited by the criteria, thoroughness and accuracy of the allocation of material to each of its sections by the bibliographer, and by the fact that some of the sections are very large and heterogeneous. Nevertheless, it gives a useful, if rough-and-ready, indication of some of the patterns in the development of community work literature in the United Kingdom.

As might be expected, the period 1960–9 was characterised by a sparse output of published materials – some 81 pieces for the whole decade. It is surprising in light of this relative paucity of material that neither the first nor second Gulbenkian reports had much to say about the development of community work's literature; an opportunity was missed to suggest priorities and to guide the development of materials and, in this context, it may be said that a particular casualty of the two reports' omission on literature was the development of community work's practice theory.

There was, in contrast, a large increase in literature in the decade 1970–9; there were some 773 published items, an almost tenfold increase over the previous decade. The output of materials doubled in 1972 and continued to rise to a peak in 1975 with the publication of some 126 items, a peak that is attributable almost wholly to the appearance of material from or about the Community Development Projects. Thereafter, output of literature declined until by the last year of the decade it was at the level achieved in 1973 – between 70 and 80 items annually.

Some 40 per cent of the literature in the 1970s fell into the three categories used by Lanning of 'Work at the local level', 'Local politics' and 'Case studies', with the majority of the latter concerned with neighbourhood work. This reflects the localism of British community work in the 1970s, its attention to change at neighbourhood level and small communities. Less than 2 per cent of the decade's literature was devoted to work at the agency level, and the amount of literature given over to some of the key concepts in community work (community, participation, ideology, for example) was relatively little – under 5 per cent of the decade's published output. There was a similar lack of interest in writing about community work's infrastructure – the materials on, for example, employment of community workers, their training and supervision and research and evaluation remained at or below 5 per cent of total output in the 1970s.

There are over 700 entries in the bibliography and less than a quarter of these were written or edited by community work teachers on community work, social work, youth work and adult education courses in this country. Of these entries contributed by community work teachers, just under half were written by the same group of ten teachers. Of the 49 people who at the time of their publication were identifiable as community work teachers, only 10 had published more than five articles/books throughout the period covered by the bibliography – 1960–79. (CDP materials and government reports are excluded in this particular analysis.) The majority of publications were written by practitioners, researchers, councillors, student unit supervisors, and academics from other departments such as sociology and social policy. The above analysis showed that some people wrote far more when they were in practice or student unit supervision than when they found themselves in community work teaching posts in colleges.

The analysis of the Lanning bibliography confirms that community work literature was largely case-study based. Both Bryers (1979) and Baldock (1979*a*) have observed that the bulk of the case studies were overly descriptive and general – 'simply stories' – with little specificity about the role of the community worker. Such specificity about the worker is necessary if the literature is to be used to develop knowledge and skills in intervention. Much of this case study literature failed, too, to prepare any analytic frameworks or concepts from the actions being described. This was a serious failure because case studies are a useful means to develop theories out of the 'home-grown' practice of community workers. What then should we look for in a case study? While this clearly depends greatly on the nature of the situation being described and the purposes of the case study, there are perhaps some broad questions which one would generally expect to be addressed. These might include:

(1)   Who identified the problem and how did they define and analyse it? What factors contributed to the problem?
(2)   Who determined the general course of action to be adopted? What alternatives were there? What would be the likely gains and losses of adopting any of these alternatives?
(3)   What influenced the forms of organisation and communication which developed? How did people and groups come to be included or excluded and with what consequences? Was the organisation appropriate for the purposes to be achieved? How was the effectiveness of the organisation built up?

(4)   What factors account for the course of the development? How did the type of population involved and the nature of the problem affect the development? What obstacles were encountered and how were they overcome? How did the broader social setting of the development affect the outcome?

(5)   What were the group's relationships with other organisations? How was conflict within the group and between the group and others dealt with?

(6)   What roles did the workers adopt in these developments? Were they appropriate to the situation and the purposes to be achieved? What specific activities did the workers engage in and how did these contribute to the development, positively or negatively?

(7)   What were the aims of the sponsoring organisation? How did these compare with the objectives of the workers and those of the groups involved? What did the sponsoring organisation hope to gain from the development? What did community groups hope for?

(8)   What benefits, if any, were gained from these developments? Could they have been achieved in other ways? What would have been the consequences of different approaches?

For the purpose of studying practice it is essential that the role and activity of the worker and the assumptions and thinking on which these are based should be given as much attention as the work of the target group or organisation and the development of the situation. This should include also a critical appraisal by the worker of his or her own approach and actions.

Ideally, the case study should include enough information to enable the reader to make his or her own interpretations of the situation. Such a mixture of descriptive and analytic material would also provide a basis for more general propositions or hypotheses about the practice of community work. This is a very demanding task. Potentially, however, case studies are not merely an illustration of theory developed for other purposes but an important source of an indigenous theory of practice (taken in full from Henderson *et al.*, 1980).

The lack of attention to the worker in case studies, together with their non-analytic character, meant that there was little in community work literature in the 1970s on the methods and techniques of the practitioners – an imbalance noted in 1982 by Eric Sainsbury who commented on the emphasis in articles on values and policies rather than 'the criteria by which, in a specific situation, a skillful community worker would select certain interventive techniques and discard others'. There was, however, more material available on the strategies open to community groups – thanks, in large part, to the magazine *Community Action*. Baldock has suggested that 'the absence of any emphasis on the "virtuoso performance of the professional" in British community work literature is one of the major ways in which it differs from the literature of other professions' (in Henderson and Thomas, 1981). This absence has had adverse effects on the training of students and the support of workers, and on the ability of community work to persuade funders and policy-makers of the details of its intervention. Where these details remain unclear and obscure (as they did for most of the 1970s) there can be little confidence that community work can contribute to the problems identified by its practitioners, by policy-makers and by community groups. An understanding of the methods of the intervention – knowing just what it is that community workers do – is necessary (together with confidence that they have the experience and expertise to do it) for the occupation to be credible. The absence of specificity about methods of intervention will, too, combine with other factors to produce inadequate opportunities for student training and in-service support.

Much of the literature is skewed towards students and trainers. It is now well known that practitioners in a number of occupations rarely read books and in many cases have difficulty in getting access to them; books are, on the whole, used more by students and their teachers. Articles may have a better chance of being read by practitioners, but this is more likely to occur when articles appear in popular weekly magazines. Table 7.1, compiled from the Lanning bibliography, shows, however, that the majority of community work articles appeared in publications coming out less frequently than weekly or fortnightly. Many of these publications are academic and international publications, designed for particular fields, with the consequence that even students, and certainly practitioners, may not have easy access to them, or even information of their existence. The weeklies that carried a good proportion of community work articles (*Social Work Today* and *Community Care*) have a largely social work readership, and are probably read more by community workers in social work than in other agencies.

It is more likely that ACW's *Talking Points* (excluded from the table) reached practitioners, but these were more likely to be confined to ACW's small membership. It is apparent from this crude analysis that the literature for community work practitioners was extremely un-satisfactory during the 1970s and trainers and organisations such as ACW and FCWTG may want to consider how to improve this element of the infrastructure during the 1980s. The other point worth making is that the skew of the literature towards the interests of students and trainers makes the paucity of material on methods and techniques even more peculiar and unsatisfactory.

The table also gives a rough indication of the 'permeation value' of community work articles: that is, their ability to influence thinking in related occupations. The table suggests how social work has had far

Table 7.1 *Distribution of Community Work Articles, Using the Lanning Bibliography, 1960–79*

	Social Work	Community Development	Local Government	Social Policy & Administration	Planning & Architecture	Education	Race Relations	Youth Work	Other	TOTAL
Number of journals/ magazines counted	12	6	4	4	7	6	3	1	15	58
Number of community work articles counted	145 / 39%	111 / 30%	20 / 5·4%	16 / 4·3%	13 / 3·5%	11 / 3·0%	8 / 2·2%	4 / 1·1%	44 / 11·8%	372
Number of weekly publications in count	2	—	3	—	—	—	—	—	1	6

more exposure to community work literature than other fields. The difference between social work and other categories may be exaggerated if the bibliographer was less able to survey journals in these related occupations, and is explained in part by the number of journals/ magazines in each field, and the frequency of their appearance. Social work has more journals, and two which appear weekly, and this has encouraged the dissemination of community work ideas. Given the complexity and seriousness of the tasks that face community work in the 1980s it is a matter of some concern that community work has been so inadequately discussed in the publications designed for local government, social policy makers and administrators, and those working in planning, race relations and youth work.

A content analysis was carried out by Harry Specht (1978) of articles dealing with social planning and community work in four American social work journals. The analysis revealed 'an intellectual lag between the realities of the field and the literature of the profession'; the increasing concern in the field and in legislation with social planning, promoting consumer participation and agency and inter-agency co-ordination was not reflected in commensurate attention in the literature to these aspects of practice, and the skills and knowledge needed to carry them out. It was not possible to carry out a similar analysis of British community work literature, but Specht's article should alert us to the existence of such an intellectual lag in British community work. A number of community work trainers felt that they were training students as grass-roots, neighbourhood organisers (using the experience and literature of the 1970s) but were apprehensive that the realities of work in the 1980s may demand skills and knowledge in addition to those of neighbourhood work.

THEORY

By theory I mean a set of tested or testable propositions, ideas, or hypotheses that contribute to our understanding of what we do, why we do it and with what effects. Our theories of the world and of community work affect how we observe and interpret the world, and, in principle, determine the basis of our interventions. These theories are as much part of the occupation's infrastructure as some of the other activities we have discussed because they exist (where they do) as a source of guidance and enlightenment. They are something to be drawn upon in the aid of practice, as much as they may be generated through that practice, and the paucity of a theoretical infrastructure can be as harmful as the inadequacy of facilities for training or in-service support.

There have been a number of very pertinent reviews of the development of theory in British community work (for example, Tasker,

1980; Bryers, 1979; Hanmer and Rose, 1980). Their conclusions are similar to many of those trainers, researchers and practitioners who took part in this study's Delphi exercise on training and research in community work: there has been little progress in the last decade in the development of firmer and clearer theory. The literature has grown but, as one respondent argued, 'most of it is commentary, description or bland rhetoric'. He went on:

> Practitioners in Britain do not, in my experience, thirst for knowledge (again there are exceptions) and neither do they set out very often to contribute to the development of knowledge about the work. There is some resistance to theorising and little recognition of the practical utility of sound theory. There is so little funded research, documentation or systematic recording of the work that it is surprising that the literature has grown as it has. Nevertheless, hard-headed commitment to the growth of the knowledge-base of the occupation (if such it is) is singularly lacking.

This knowledge-base may be separated into two main categories, practice and explanatory theories. Practice theory is 'how-to-do-it' theory that helps people understand the numerous tasks in the doing of community work. Practice theory is sometimes called 'the tricks of the trade' or practice wisdom, the gradual refinement of skills that are needed to accomplish a wide variety of tasks. Practice theory is developed essentially from experience, but also from the selective application of social science knowledge and the use of the findings of research. At the beginning of the 1970s practitioners' theories about their interventions were dependent on limited American literature, and on material that had developed through experiences in former colonies. Workers proceeded less on the basis of practice theories and more through intuition, trial and error, though the conclusions of this 'learning through doing' process were only inadequately passed on through the occupation. By the middle of the decade, when there was enough field experience to bring people's own learning together into some codified structure of practice theory, the occupation became preoccupied with the implications of the reports from the CDP projects which were concerned more with explanatory than practice theories.

The first Gulbenkian report recognised that the principles and methods of community work 'have only been conceptualised to a limited degree in this country' and suggested that the development of a theory of practice was primarily the responsibility of community work trainers. The second report in 1973 said virtually nothing about practice theory, and at the end of the decade Phil Bryers was pessimistic in his assessment. 'At present there is a limited body of practice theory with considerable variations in degree of sophistication between different areas, and from one worker to the next . . . This must be seen as an unsatisfactory state of affairs.' He went on to conclude:

> community workers have not given priority to the recording and transmission of practice theory. It is also a commentary on the transitory nature of many of the publications in which practitioners publish their views – they are read at the time of publication, but are very soon lost or forgotten. The task of keeping up with articles and papers from a bewildering number of sources is beyond the average practitioner who has probably settled upon a limited range of magazines to read, and does not possess the facilities to track down relevant material from other places.
>
> This state of affairs suggests a situation in which new community workers soon pick up a general idea of the 'ethos' or norms of community work, consolidate this by reference to one or two texts which outline useful models of practice, and then develop techniques in their day-to-day work of 'getting by'. This may be as much as can be expected – and is possibly more than can be said of other groups of self-professed 'professionals'! If, however, we aspire to more than this we must conclude that over the next decade community work must find ways of disseminating what has been learnt about practice theory much more effectively. A corollary to this is that community workers must accept the discipline of looking at their practice systematically and analytically. (1979)

Explanatory theories provide knowledge about why things are as they are. They try to explain the existence and operation of social and political structures, institutions and processes. These theories deal with a wide range of phenomena from the workings of the state to processes of change in small groups and individuals. British community work has been affected by two 'traditions' in the development of explanatory theories. First, the sociological tradition, with a considerable reliance on the American social sciences for knowledge about, for example, processes of change in large and small groups. This was a tradition mediated through the expanding sociology departments in British colleges, from which many of the recruits to community work came in the late 1960s and early 1970s. The second tradition was political, linked to the student and ethnic 'revolutions' of the late 1960s, and associated in this country with groups such as the International Socialists. The theories of such groups about the state, capital and labour were at the top of a scale that descended through varying levels of ideological development to countless community workers who simply 'felt strongly' about the maldistribution of power and resources, and who also wanted to do something to achieve a more participative democracy.

The variety of ways in which the sociological and the political were mixed in individuals produced a heterogeneous set of assumptions amongst those practising community work. People in community work were independent and possessive about their view of the world that had come about through the particular mix in them of the sociological and the political. It was not until the middle and late 1970s that articulated and developed points of view offering explanatory theories began to emerge. First, there were the views of a group of staff that emerged from some CDP projects with a materialist theory, providing, as Baldock indicates, 'a rather empirical sort of Marxism, providing a series of examples of exploitation rather than developing a Marxist theory of poverty and urban deprivation'. Much of this analysis evolved through a process of doctrinal extension and not through reflection on the experiences of community work and the characteristics of urban working-class communities. Secondly, there was the Christian view, ideas that were given extended expression in the William Temple Foundation report in 1980 and which offered a theory of society constructed around a number of political and theological conceptions about 'involvement in community'. Thirdly, socialist feminism that emerged from the experiences of women community workers or group members. No other positions were as well articulated or published as these three, and it is only the last two that offered a synthesis of handed-down theories with what people had learnt through their experiences in the field during the decade.

I shall now examine more closely what explanatory theories have developed from community work practice, and I shall use three categories to do this: policy theory; political theory; and sociological theory. Whilst community work has drawn in each of these areas from other disciplines and occupations, what can one say, after more than ten years experience, that we have learnt in each of these areas from the *practice* of community work?

(1) Policy Theory

This term was first used by Tasker to refer to theories that describe 'where community work fits in an overall strategy of services to and control of society'. Policy theory is the theory that locates community work as a helping occupation or as a social movement, or as both. Policy theory is a way of conceptualising community work as an intervention within a wider framework of welfare and political activity. Policy theory provides a theory of change, relating both to social change and change to individuals who take part in collective action. The importance of seeing community work as part of a wider strategy has been emphasised throughout this report; it is important not just to achieve effectiveness in using scarce community resources but also to relate to and hold one's own with policy-makers in politics and other occupations:

> There is a great temptation in a helping profession to pre-occupy oneself with the individual person. Policy makers, however, do not suffer this constraint, and they direct welfare services according to well thought out policy theories of their own. To fail to do likewise on the part of community workers incurs two risks. First, they fail to match their own arguments for the provision of the service against those put forward elsewhere in public and professional life. Secondly, they risk manipulation through a lack of awareness of the type of scheme into which their projects are intended to fit. In fact community workers need to be better social-policy theorists than others because of the extreme political sensitivity surrounding their profession. (1980)

Tasker's review concludes that there is an 'inadequate level of policy theorising in community work. Neither the training system nor professional organisation within community work are geared to establishing a tradition of that at this level . . .' In the late 1960s and early 1970s community work's policy theories were a naive mixture of revolutionism and anti-officialdom, bent on prising resources from local authorities. The various theories of social development associated with colonial development and the new women's movement had been rejected, or, even worse, not even known about. The emergence of materialist ideas via the CDP projects enlarged the conceptual map with which community workers had been operating, but their analysis said little about where community work fitted in a theory or strategy of social change.

Another way to view policy theory is to see it providing the justification for the existence, and continued support, of an intervention. Tasker argues that community work never provided its own policy theories to explain its work because it saw the 'helping' of the helping professions with which it was bound up (social work, youth work, education, and so on) as adequate justification for its own existence. When community work was asked to justify itself, and to explain how it fitted within policy concerns, it invariably responded with an analysis that justified itself as part of a host occupation. What has been lacking are theories about community work that locate its contribution within processes of structural and individual change, and which thus provide the overall strategy which legitimises the work of community workers within the helping professions and social movements to which they are linked.

(2) Political Theory

It would not be unreasonable to expect that our experience with community work would have resulted in some contribution to political theorising. Community work has been involved in questions of the distribution of resources and power; it has attempted to influence and be part of political as well as professional decisions. Many of its practitioners came to it with a dissatisfaction with the workings of local government, and the desire to achieve a more participative democracy. It is connected to political parties and to social movements and as a matter of priority gives its attention to the working class; this fact alone makes us look for a contribution to socialist thought. But what is most striking about political thinking in community work, particularly in the early and mid-1970s was its naivety and crudeness, a point well put by Raymond Pringle:

> One of the main characteristics of community work over the last decade has been the fact that it has lacked an adequate theoretical framework. Community workers have operated with a simple analysis of urban society and equally naive prescriptions for practice . . . The grandiose claims, the heady optimism, the intense ideological debate and the radical posturing of those halcyon days that followed 1968 are now seen to be fallacious . . . Instead of a theoretical perspective and concrete analyses there was idealism, radical chic and frenetic local activity. The disadvantages of this lack of theory were to be recognised as the inadequacy of ideological rhetoric and the limitations of uninformed practice became increasingly apparent. This was particularly noticeable after 1974 as a retrenchment in the welfare state steadily increased. Our failure to develop a theoretical analysis of the urban context has had major political consequences. The local state has been portrayed as a monolithic organisation that simply acted in the interest of the ruling class . . . We have had little grasp of the complexity of the political and economic imperatives that limited the autonomy of the state. We assumed that change would only occur by organising urban protest against the local state. Consequently we exaggerated both the potential of community work and the role of urban protest. (1981)

The structuralist analysis of some CDP staff was partly a restatement of ideas current in revolutionary left groups since the late 1960s and suffered, as did other attempts at theorising, from the general inability of the left to generate contemporary indigenous theoretical frameworks that were born of the events and experiences of the 1970s. This argument is developed at length by Taylor in an article on Marxist inertia (1980), in which he recognises the emergence in the late 1970s of more thoughtful works reflecting on British experience. This theorising included socialist feminism and, perhaps, some of the British students of Castells and the critical social policy caucus; it was taken up by community work as refinements of the former structuralist analysis, but it owed little in its development to the thinking and practice of British community workers and trainers. Whilst the structuralist analysis of some CDPs was not an altogether original contribution to British political thought, the publications that examined the political economy of the inner cities were important to debates within and about social policy; as such, those publications are much closer to the interests of social planning (and hence the original Home Office remit for the projects) than has been appreciated. These political economy reports, with their continuing emphasis on the control and direction of the housing, employment, welfare and money markets, came at social planning through a political analysis, and thus complemented the more technical and administrative perspective on planning that was characteristic, say, of the approach of Americans such as Perlman and Gurin or Gilbert and Specht. British community work responded to the reports' structuralist framework rather than to their concern with planning, and it was the ideological cast of the reports that inhibited policy-makers from attending to what was being said about the political economy of the city. As Lees points out, similar conclusions about the primacy of structural economic factors were being accepted by government as a result of the differently packaged and argued Inner Area Studies (1980).

The failure to contribute to political thought is not simply a failure of the Marxist left in community work. Little has been offered from community work experience that has enlarged our understanding of democratic processes. The involvement of community workers in helping people join and stay in collective action, the contact with the representative system of government and the espousal and, less frequently, the design of new measures of participation, have not resulted in community work practitioners and trainers adding to our understanding of how best to improve democratic political practices.

(3)   Sociological Theory

Two key concepts in the development of sociological thought have been those of *community* and *class*. Both have been central in the thinking and practice of community workers − it is an occupation carried out in a variety of communities, both territorial and functional, and largely with members of the British working class. Tasker rightly criticises the tradition of class analysis in British sociology as being static, and tending to highlight features of working-class communities 'for better administration rather than for their potential for change'. He goes on to argue that 'the most important thing to recognise in assessing the state of theory in community work is that community work is about class. The efforts of community workers are concerned with certain kinds of under-privilege among working class people . . .' He suggests that work with this class 'is not really possible so long as there is insufficient understanding by professional workers of the rest of the culture in which they are working, into which they are trying to introduce new skills and attitudes, and from which they are trying to encourage particular kinds of initiatives'. He continues that better comprehension of the cultural context of a class and its reaction to various aspects of practice is perhaps the greatest need in the theoretical development of community work: 'only when customs and values of a community and their relation to practice theories are understood can the potential for change within it really be evaluated'.

British sociology (in contrast, perhaps, to German and French) in the 1970s offered little that was new to community work in its understanding of class and community, and community work itself has contributed little in the other direction. Theories of class developed from community work experience have been particularly inadequate, and the opportunities of feedback of experience into the sociological mainstream have been negligible. The reasons for this include the lack of theorising within community work on these two concepts, the distrust of academia endemic in community work and the indifference to the phenomena of community action amongst the major social science disciplines. Another factor is that the intolerant culture that grew up in the 1970s in community work made it inevitable that few people would publicly express dissatisfaction with the aridity of some of the thinking about class, and to offer their own formulations in an attempt to develop the field's thinking. Class was a sensitive issue, and most people preferred to say nowt; this was infinitely preferable to being publicly attacked for being 'unhistorical' or 'misguided' or 'conservative'. If anyone doubted how they might be dealt with, then the shameful treatment of Harry Specht at the 1974 ACW conference (when he was abused by a group high on dogma and beer), and of members of the women's caucus at the 1980 conference in Birmingham, indicated that community work was not a culture in which it was safe to take intellectual risks and to enter into dialogue.

A number of articles that Tasker has written on the issue of class in community work are important; whilst holding a materialist view of society, he has also been able to see how this is quite an insufficient base for comprehension of the life and culture of the working class. Likewise, Pringle has exposed the naivety of theorising on class, and the continuing inability in British community work to appreciate not just that class's life experience but how unorganised, divided and politically inactive it has been. There has, of course, been much talk and sloganising about class in British community work but it is, unfortunately, all too easy to encounter workers and trainers with a sophisticated class analysis but with little understanding of the cultures and values of the working class. The critical theoretical failure in British community work has been its inability to use its involvement with the working class to produce a phenomenological account of that class – that is, an account that shows us what it is like to be a member of that class, and to experience the opportunities and constraints of its own values, and the more materialistic constraints imposed by the rest of society. Without this understanding of the meanings that people in that class give to their experiences, we run the risk that our increasing competence as community workers may prove to be mechanistic and epi-phenomenal rather than rooted in the social meanings and political aspirations of working class life.

I have concentrated on community and particularly class because they are central both to sociology and community work, but there are other areas where community work's sparse contribution to sociological thought is equally apparent. For example, community work has offered the opportunity to re-evaluate social science knowledge about group processes, and to throw up further insights based on the work of 'natural' and not laboratory groups. With few exceptions (such as the book by Butcher *et al.* (1980)) there has been precious little material on this theme. Likewise, the involvement of community workers in work within and between organisations has not resulted in material that adds to, or critically reflects upon, the range of publications on organisational theory that was a product of the American social sciences during the 1960s and early 1970s.

RESEARCH AND THE PROCESS OF THEORY DEVELOPMENT

It is reasonable to reflect on these criticisms and to say: you are expecting too much too soon. Community work practitioners and trainers have worked with limited resources; community work is still a relatively young occupation, and it is unrealistic after ten years to expect too much in the way of theory development. There is now much more material available than ten years ago, and considerably less dependence on American literature. There is far more appreciation today of the usefulness of theory as an aid to practice, and less dependence on intuition, charisma and luck in day-to-day practice.

As important as the amount of theoretical material is the process through which it has been developed, and there are a number of points to be made here. First, that it was only relatively late in the 1970s that community work began to generate its 'own' materials. The period from about 1968 was dominated by three sources of intellectual energy that were largely outside, or on the boundaries of, community work, and whose cumulative effect was to overshadow thinking that came out of community work experience itself. At the beginning of the decade there was the influence of the politics of the New Left and the student revolutionaries; in the middle of the 1970s the combined effects of the CDP literature and the unitary theorists in social work were to dampen intellectual curiosity within community work: the CDP influence took attention away from the process of community work intervention to the larger political and economic structures within which it worked. The social work theories of unitary methods, by presenting a theory of social work in which community work was conveniently an integral part, absolved community work practitioners and trainers of the need to produce their own theories of community work. At the end of the decade it was socialist feminism that was beginning to influence thought within community work, continuing the cycle of extraneous intellectual influences on community work that, whilst of considerable value in many respects, were to the detriment of indigenous ideas and frameworks. Throughout the 1970s, workers and trainers struggled to keep up with and integrate these and other external knowledge systems, and what was generally sacrificed was the production of material that came directly out of British community work practice.

The process of theory development in community work was, on the whole, non-accumulative: that is, writing, and particularly the small amount of research that was being carried out, proceeded with little reference to what had already been described. The findings of articles and books were rarely used as the starting-points of subsequent pieces of work. It was difficult for researchers and authors to meet with colleagues to discuss their ideas, and it was a common experience for there to be little oral or written feed-back on published work. Theory development in community work proceeded along almost 'sectarian' lines. Because community work was populated by practitioners and trainers from a diverse range of academic and occupational backgrounds then it was inevitable that writers and researchers would bring the intellectual traditions of their own provenance (as well as their own political views) to the study of community work. In addition, the number and complexity of variables to study in community work are so great that it may be inevitable that people will abstract those that interest them (or their funders) and study them in isolation from research and theory about other aspects of community work. There were, too, the divisions in community work that were discussed in an earlier chapter that ensured that different kinds of theories were produced by different groups of workers and trainers; practice theory, for example, tended to develop separately from contextual theories about the social and political environment within which community work operated. The absence of any substantial interest by academics in other disciplines such as sociology or political science meant that there was a paucity of 'outsider' views that could encompass, if not knit together, the various theoretical tendencies within community work itself.

The place of research in theory development is an important matter, and I want now to say something briefly about this, and then go on to the larger issue of the contribution of research in the development of community work as an occupation. This will be to treat research as part of the infrastructure of community work practice. Much of the research in the 1970s was in the form of case studies or action research studies; whilst they offered insights into practice they had the disadvantage, as one correspondent to the study noted, of being 'insider' and often partisan views and that 'it was hard to generalise from their results since the wider implications tended to get lost in descriptions of the incidentals of the particular situation . . . there was little research into what community workers actually did. Neither was there much evaluation work, or comparative research into its achievements in different settings . . . Embarking into the 1980's, therefore, those who have an interest in the continued growth and development of community work find themselves with a poor research base on which to act.'

The scepticism about research that is evident within community work should not be lightly treated. It helps us to ask: is community work an occupation where research need be no more than a marginal activity? To make it anything more, it might be argued, would be an investment on which the return would inevitably be disappointing because of some limitations of research methodology and the peculiar character of community work. Does effective practice in community work require the kind of systematic evaluation of data associated with research? It can be argued that not so much is at stake in community work as there is in medicine or even education. Here research is needed to guide the critical decisions of doctors and educators. Does it really matter that community workers muddle through, learning by doing, making mistakes as they proceed? What harm can there be to community residents that cannot be avoided by effective supervision? This casual approach must be rejected: it is callous about the hopes and ambitions that people invest in collective action, ignores the pressing need for dealing with many neighbourhood issues, and underestimates the complexity both of the issues that groups try to grapple with as well as the task facing the worker in helping people to join in group activity.

It might be argued that research is only one way of divulging knowledge useful to practice, and, furthermore, it is limited by the narrow forms that are available for dissemination. As important as research may be the incremental and necessarily slow development of 'theory out of action'. Practice wisdom is distilled from experience and as it is refined and communicated orally between practitioners. This accretion of knowledge and its transmission will depend in large measure for its effectiveness on viable links between practitioners, and their ability to reflect critically on their work. The availability of competent supervisors and consultants, as well as resources for in-service training and the space to read, reflect and write, are also important ingredients for making 'theory out of action'. I believe this approach has much to offer, especially as a complement to, rather than a substitute for, social research. Its effectiveness in Britain in the last decade has been vitiated by the tenuous links between workers, and the poor infrastructure of supervision and consultation – not to speak of the effects of the distaste for theorising, no matter how home-grown and empirically derived.

My conclusion is that there is a useful role for research to aid our thinking about practice, administration and training but it is not necessarily more or less important than other ways of generating knowledge. Its advantage over other forms such as 'theory out of action' is that its dissemination and applicability can be given a national character; it provides critique and scrutiny; it informs non-community workers such as managers and students; and provides a clearer way of developing cumulative knowledge. The place of research in community work is well described by a respondent to the study:

> Despite the difficulties, research can be a useful tool for community work as it develops its methods and argues for its survival. The scope of the issues encountered demands constant analyses and rethinking. Methods need to be systematically and dispassionately reviewed. Evidence is needed on the impact of intervention. There is a particular gap between rhetoric and day-to-day practice which needs to be bridged by grounded, or practice, theory. The precision of a researcher and his or her commitment to questioning assumptions, translating broad statements into operational terms, seeking evidence to support beliefs is a valuable resource. There is useful work to be done bringing together experience across the field – on organisational forms, individual motivation for sustained involvement, the promotion of ideas and awareness, techniques and tactics which draw together ideas about the structure of the problems facing the community with ideas for action. And experience and ideas need to be expressed clearly and shared widely.

But the role of the researcher should not be confined to putting community work under a microscope and generating practice theory that is both testable and generally applicable. It is equally important for researchers to help practitioners make theory out of their own action, aiding the gradual accumulation of practice wisdom, of improvement through performance as well as through systematic inquiry. Researchers can facilitate theory from action by:

- helping practitioners to reflect and write;
- raising the self-awareness and analytic capacities of workers;
- if theory is to emerge from action by being communicated from worker to worker, then we need research on:
  (i) communication networks in community work
  (ii) the types of management and supervision structures that facilitate cross-fertilisation of ideas and experience
- desk research to distill practice theory from existing materials;
- the replication of social science research (for example, about group processes) in the natural settings to be found in community work practice.

The first two tasks indicate the enabling or educational role of the researcher, and this is exemplified in the work of the research staff of the Community Projects Foundation during the second half of the 1970s.

Our experience in the 1970s suggests that not only has research an important place within community work's infrastructure but its contribution may be categorised in the following way:

- research as a *tool* in community work, practice, teaching and administration;
- community work practice, training and administration as an *object* of research.

I want to look at these two categories in further detail, and, in doing so, I will extend a previous paper in the *Community Development Journal* (1980).

(1) Research as a Tool in Community Work Practice, Training and Administration

Here research is an aid to those in the practice of community work, and those who teach it and have responsibility for the employment of workers. It has been described as *service research,* and it comprises three overlapping but often distinctive elements:

(A) INVESTIGATIVE RESEARCH

The emphasis is on obtaining guarded or privileged material about organisations who are the targets of the community work activity. This kind of research is perhaps best exemplified in the work of *Counter*

Information Services and in *Community Action's* 'Investigator's Handbook'.

(B) INFORMATIVE RESEARCH

This kind of research helps community workers to make decisions about goals, priorities and strategies in their work. At one level, it comprises such research as local needs assessment, and research that is specific to the interests of a particular community group. At another level, this research comprises the documentation of the extent of social problems in the specific neighbourhood, community, or region of the community work intervention. This is sometimes called political economy research that presents a multivariable analysis of the political and economic factors within or affecting a particular area. This level of research also seeks to disseminate its findings to a wider public on the basis that either the local problems or issues are structurally caused (and are therefore not purely 'local' matters) or there are other parts of the country experiencing similar problems. Examples of this research are to be found in many of the CDP reports, particularly the local project reports such as *Workers on the Scrap Heap* (1975), and in the more national publications like *Whatever Happened to Council Housing?* (1976) and *The Costs of Industrial Change* (1977).

(C) ACTION RESEARCH

This is probably the most commonly thought of aspect of service research; action research is defined by the planned interaction between researcher and practitioner and by the simultaneous involvement of the research activity in both studying the community work intervention and contributing to its development.

Service research has been the least problematic area of the relationship between community work and research. In each aspect of service research, the main issues seem to be about the research skills of community work practitioners – skills that help them carry out their own research, relate more comfortably to researchers, enable them to consume research material and see the relevance to their practice, if any, of political economy research. I am not convinced that training courses have done much to develop practitioners' research skills, or to encourage a sympathy with research interests and procedures.

(2) Community Work Practice, Training and Administration as Objects of Research

What community workers do, and what community work projects and programmes have contributed, are themselves objects of research. Research that examines community work practice, training and administration may be classified as either *evaluation* or *knowledge-development* research.

(A) EVALUATION RESEARCH

This seeks to monitor the activities of a community work intervention, and to assess the outcomes of such interventions. Its purpose is fourfold: to aid discovery; to ensure the accountability of workers; to help workers clarify goals and priorities and to plan their work; and to develop their skills and knowledge. In America evaluative research in community work, social work and social action programmes has been extensively carried out and written about. In Britain, however, little evaluative research has been done in community work or related fields. Moseley came to the opinion that 'people working in the field of community development place little value upon formal evaluative research, and show in their writing little awareness of the thought habits which its practice encourages' (1971). These thought habits are easy to recognise but difficult to define. There is a certain quality that one finds in the thinking of good researchers and statisticians. It is a cautious, analytic style, a little clinical but certainly rigorous, and an ability to ask questions that startle previously held assumptions. It is a questioning, objective, take-nothing-for-granted approach. Community workers, on the other hand, are enthusiastic, committed, passionate, partisan and subjective when it comes to their own work and that of community groups. And so they should be. The tensions between the frames of the evaluative researcher and the community worker have been well described in detail by Jack Rothman (1974).

Another way of describing these thought habits is to describe them as systematic. One might say that traditional evaluative research encourages one to think logically along a sequence that runs something like needs – goals – priorities – action – and evaluation. Thinking like this is an excellent practice, particularly for planning purposes, but it has long been recognised that in community work it is often neither feasible nor desirable to keep closely to previously identified goal statements.

These thought habits of evaluative research do not usually come intuitively or magically. For most people, they have to be acquired and developed. But how can we expect this to happen? There are only a handful of community work and social work courses in Britain that have offered studies in research methods – and what was offered has usually been quite rudimentary. We have simply not trained our community workers to engage in evaluation: to ask them to evaluate is to ask them to do something for which most of them have had no training or experience.

Likewise, those people who ask for evaluation – councillors, managers and supervisors – have usually had no training in evaluative research and – what is more – little guidance or experience in consuming the outcomes of evaluative research.

No doubt the formidable methodological problems have deterred many practitioners from evaluating their interventions. But there are also other factors which help to explain the virtual absence of evaluative research in community work in the United Kingdom. First, neither sponsors nor agencies seem to have accorded much value to evaluation; thus the climate in which community work has developed has been relatively free of expectations that evaluation was a likely or desirable conclusion to community work interventions. Evaluation research often lacks the ability to affect decisions about services because too many people and organisations acquire vested interests in the continuation of those services. The breadth of sponsorship of community work, and its sheer diversity, have both inhibited comparative studies and the transferability of knowledge. Practitioners have been suspicious of evaluation, and cynical about its supposed benefits: is it yet another way to make money out of poverty, for it is through evaluation that academics have become most involved in community work projects. There is an especially deep suspicion that evaluation techniques are reductionist, that they simplify, for the sake of measurement, the complex world in which the worker operates, and in the end they can only measure the tangible and the concrete.

The only British publication of any merit on evaluation is that produced by the Community Projects Foundation (Key *et al.*, 1976).

(B) KNOWLEDGE-DEVELOPMENT RESEARCH

The purpose of this kind of research is to generate theories and generalisations about community work interventions. As importantly, it would seek to examine aspects of the administration and training of community workers. The kinds of research interest within these three areas are shown in the following list, taken from Maas (1966).

These are only some examples of areas where knowledge-development research is needed, but has been lacking in this country. The failure is a compound one. Not only has there been insufficient research of this kind, but we have failed to tap adequately two important sources of practice theory: first, the experience of practice (theory out of action); and secondly, knowledge that comes from fields outside of community work – sociology, political science, group work, and so on. The research task here is to gather this material, to order it and to help practitioners apply, refine and test it in practice, eventually to be incorporated or discarded. This is often called desk research, but little has been done to transform such research to make it applicable within

Practice		*Administration*		*Training*
(1)	People and groups with whom community workers work – their characteristics, motivation, experiences, and so on	(1) Organisation of community work services – the different ways of deploying and supporting workers	(1)	Analysis of content of training
(2)	Methods used by workers in their interventions	(2) Policies of agencies re community work	(2)	Value of placements
(3)	The practical problems faced by workers in day-to-day work	(3) Funding arrangements	(3)	Influence of training on values
		(4) Numbers and profiles of community workers		

day-to-day practice. Such a task might be seen as the job of a national clearing house, or of locally based consultants who can help workers deal with the local applicability of externally derived research material.

The consequences of this compound failure in the relationship between research and community work was elegantly summarised by one contributor to the study: community work 'is not so much enriched by a variety of mature approaches as confused by a plethora of disconnected theories and practices. There is a lack of intellectual rigour (not to mention results) and an excess of naive optimism wrapped in mystification.' In the next section I want to suggest some of the reasons for this state of affairs.

(C) THE DEVELOPMENT OF EVALUATIVE AND
KNOWLEDGE–DEVELOPMENT RESEARCH

Little progress has been made in community work in the last two decades in Britain in the development of these two kinds of research. One indicator of this is the near-absence of such research from the lists of on-going research projects provided by INLOGOV, the Social Science Research Council and the Central Council for Education and Training in Social Work. The 1972-6 INLOGOV cumulative index, for instance lists only one piece of community work research. Of the 514 founder members of the Social Research Association, 49 list 'Community Development' as a research interest in the 1979 Directory but only six of these can be said to be researching community work. A similar dearth of research is apparent in the DHSS Handbook of Research and Development throughout the 1970s and in the British Library's listing of research in British universities, polytechnics and colleges (15 in 1974–5 and 11 relevant entries in 1980, only a few of which are directly concerned with community work interventions). It is apparent that the large population of academics in community work, social work, social administration, social policy, political science and sociology has shown little research interest in community work. The reasons for this are quite complex: community work is still not a central method of intervention in social work and even less so in other occupations. It has thus been given little priority by researchers and research sponsors, and it has not sufficiently established itself to generate its own research culture and expectancies. Those academics who have shown interest were usually syphoned off into evaluative research, and particularly into the ill-fated CDP research teams. Additionally, research interests have been turned aside from the challenge of elucidating fieldwork in order to narrate the political economy of the United Kingdom, that is, research interests have followed the ideological dispositions of the researchers rather than the needs of practitioners for help with the day-to-day problems of doing their job. Community work must also have seemed, especially to those in sociology and politics departments, quite uninteresting and unimportant compared to some of the political and social changes that were taking place in the 1970s; and as it was not established within, or as a separate, occupational system, research in community work must have seemed, suggests one respondent, 'instant professional suicide', the more so because it called for innovation in research techniques and attitudes. Academic diffidence about community work would have been exacerbated by the radical pessimism that was apparent within community work; if there was little point in community work, there was less point, and little future, in researching it, particularly as many community workers themselves began to doubt whether community work would survive within the budgets of sponsoring agencies.

A further difficulty was that there were no clear sources of funding for community work research. The DHSS allocations, for instance, were dominated by medical and, to a lesser extent, social service, research interests. Established social science research funds were, or were thought to be, tied to conventional positivistic research designs that were felt to be inappropriate to community work research. This demanded a different attitude on the part of the researcher, an attitude that resisted imposing predetermined frameworks on the complex and messy world of the community worker and which understood community work as 'a mode of action which depends on interpersonal skills and pragmatic/political divisions . . . the researcher must then devise a way of ordering the information which retains its essential looseness and flexibility'. But even with the best of innovative research designs there would always be a tension between researcher and worker: the researcher's interest is in rigorous procedures, explicit goals and objectivity; the community worker's commitment is to flexibility and intuition in the field, non-specificity and openness of goals, and subjectivity and self-interest in documenting the success of his work. The slower pace of research, its costs in time and money and its usefulness to power-holders (as well as their disregard of it when it is politically or economically opportune) aggravated suspicion between researchers and workers; the latter were also critical of the remoteness of research and the risk of researchers harming through their intervention the relationships established by a worker within a community. Workers distrusted research as a source of knowledge, and few had been socialised towards its usefulness as part of their training. Writing of the anti-theoretical and anti-professional ethos in community work, one contributor suggested that

> The level of information skills in the field must inevitably inhibit the development of research. The tendency of workers to fail to record their own work places substantial restrictions on the development of research. They also inhibit the development of knowledge, although there remains the problem of how that knowledge is developed. To date the field is demanding that knowledge is developed solely from the field and there is an inherently conservative attitude to the development of knowledge. Linked to this is the ambiguity of training in community work. While the transmission of skills is accepted in the context of field placements, the role of the academic institution in training is generally rejected in part at least because of the anti-professional ethos of community work. The utilisation of research is linked to the development of training.

Community work was also a 'transient occupation' in the 1970s. There was a high turn-over of workers and few stayed long enough to see the value of research-based material in their work, and to improve their research consumption skills as part of their in-service development. There was, too, insufficient commitment on the part of practitioners and community work teachers to theory in community work, and a consequent reluctance to theory-build. Any field that fails to generate sufficient interest in the theoretical propositions for its work will carry out little research. The concern with ideology and political economy issues dampened the appetite particularly for practice theory, especially as practice theory seemed to cut across powerful sentiments in the decade that community work was essentially about commitment spontaneity, intuition and personal characteristics. Where there was too, little interest in skills teaching, there could be little research into the methods of community work. Amongst community work teachers who might have been expected to carry out research, there was often little experience of community work practice, and even less of the skills necessary to carry out research. We have already noted the factors that made it difficult for community work teachers to write and to do research – heavy teaching loads, doing some community work themselves, promoting the interests of community work in bodies like ACW, acting as consultants to local workers, and so on. In addition to these constraints they were also members of departments – social work and youth work are good examples – which themselves produced little research and gave low value to the place of research skills in practice and training.

I have already referred to the dearth of cumulative or additive knowledge in community work, and given some points of explanation. Cumulative knowledge depends in part on the presence in an occupation of opportunities for dialogue and a willingness to learn from, and build upon, others' experiences. Several contributors noted the paucity of dialogue between researchers through journals and conferences, and between them and trainers and practitioners. What little research there has been has occurred through the incremental expressions of individual interests (rather than, or in addition to, the systematic analysis of existing theories and hypotheses), and has also followed on opportunistically from the interests of research-funders. The preferred way of working, suggests one respondent, is that 'research should feed other research. The prime beneficiary should be a body of knowledge into which each new study can be fed and related to others . . .' What has happened, however, is that the body of knowledge that was established in the 1960s and early 1970s (through the work, for example, of Batten, Goetschius and Ross) has remained relatively unexplored and unmodified by evaluating it against British experience in the last decade.

While it is lamentable that the opportunities for dialogue about research and other matters did not develop, one must remember that they would have appeared only if people felt the *need* for them. Research is an aid to learning and, one would hope, to better practice. In order to learn, one has to be prepared to listen to other people, and to discuss issues with them critically, but openly. To do this, there must at least be some acceptance of the value of diversity, and a sense of trust or acceptance between people with different or uncertain or even inconsistent views. In an occupation such as community work, there must follow from youthfulness a feeling that we are engaged in a process of mutual exploration where there can be no fixed and eternal verities.

We have also been uneasy about the consequences that research was *critique*: it invariably involves scrutiny of goals and practices in which there has been considerable investment. A contributor to the study suggested that community work as an occupation never developed the *self-assurance* to tolerate the scrutiny that systematic research would have thrown upon it. It has an ambiguous and often insecure place in the minds of funders, policy-makers, politicians and its employing agencies; it carried a self-inflicted and potentially lethal sense of modesty and pessimistic denigration of its contribution. It remained overawed by and inarticulate about the political and social movements of the 1960s and 1970s, and was unable to contribute anything of substance to the major reorganisations of the decade that affected the whole range of welfare services. Community work emerged from the 1970s as unclear as it entered it about its purposes and principles, and just as unsure and covert about the methods of its interventions. Its sense of self-image and identity took on no organisational forms, and relations between practitioners remained tenuous and unstable. Loyalties and interests of practitioners were essentially local and parochial; there did not develop a pattern of national affiliation and identity with a set of common principles and purposes, made manifest by an organisational centre that held together the interests of the occupation, and helped to develop and promote them. No wonder there was so little research: we were part of an occupation whose sense of assurance in what it was doing and how it was doing it was low; it could tolerate doctrinal and ideological debate, and differences over political and economic issues but not close scrutiny of its purpose, role and methods of intervention. Indeed, the former whilst of value in their own right served also as a way of avoiding the pain and challenge of the latter.

What does this mean for the 1980s for the place of research as part of the infrastructure for community work practice? The contribution of research in the coming years may be summarised as follows:

- systematic reflection on practice in relation to aims and objectives;
- the operationalisation of ideas and rhetoric into clear expectation for action;
- the development of frameworks against which ideas and action can be more clearly understood;
- providing systematic feedback on action.

Research and theory development can also help to sustain the *confidence* of community workers in their occupation. Investment in research (and in other areas of the infrastructure) provides a sense of worth; the interest of researchers can be seen as a validating activity – confirming both the field as a whole and the endeavours of individual worker within it. Research investment shows evidence of interest and commitment by sponsors and by government (however ambivalent community workers may feel about *that*). More specifically research outcomes can promote occupational confidence by evaluating methods and outcomes in practice, enhancing understanding about the skills and knowledge of the occupation, and building up awareness of common interests between workers.

The priorities for the 1980s that emerged from trainers, researchers and practitioners, and which were confirmed by those taking part in the research Delphi exercise, may be summarised as follows:

(1) To develop theory and knowledge cumulatively by building on previous work and by providing the means for dialogue between researchers and between them and practitioners, trainers, managers, policy-makers, community groups and the public at large. There is a need for fuller and faster dialogue and closer operational relationships between these parties. There have been a number of suggestions as how to facilitate this, including the setting up of a research liaison group in community work to bring researchers together and to act as an influence on such matters as research funds and priorities. The issue of funding is central, and besides the general question of better access to research funds for community work, funders must be persuaded to extend their support to researchers not based in academic institutions, and to those who want to move away from classical empiricist research designs – the intervention of researchers in a field such as community work provides a learning opportunity within social research to extend traditional research methods. The concern with research might also be part of the responsibilities of a national community work body. Its function might be the promotion and dissemination of research; the support of trainers and researchers; and to provide a stimulus and initiative for local networks of practitioners and researchers. This issue is discussed at the end of this chapter.

(2) For research that develops theory relevant to community work practice, training and administration. Contributors to this study have stressed the need for research into the processes of doing community work – practice theory. The areas of practice theory given special emphasis were:

- the strategies of workers with groups and agencies;
- the processes of group origins, formation and development;
- the interventions of groups with the local state, and within federations and alliances;
- the range of transactions between workers and group members.

The enhancement of practice theory is also seen as a useful way of testing 'rhetoric against reality' and of assessing the fit of various models of intervention available within community work.

The priority to be given to practice theory should not, however, detract from the continuing need for research into other aspects of community work, and those singled out by contributors to the Delphi exercise include consumers' views of community work; definitions of community work practice, its boundaries and its purposes; evaluation of its effectiveness and outcomes; the different employment arrangements for workers and the role of the worker in different settings; and the continuation of political economy research. Particular importance was given to the need to carry out an analysis of existing community work literature in order to derive general principles about the process of practice, as well as its purpose and effectiveness.

(3)   To enhance the research skills and interests of practitioners to help them become better consumers of research; to carry out their own research interests in practice; and to work collaboratively with research staff in local agencies, particularly those with experience that may be needed by local groups.

I want to complete this section by discussing briefly the information needs of community work, an element of the infrastructure which may be taken to fall within the category of service research. The information role is important in community work, both to realise the goals of community groups and to facilitate people's competence and confidence in themselves, in the work of the group and in the value of collective action. The information role is part of each worker's relationship with a group or agency, but it has also been institutionalised in the form of community newspapers, welfare and legal rights pamphlets, neighbourhood information centres, advice centres, resource centres, unemployed workers' centres, and in more specific developments such as the Tyneside Trades Union Information Unit. In most of these developments information is provided as much to engage with people in collective action as a service or need in its own right, and Streatfield has helpfully looked at some of the opportunities and difficulties of advice centres within community work (1980a).

The minimum information needs of community workers relate to information about their agency and other services, about the neighbourhood and about the substantive issues of concern to residents, and about ideas and developments within community work and related occupations. Following Streatfield, these information needs may be classified as follows:

Category	Purpose
	Enables the worker:
(*a*) Information required by the community worker (e.g. job description; administrative information; report on progress of a project)	(i) to function within his employing organisation (or the group to which he is committed); and (ii) to keep abreast of developments in the theory and practice of community work;
(*b*) Information on the community (e.g. names, addresses and assessments of local community leaders; demographic data)	(i) to understand 'his' community; and (ii) to build working relationships with groups and individuals locally;
(*c*) Information required for community groups (e.g. how to obtain a grant, appeal against a government decision, run a play group)	(i) to develop credibility within the community; (ii) to provide support for local groups; and (iii) to lead groups towards self-help; that is, by showing what information is available and now to get it he should be able to encourage groups to seek out their own information;
(*d*) Information required for campaigns (e.g. planning information on an area; advice on public health law)	(i) to maintain credibility within the group by helping it to achieve its aims; or (ii) to become an active participant wholly committed to the campaign;
(*e*) Information required about ideas and developments in community work in this country and elsewhere	(i) to support and confirm the worker in his ways of working; and (ii) to keep his practice up-to-date and as relevant as possible to the needs of a neighbourhood.

(taken in part from Streatfield, 1980*b*)

The needs of community workers are wider than that of simply having to *have* information; they need skills in extracting information from its holders; and in storing and retrieving it. They must be able effectively to publicise its availability and have education skills to pass it on to residents and group members. They must be able to consume technical and legal data, and be able to analyse, interpret and advise on it in ways in which local people can understand and which strengthen their independence and confidence.

The *minimum* information service required for the effective performance of community work, suggests Streatfield, includes adequate organisational information services, a well-developed 'grape-vine' linking the community worker and her community, and access to a library covering community work and social policy literature. To this we must add: an occupational grape-vine that keeps the worker informed of what is happening in the broad field of community work. Streatfield's conclusion, however, is that 'at present many community workers, including the majority of those employed in social services departments, are poorly provided with information services by their employers and have only limited access to community work and social policy literature'.

It is likely that there are variations across the field; the information capability of, and services to, departmental community workers are likely to be less well developed than to workers in the other two streams; many project workers will be based in advice centres where information has a more prominent status, and programmatic workers will likely be better off as a result of being altogether better resourced within their programmes and sponsoring agencies. Even so, Streatfield has been critical of the quality of information services provided by neighbourhood information projects. He writes:

My own experience of visiting NICs and other advice agencies is that use of out-of-date reference works is commonplace and that the information services which are potentially available, such as the Disabled Living Foundation service or the CAB information packs, are usually not used by these centres. Under-financing of information centres makes this state of affairs inevitable, but perhaps more serious is the cheerfulness with which some information centre staff contemplate this situation. A similar 'slap happy' attitude to the accuracy of information is sometimes carried over to other areas of the work of information centres.

A further difficulty may be masked by the apparent indifference of some information and advice centre workers to 'information', by which is usually meant published information. Little attention has been paid to the extent to which available published material in existing information centres is used by the staff. My impression of work of this kind, supported by comments from a few other observers and practitioners, is that staff tend to make minimal use of publications, preferring to rely on their store of knowledge supplemented by contacts with colleagues in other agencies as required. The nature of the knowledge held by centre staff, particularly in NICs and centres providing 'specialist' services in relatively confined areas of information (such as housing action centres or consumer advice centres) usually appears to be what Schutz defined as 'recipe knowledge', that is knowledge of procedures which can be trusted even though they are not clearly understood. Schutz contrasted recipe knowledge with expert knowledge and, to the extent that this generalisation about the information offered by neighbourhood information centres holds true, it may be inferred that centre staff do not need much of the published 'expert information' available to them. (1980*a*)

These comments have been disputed in a reply from the National Co-ordinating Group of the Federation of Independent Advice Centres. Their spokesperson questions the evidence for Streatfield's conclusions and suggests that some information services, such as that of the CAB, have proved inadequate, and that the Federation's members are engaged in redesigning existing information systems to make them more suitable, as well as initiating a project to lay the foundations for appropriate types of information and training for neighbourhood advice workers.

It would not be surprising to find some basis for Streatfield's analysis: information services may take second place in advice centres where the primary concern is to use information-giving as a means to helping people organise around issues. The pressure of work in neighbourhoods, the shortage of staff in most advice projects and the general absence of in-service training for them will combine to make it difficult for staff to maintain the quality of their information service − particularly in areas where legislation and services are complex and in the process of revision.

But it is sufficiently clear that whether it is to make better use of existing information systems or to design and experiment with new ones, community workers will require continuing support to develop the information aspects of their role. Streatfield has suggested the establishment of a national urban documentation centre. This centre would be charged with gathering information on developments in community work and in related professions and areas of knowledge, and 'to promote social education through seminars, conferences, training courses and other means'. I want to look at this matter in the next section; I wish to say here only that I believe that any national centre is well suited to meet the need for occupational information, that is, to act as a clearing house and dispenser of information about ideas in community work and in other occupations and movements. But I suggest that the information needs of workers that relate to local government, their agency, the neighbourhood and the issues that are being worked on are largely, but not wholly, best met at a local or regional level, through consolidating the work of resource centres and through extending the consultancy role of existing organisations such as CVSs and student units as development centres. It might be added that a national clearing house would also be an appropriate way to respond to the information needs of community work teachers and researchers, and to facilitate an exchange of, for example, teaching materials and bibliographies.

A NATIONAL BODY FOR COMMUNITY WORK

I shall end this chapter by looking at the issue of a national body which can be seen as part of the infrastructure of practice but with responsibilities to develop that part of the infrastructure concerned, for example, with research, training and information. Interviews and meetings during this study have indicated that the need for such a body is now recognised within community work (and it was a particular point of discussion with trainers and researchers), and is perhaps an inevitable extension of the support for a national body on training expressed in 1976 to a working party that examined the matter at that time.

A national body was seen as something that would fulfil some specific functions and would be a source of energy or holding point at the centre of community work, a point of reference that would help to establish a sense of identity amongst all those involved in community work. Acceptance of the usefulness of such a body has probably been helped by the development in recent years of local and regional networks, particularly amongst practitioners, that might be used and further strengthened to contribute to the management of such a body, and the clarification of its policies and work programmes. Whilst there is support in principle for a national body for community work, there are still different views about such matters as its functions, funding, staffing and constitution.

A national body may be seen as filling the vacuum created by ACW's refusal (and inability because of inadequate resources) to be a consultative body, speaking for community workers and helping in the formulation of policy at local and central levels. ACW is also a membership organisation, serving mainly the needs of its members, who form only a small proportion of those involved in the practice, training, research and administration of community work. The need for a national body reflects, too, the fact that other national organisations have not been interested in servicing community work and, if they had been, probably would not have been allowed to do so by an altogether suspicious occupation. The same might be said of the Community Projects Foundation and the CDP (particularly its information and intelligence unit) which did not address themselves to the practice, research and training needs of the whole of the occupation but (with the exception of their publications) kept largely within their own programmes. Indeed, the possibility of acting as a general resource to community work was put specifically to the CDP information and intelligence unit and they rejected it.

It was put to me that community work is now one of those few occupations which do not have a national body of their own concerned with information, training, research and the promotion of the occupation's interests and ideas. Besides the information and advice-giving services of pressure groups (such as MIND) in the social welfare field, there are specific institutions or services set up to meet the needs of particular groups of workers – examples are the National Youth Bureau, National Children's Bureau and the Volunteer Centre.

The idea for a national body has been germinating through the 1970s and several initiatives have been taken during the decade. The first Gulbenkian report in 1968 discussed the setting up of an 'independent committee' as an interim measure, whilst a national council for all forms of social work was being set up. In the previous year the European Regional Clearing House for Community Work had been set up in Holland, and there also existed in that country a national institute for community work (NIMO) concerned largely with research and development. The next events of any significance occurred in 1973: a Community Work Information Centre for Wales was opened and stayed in operation for some two and a half years. In the same year the second Gulbenkian report appeared, and recommended a national resource centre:

> A compact, flexible clearing-house is proposed, with a small staff of high calibre, to link and support the area resource centres. It should on no account store or provide information or resources already available but rather be ready to refer enquirers promptly to the right source; it should process and distribute information in the most useful form and offer technical advice and equipment to area centres, teachers and others. It must be geared to responding quickly to enquiries. The centre should also encourage and publicise facilities of all kinds for community work training; stimulate evaluation and research likely to be fruitful; arrange or sponsor discussion and exchange of views; and generally promote initiatives and experiments in community work.

The Information and Intelligence Unit of CDP was also opened in 1973 and was closed in 1975, the year in which the Northern Ireland Council of Social Service began its Community Information Service, following on the initiative taken in the previous year by Muintir na Tire in Eire to run a Development and Service Unit. 1975 saw, too, the appearance of a proposal to establish a community development agency for Wales, offering consultancy and development services to those involved in community work.

These largely Celtic initiatives were matched in 1976 by the Association of Community Workers, who prepared a position statement on training that recommended 'the creation of a new body concerned with training for community work'. Its aims were:

(i)   to sponsor, support and evaluate a range of methods of training giving particular emphasis to the development of new methods of training;

(ii)   to maintain close contact with existing training schemes for the purpose of mutual exchange and debate about methods of training.

Another consultative document appeared in the same year prepared by a working party of practitioners and trainers nominated at a meeting of teachers of community work and representatives of regional groups of workers. It concluded 'that the present and future needs of community work training will only be met by the creation of an independent body with responsibility for the development of training at all levels'. Consultations of this report led to the setting up of the Interim Central Training Group and to the Federation of Community Work Training Groups.

Around the same time the Calouste Gulbenkian Foundation was preparing to act on the recommendations of the 1973 Boyle report. Lack of government support had put an end to the idea of a national resource centre, with a system of area resource centres. But support was expressed for one experimental area resource centre and a national forum, and in 1976 the Foundation established its Area Resource Centre and National Forum Advisory Committee. The proposals for a national forum, however, were soon dropped: it became clear that there was no money available for such a forum from the Voluntary Services Unit, the EEC, or the Foundation itself, whose consultation day on the forum was boycotted by the Association of Community Workers. The Foundation's efforts to provide advice and support to the field nevertheless continued in other forms: we have already noted how much of its grant allocations were given to develop community work's infrastructure (particularly its training, research and publications) and it also established in 1977 the inner-cities support programme with its own co-ordinator. In 1978 it established the Community Resource Unit for a three-year period. The final report in 1982 of the Foundation's Advisory Committee also recommended that steps should be taken to establish a national community work organisation, and a working party, chaired by Hywel Griffiths, was set up to take the idea forward.

There were several other initiatives taken in the latter part of the decade that imperfectly expressed and fulfilled the need for a national body; some of these, like the forum of community work trainers in Scotland, were regional, but of national importance was the Federation of Community Work Training Groups. Whilst this was constitutionally and ideologically a non-centrist body, it began to act and think as if it were a national organisation, promoting community work's interests and taking part, as did ACW, in discussions about community work training with other national bodies such as CCETSW. Such forms of 'covert centralism' were becoming more evident: the 1978 workshop in Bristol organised by the National Institute for Social Work and ACW was a forum-type activity that brought together practitioners, trainers, managers, researchers and funders of community work. The National Institute itself may have performed many of the functions of a national community work body through its training programmes, research, publications and consultancy service. Although based in London, its community work staff operated across the country, and with community workers and trainers from most of the settings in which community work was being practised.

Discussions held during the process of this study suggest that the support for some kind of national body identified by the 1976 working party of practitioners and trainers has grown stronger. There is acknowledgement of the potential usefulness of such a body amongst trainers and researchers. Amongst practitioners I believe there is a small group who would favour it, and a similarly small group who would be quite opposed; in between lies the large majority of practitioners who are neither for nor against but are prepared to see that such a body might be valuable but that this would depend on a number of factors such as its constitution, staffing, funding and terms of reference. The attitudes of this group would be determined by what such a body did in practice – if it provided a useful service it would be supported, but if it failed to reach out to practitioners then it would not be seen by them as being relevant or important. Such a position was summarised by the 1976 working party:

> Most of the responses to the original questionnaire stress the importance of control from the periphery rather than control from the centre. None, however, completely rejects the possibility of some national body though there is a considerable variation in the degree of saliency given to it. Some see it as a fairly immediate objective while others regard it as something which might emerge over a period of time.

There seem to be four primary functions that a national body might carry out: training, research, information clearing house and consultancy. In writing about these functions, I am indebted to a number of previous papers on the subject, some of which are referred to above.

(1)   Training

It does not seem appropriate that the national body should provide full-time basic or post-qualifying studies in community work. Its concern with training might be:

● to provide developmental seminars and workshops for those inside and outside of community work, according to needs and priorities current in the field;

● to provide information on training opportunities, in association with other relevant bodies;

● to monitor and support existing training opportunities and particularly to help in the innovation of new ideas (for example, apprenticeship schemes) and the development of curricula and teaching methods:

● to assess training needs for particular groups of workers and to assess gaps in provision;

● to facilitate co-operation between fieldworkers, not only in community work but in related disciplines, in exchanging knowledge and experience;

● to support with others a network of training resources using existing agencies, workers and trainers;

● to offer help and advice to community work teachers on all kinds of training courses;

● to liaise with government departments, local authorities, training councils and courses about community work training.

(2)   Research

It would be appropriate for the national body to carry out research, but the extent of this would depend on the staff and other resources available. But there is an important role to be played in the promotion and dissemination of research, and in the support of researchers and trainers. The specific functions might include:

● to enable researchers, practitioners and trainers to meet, discuss and develop ideas together; to provide a structure for dialogue and the dissemination of research;

- to provide a pool or network of researchers who could service groups and workers on particular issues;
- to attach research resources to networks of practitioners to enable them to share experiences and explore issues, and to provide research foci for the researchers;
- to ensure a balance is maintained between different kinds of research, for example, action and evaluative;
- to communicate research findings and to encourage the taking up of new ideas;
- to encourage differing research initiatives in order to throw light in a systematic way on the activities of community work and community action.

The national body might also identify areas of practice or training in community work where research is needed, and provide advice on research proposals and the available sources of research funds.

(3) Information Clearing House

There is clearly overlap between this and some of the other functions; many of the research and training activities would involve the collection and dissemination of information and ideas. The specific functions might be:

- to act as a clearing house for the distribution of materials to community workers, researchers, trainers, funders and employers;
- to publish papers, pamphlets, books and video tapes that assist in the development of practice, training and research;
- to publish a community work journal;
- to act with others as a forum, bringing together in conferences, workshops, and so on, all those involved in community work (whether practitioners, trainers, researchers, funders, or employers) and bringing together those in government and related occupations with an interest in community work, including elected members.

(4) Consultancy

Functions here would be:

- to provide a limited consultancy service to community workers, trainers, researchers, funders and employers;
- to help establish local and regional consultancy networks, to keep a directory of consultants and be able to refer workers to people on that directory;

● to be a source of advice and information on community work to staff in other occupations, and to staff in government, and to elected members.

Discussion of a National Body

Clearly, these functions may not all be seen as equally acceptable or important and thus the work of a national body may be narrowed down to a selection of these functions with, indeed, others added. In any case, it is doubtful that a national body would have the resources to carry out all these functions, and priorities would have to be established. There are two further functions that are a matter of controversy in community work – validation and accreditation of training courses, and the representation of community work's interests. There seems to be little need, or support, for a national body to validate and accredit courses, though it may be that in the very long term this will be seen to be a useful function for a national body to carry out. The matter of representation is more contentious. It is plainly difficult for any one organisation to claim to represent community work, or to be seen by others as doing so. Community work is too heterogeneous for this to be a viable role of one organisation. However, it could be an important function of a national body to promote and to be consulted about the interests of community work, and to be consulted, and to make representations, about matters of social policy and welfare. It must be clear that in acting in this way a national body would not be speaking for community work but only for itself, and this may well prompt other bodies in community work likewise to put their views forward on the issue in question. In this way, a number of representations from community work can effectively be made, and the variety and differences in the occupation made clear.

The range of titles for a national body are subtle indications of the sensitivity of the issue; the label attached to a national body will say a lot about its status, and will affect people's perceptions of it. Amongst those suggested were the Council for the Development of Community Work; the National Institute for Community Organising; the National Community Work Forum/Council; the Community Work Clearing House; and the National Community Work Bureau. This last reflects the feeling that such a body might be modelled along the lines of the National Youth Bureau and that its functions might be summarised as 'a national resource centre for information, publication, training, research and development, and as a forum for association, discussion and joint action in the broad field of community work'.

The users of a national body are indicated in the above description of its functions: community workers, groups, trainers, researchers, funders and employers of community workers; local and national government departments; staff and trainers in other occupations; and elected members. Again, some priorities would need to be established so that some categories of users are given more emphasis, though these priorities will change over time. A national body would be an independent body, and this independence would in part be determined by its sources of funding. The general funds of a national body, which may be supplemented by monies for particular projects, might come both from trusts and governments, and to the extent that community work is relevant to the interests of several departments of government it may be desirable to seek support from more than just one department. This mix of government funding would also go some way to ensuring the body's independence and stability.

The range of functions to be carried out by a national body, even when they are reduced by clear priorities, cannot be adequately fulfilled by one person and administrative support. To attempt to do so would be to bring a national body, and the whole idea of a central body, into disrepute and to risk the burn-out of the staff group. To meet the needs of the field, to have an impact on its practitioners and trainers, and to be a voice in matters of policy requires both adequate and long-term resources.

The difficulties in establishing any form of a national body are considerable, even with the support that is evident. There are fears that a national body would become bureaucratic, hierarchic and remote from the field; that the sort of people to be involved in such a 'prestigious undertaking' might not be predominantly fieldworkers and that, as Streatfield has suggested, such a body might reflect and exacerbate any distance between theorists and practitioners in the field. There might be those who would see a national body as a step towards a restrictive professionalism in community work, promoting 'spurious academic pretensions, irrelevant institutional hierarchies, and surreptitious aspirations towards professional elites'. Another correspondent said:

> The very idea of a national body conjures up a nightmare of political infighting. It will be difficult to carve out the central ground without treading on someone's toes. It is going to be colonised by one or other part of the community work world, and consequently vetoed by others – particularly by self-styled leaders in the field who don't get the jobs . . . I agree the debate should be reopened but I'm a bit nervous of what will result.

A major point of negotiation will be the constitution of such a national body; there is certainly a strong feeling that any national body 'ought to have strong roots in the field'. What constitutes the field, and the precise nature of these roots, remain problematic, not least because 'the field' can include those engaged in interagency work and planning and those involved in the direction of community work agencies and services.

There seem a number of interests that ought to be part of the constitution of any national body:

(1)   consumers of community work;
(2)   community work practitioners from each of the settings where it is practised;
(3)   community work trainers and researchers;
(4)   community work funders and employers;
(5)   organisations such as FCWTG and ACW (as examples);
(6)   local and central government departments;
(7)   representatives from related occupations with a real interest in community work.

There are considerable difficulties in implementing this kind of wide representation, including that of deciding whether the field is taken to be local (at least city-wide) or regional, and what kind of representation is obtained for the four countries of the United Kingdom. It would be necessary, too, to ensure that the representatives or delegates to the board of a national body reflect the interests and diversity within community work and do not become dominated by any one grouping or setting for community work. In addition, this kind of arrangement is only as effective as the local groups and structures that send people to the board. This is a problem that goes wider than the issue that in many areas community work groups are weak or non-existent, but that local groups of workers can themselves become unrepresentative of the community work interests in their locality. Practitioner groups also suffer from turnover in their membership, and often limited commitment to them by local workers where, for example, they find it difficult to give up time and energy from the demands of fieldwork. These considerations are provided only as illustrations and they serve to indicate that whilst adequate representation of fieldworkers on any national body is a good principle, it is one that is not sacrosanct and one that must be assessed, in the weight given to it, in the light of the credibility and effectiveness of practitioner networks. This suggests another important point: the constitution of any national body, and particularly its relationship with the field, will need to be worked on, and to be changed with experience and as community work itself changes. We may have to begin with a less than perfect arrangement but it should be part of the remit of any national body to support local networks so that they can play as effective a part as possible in the constitution of the national body.

These matters are pertinent to the consultations and discussions that will need to be held about the proposal for a national body.

Although it will be essential to have practitioner representation on the national body, it cannot be assumed in consultations about a national body that the views of fieldworkers are the only or the most important to be taken into account. The vested interests of community workers as a group are only one consideration; it is important to remember that community workers comprise a very heterogeneous group so that there are likely to be a variety of vested interests within it, not all of which will be represented in established or informal groups that will claim to be acting 'on behalf of community workers'. Community workers are in the field doing the work – and they will speak from that experience and perspective; this experience is important and must be present within the constitution of a national body; but in consultations about a national body some people will claim in arguing for and against a national body that their arguments are given a special status from being in the field'; this claim must be evaluated cautiously. The fact that someone is in the field does not of itself give their views a special importance or weight, and there should be no place in consultations for excessive and uncritical deference to views from the field.

Much the same can be said about the opinions of other interests. It may be, for example, that government departments and employers may be slow to recognise the needs for a national body for community work, and even slower in coming forward with funding for its establishment. The indifference or antagonism of any particular department or sector would be unfortunate but should not delay unduly the consultations about a national body. The experience of community work in the last decade indicates that there is a need for workers, trainers and others directly involved in community work to co-operate with trusts and other funders to innovate, and to bring others with them once the benefits of the innovation become apparent during its operation.

It must be stressed that a national body will depend for its effectiveness on the existence of other organisations, and must be expected to sit alongside local and regional initiatives. More immediate and less ambitious proposals must be continued with, such as those for a research liaison group and a network of community work trainers that can offer members support, advice and the exchange of ideas and materials. The continued growth of regional networks, such as the regional training groups, is essential; the FCWTG has a key role to play in the future development of community work alongside, or as the basis for, any national body. The role of regional training groups might include:

- consultation with full-time training courses;
- releasing the resources of these institutions for regional training needs;

- facilitating joint appointments between the college and the field;
- creating regional forums for community work training;
- creating and sustaining relations between workers, employers and trainers;
- providing training and support for workers and voluntary activists, and persuading employers to develop means of recognising workers without formal qualifications.

It is evident from these examples that local initiatives are not only compatible with the work of a national body but must also support, and be supported by, such a body, which can only be fully effective if there are concurrent local and regional arrangements.

8 *From Being to Being More*

> The passage from the individual to the collective
> is the crucial problem of human energy.
>
> *Teilhard de Chardin*

The purpose of this last chapter is to provide some concluding thoughts on some of the matters discussed earlier. It begins with de Chardin's sentence because it captures many of the themes of the book. Community workers try to help people come together, to pool their resources in order to achieve common goals. Each incident of action by the community is a statement about the passage from the individual to the collective, hinting at the promise of more fruitful relationships between people.

But community work itself faces this journey to the collective. It must continue to tidy up its ideas into some form of *intellectual coherence* that both accepts and relates to each other the differences that exist within the occupation. This will require more clarity about the relation between community work's distributive and developmental goals. These goals accommodate a great number of views and contributions but also transcend them by providing a broader rationale that can belong to the occupation as a whole rather than to people and sub-groups within it; they are goals that have some independence of, first, the specific and different views of agencies, individual practitioners, trainers, and so forth; and, secondly, the uses to which community work is put in particular situations.

The passage to the collective will also be facilitated by a growing confidence within community work about the skills and knowledge that are the basis of its credibility as an intervention. The acceptance in the 1980s of community work as an important intervention will depend in large part on the willingness of its practitioners and trainers to convince those outside community work that the occupation has become more sure about the expertise that it has to offer. This will involve further development of training opportunities. I have mentioned the value of a single form of qualification, the need to differentiate between the content of various kinds of community work courses, and the possibilities of a period of supervised learning following threshold training. Just as relevant here are the provision of resources to in-service support, and the potential of some student units and councils of voluntary service to become regional development centres, providing training and consultancy to both workers and project management committees.

The effect of the resources that have been put into community work in the last two decades has been diminished because interventions have been conceived and implemented in an ad hoc, piecemeal manner. Perhaps this was inevitable, and characterises any innovation as it tests out what is possible in practice and to win recognition. We now know more about what community work has to contribute, and it is no longer appropriate to regard and resource it as an experiment. We should develop regional or city-wide policies for community work, conceive of it as a programme and try to relate the various community work initiatives in an area to each other within the framework of this programme. This involves linking community work to other interventions within community action, community development, social planning, community organisation and service extension. Here, transformation towards the collective requires greater *operational coherence* in the implementation of community work, as well as the resources to develop the infrastructure that is necessary to sustain practice. Community work will not be able to contribute fully to the agenda of work described in Chapter 4 unless there is a degree of co-ordination between projects and workers in an area, and an acceptance that their efforts must be supported by adequate training opportunities. I have referred to the role of community work committees in local authority areas, the place of regional trust funds and the development of policies and planning within the framework of *reconstruction, renegotiating status* and *realising the community*.

In the first chapter about community work in the 1960s and 1970s I described its development as 'a disjointed occupation, showing low coherence and characterised largely by disjunctures between its various parts'. I suggested a number of reasons why little energy had been put into helping community work to develop a more corporate identity as an occupation. The need for *occupational coherence* is the third aspect of community work's journey to the collective, a coherence that can be both achieved and expressed through organisations such as ACW and the FCWTG, and the development of a national body with the training, research and information functions described in Chapter 7. What might be called the 'psychological' aspects of occupational coherence would be the growth of a sense of common purpose that transcended the goals of individual workers and projects, and through which workers felt 'joined' to each other, and part of an occupation with a past and a future. There are a number of difficulties about this, not the least of which is that community workers tend to reject narrow ideas of professional boundaries and interest. One of the tests for community work in the coming years is to develop some occupational coherence whilst at the same time remaining inclusive.

Community work has come of age as a comprehensible form of intervention, with defined tasks and an emerging practice theory.

Community work has made the passage from being an 'approach' or philosophy to being an intervention of considerable promise. It is a method not a dogma, and there is evidence that the truth of this paraphrase is increasingly being appreciated within the occupation itself. The 'fetish of ideology' that had its peak in the mid-1970s has lost its potency and has been replaced by both a cooler appraisal of community work's goals and possibilities, and by a concern with effectiveness in the job.

An understanding of community work as a method is as apparent in other occupations. The government-sponsored Barclay inquiry into social work has hinted at the importance of community work within the personal social services, and to the contribution of 'community social work': social workers must understand the community in which their clients live, and be able to use and support informal caring networks of family, neighbours and friends. This is a direction in which other 'people-professions' are moving, not least because the recession in capitalism that has created a growing number of social problems has also led politicians to limit the resources made available to help with them.

This recognition of community work as a method is to be welcomed, though many will see it as evidence for Paul Waddington's prognostications about the institutionalisation of community work that were discussed in Chapter 4. There are, however, other dangers, particularly to the development of more intellectual and occupational coherence in community work. The appreciation by other occupations of community work as a method threatens, first, community work's status as a specialism. I believe there is no basis for this threat because community work as a specialist role or post will still be necessary as others use community work as a method within their own roles; indeed, the community work specialist will be needed to train and support these other workers. This threat is less important in reality than in the apprehension it will create amongst many community workers, and the consequent attitudes they will adopt to the diffusion of community work methods.

The second threat will be to community work's identity and self-image, something that has always been a problem in the past. Some of the issues to do with identity were discussed in Chapter 1. Attempts by community workers to develop an identity that is separate from that of host professions such as social work and education will be made more difficult as those professions accept its legitimacy as a method to be used by non-community work staff. There is, here, an intellectual and practical problem that has rarely been confronted in community work: how to develop the distinctive nature of community work as a method whilst at the same time being secure enough to disperse skills and knowledge to other people, not just those in community groups but also those in other occupations. I suspect that this tension between building-up and distributing expertise will remain with us in the years to come. Some of the difficulties are already becoming evident as people like probation officers and social workers begin to use community work as a method in their work. Community work has always contained people who were not designated community workers but did some community work as part of another job. There were few problems for community workers where these people were, for example, secretaries of councils of social service or community relations officers; but the advent of staff with a more obvious social control function is liable to produce an identity crisis in community work, that will be particularly evident when such people wish to join organisations such as ACW or attend training courses alongside 'proper' community workers. The greater use amongst other occupations of community work as a method may lead to a backlash amongst community workers themselves. It is hardly likely that this will lead to community workers reshaping the occupation as a tighter, less open group, though there is certainly the possibility that this might occur. The backlash may take the form of putting community work on a pedestal in the hope that a pure and uncontaminated model of community work can be defined that is distinguishable from that done by non-community workers in other occupations. The involvement of these other workers 'in the community' would then be grudgingly accepted, but they would be dismissed as not doing 'real' or 'pure' community work. The search for a pure model is, of course, illusory and any definitions that assumed that only full-time community workers could do 'proper' community work would be flawed. The attempt to establish such a model must be recognised as a device that some community workers may use to have the best of both worlds: that is, maintain the appearance of community work as an open occupational group, and to keep at arm's length those in other jobs who wish to use community work methods. The notion of a pure form of community work may also be used to preserve what might be called 'the naive radical illusion', and to avoid facing up to the fact that the dispersion of community work as a method amongst other occupations is yet another indication of the establishment of community work within many parts of the local state.

The use of community work by other workers should not be evaluated against some pure or ideal form of community work practice. It seems better to evaluate such work against the salient principles outlined in Chapter 3 which, broadly taken, may be used to distinguish community work from other interventions. As importantly, the work of other professionals in the community is ultimately legitimised not by whether such work stands up as community work or not but by the contribution it makes to 'development of community' through the five approaches discussed in Chapter 3 of community action, community development, social planning, community organisation and service extension.

Having said all this, there still remains some basis for apprehension about the use of community work as a method by staff in other occupations. Community workers and residents are right to be suspicious about any moves 'into the community' that seem inspired by fad or the need to gloss over the loss of resources during public expenditure cuts. The use of community work by other workers must be informed by some training as well as by adequate supervision. A weakness in the position of those who advocate more community-based work is that their understanding of community is often naive. They ignore the deterioration in the social fabric of many urban neighbourhoods and the fact that the appearance of, for example, more caring communities is more likely to be the outcome of a process of development than its starting-point. Those who call for 'a return to the community' may have an equally naive view of community work, and may underrate the skills and resources that are needed to do it effectively. Community work is also far broader in purpose than specific attempts at reform in welfare and other services. It is part of the development of a participative democracy; whilst the issues with which community work is concerned are important in their own right, they are also the means to renegotiate the relationship between those who govern and those who are governed. It will be too easy for professionals who are innovating with community work as a method to forget its developmental functions.

Another possible cause for concern is that efforts to establish community work as a credible form of intervention may lead to a preoccupation with method or instrumentality to the neglect of the *purposes* of community work and the social concern that has been a valuable part of its contribution in the last two decades. Effective community work depends a good deal on factors such as the inventiveness, spontaneity and commitment of the workers, as well as other personal characteristics and the ability flexibly to make use of opportunities as they occur. These can be jeopardised by a narrow concern with method, but it is equally true that such personal attributes are likely to be less effective without attention to process and method.

I have suggested that the developmental goals of community work are the promotion of political responsibility and communal coherence. In Chapter 3 I wrote that political responsibility comprises political significance and competence, by which terms I referred to the existence amongst people of a sense of worth in, and identification with, political processes, and the aptitude and skills to contribute to them. I placed this enhancement of political responsibility within a wider process of franchisal development. As a way of preventing undemocratic political practices, franchisal development has two elements. The first and oldest of these is particularly associated with Harold Laski; vigilance, participation, knowledge and interest in political matters is a basic operating check on those in government, and a defence against the intrusion of the state, in whose workings one can discern two temptations described by Senghor as *'assimilation* and *imperialism,* for it is by nature a conqueror' (1964). The only 'true safeguard' available to people, argues Laski, is 'the knowledge that our invasion of liberty will always meet with resistance from men determined upon its repulsion . . . a certain penumbra of contingent anarchy always confronts the state; but I have argued that this is entirely desirable since the secret of liberty is always, in the end, the courage to resist'. Courage, however, is not in itself sufficient, for Laski argues the importance of the determination and knowledge to make political mechanisms work. This necessarily involves participation, for

> the greater the degree in which the citizen shares in making the rules under which he lives, the more likely is his allegiance to those rules to be free and unfettered. Nor is this all. The process of being consulted gives him a sense of being significant in the state. It makes him feel that he is more than the mere recipient of orders. He realises that the state exists for his ends and not for its own. He comes to see that his needs will be met only as he contributes his instructed judgment to the experience out of which decisions are compounded. He gains the expectation of being consulted, the sense that he must form an opinion on public affairs . . . He comes to have a sense of frustration when decisions are made arbitrarily, and without an attempt to build them from the consent of those affected. He learns vigilance about the ways of power. Those who are trained to that vigilance become the conscious guardians of liberty. (1930)

It was argued in Chapter 2 that large sections of the population no longer have the knowledge, the interest, or sense of worth to make political processes work in the way described by Laski as a 'safeguard of liberty'. And here we come to a limitation of Laski's position: it often lacks a creative perspective, an idea of mechanisms and practices, and the assumptions behind them, adapting to the circumstances of different times and interests. This brings us to the second element of the development of political responsibility: it is associated in particular with the struggles of black people in America to reshape political processes to take account of their interests and needs. This element of franchisal development might be described as 'political modernisation', a phrase used by Stokely Carmichael to include three major concepts: questioning old values and institutions of the society; searching for new and different forms of political structure to solve political and economic problems; and broadening the base of political participation to include more people in the decision-making process (1969). Awareness of political modernisation has developed through the experiences of groups such as black people, feminists and gays, but its importance derives from the circumstances of many other sections of the population. Laski was right to draw attention to the need for determination to make political mechanisms work, but this necessarily involves persistence and creativity in helping them develop over time, and in response to factors that adversely affect people's political significance and competence.

The issue-based and campaign nature of much collective action in the late 1960s and early 1970s when local people organised against local authorities was itself a statement about political modernisation, that was more complex than is commonly supposed. It was not simply a reaction to the arbitrary decisions and intrusions of the local state, nor just an expression of dissatisfaction with the moribund nature of much local party politics, though it was both these things. It also contained elements of an attempt at a local level to renegotiate relationships within and between classes and sexes. This phenomenon may have been more evident in disputes between working-class groups and the politicians of middle-class Conservative and Labour Party councils; but it was as much a factor in negotiations both with councils dominated by conservative, paternal, working-class Labour politicians, and with middle-class officers whose numbers and power were increasing through most of the last decade. The involvement of considerable numbers of women in collective action was an expression of discontent with the extent to which decisions about people's well-being were almost exclusively in the hands of male councillors and officers. Very little, if any, of this participation by women was informed by a feminist analysis but it is to be recognised as a means through which some working-class women renegotiated their status within political decision-making and, often, within their own families, neighbourhood and workplaces.

The need for political modernisation, for which local collective action was also a model, goes beyond the kind of participation in decisions mentioned by both Laski and Carmichael. This type of participation is necessary but not sufficient; arrangements can be made to incorporate people in participations about, for example, local authority decisions but these, whilst important in their own right, may leave untouched the structural relationship between governors and governed. This is most evident in the United States, where there have been legislative requirements for citizen participation. These extensive provisions have not only absorbed and stultified local community action but, more critically, they have done very little to affect the balance of political interests, power and knowledge in the process of government.

Much of Chapter 2 in this book discusses how to give substance to the notion of political modernisation or franchisal development. There was a reference to the relationship between political significance and competence, on the one hand, and, on the other, the development of local communities as effective social systems that provide the opportunity for people to interact with each other in a variety of roles and networks. This concern for the interaction between political responsibility and communal coherence as a basis for political change has been paralleled in the women's movement ('the personal and the political') but given its fullest expression amongst minority groups. The black power movement in America, for example, was described by Carmichael as an assertion of a 'sense of community' among black people, based in part upon common colour, economic exploitation and the experience of racism, and was linked conceptually to what Senghor has called the common denominator of all negro Africans, *negritude*.

The development of a 'sense of community' amongst minority groups has been analysed by Rivera and Erlich who define them as *neo-gemeinschaft* because the 'primary cultural, social, political and economic inter-relationships of such communities are of fundamental importance' in surviving in a hostile environment and social order. The evolution of social networks within these communities to provide mutual support, access to new and diverse information and social contacts, communication of expectations, evaluation and a shared world-view, and a way of getting things done, are part of the characteristics of neo-gemeinschaft communities. Rivera and Erlich warn that intervention in these communities must go beyond many of the traditional models of community work:

> The so-called mobilisation style of organising (set up shop in relation to a particular issue, mobilise around it, win what you can and get out) will not work. Developing the trust necessary to fully understand, appreciate and gain access to social networks is going to take a lot of time and patience, much of it beyond the normal work day. Some activities border on the quasi-legal and involve economic exchanges that keep money in the community rather than flowing to outsiders. One organising key will be to figure out ways of building up existing social networks rather than generating new structures that will undermine these networks – as some of our community action agencies did during the 'War on Poverty'. Rather than beginning with the problems, weaknesses and inadequacies of these communities, our analysis suggests that strengths are to be noted first and foremost, and looked upon as the basis for organisation-building. (1981)

This is a point I have made in this study in relation to community work in all types of communities in this country: I have criticised the limitations of 'smash-and-grab' collective action because, although it has been necessary and has achieved much-needed benefits, it does not on its own provide an adequate analytical and practical base for long-term development work for political responsibility and communal coherence.

I have mentioned these matters that come out of the struggles of black people because the experiences of minority and sectional groups are often a mirror in which we see reflected issues that are of relevance to the whole. In this particular case we see the value of making the connection between political development and social development, and thus the need in urban areas in this country to extend social networks and roles as a good in itself and as the basis for political progress. We are being pushed, particularly by feminist community workers, to value not just what a group can gain by way of resources, or the services it can provide for its members, but also the opportunities it offers for transforming the individuals within it, as well as the extent and quality of the relations they have with each other, and with others in the community. This feminist analysis is a restatement of community work's process goals that takes us further by identifying personal change as the beginning and the process of political development, both of the individual and of existing structures. The development of, say, mothers and toddlers groups is equally, if not more, relevant here as campaign-type action groups, provided that the workers are operating within some kind of long-term developmental perspective that acknowledges the relationship between the personal, the communal and the structural.

In one respect, the United Kingdom is a reflection of many Third World countries — there exists an imbalance between economic development, on the one hand, and social and political development, on the other. The reflection is inverted, however, because there is in the United Kingdom a well-developed economic system alongside a stunted polity and, in so many urban communities, an unsatisfactory social structure. The current crisis in the economy may lead us to question the depth and permanence of the country's economic maturity, but it is not my task to discuss that issue here. My point is that in a flourishing economy, where energies are directed primarily to the production and consumption of wealth, there will be little awareness of the functioning of social and political mechanisms. But as the economy declines, and fewer resources are made available for housing, schools, health, and so forth, the stresses within social and political processes become more serious, and the imbalance between the economic and these other spheres more apparent. Political mechanisms and procedures, to which neither government nor the people gave much attention in years of prosperity, become experienced as inadequate both for expressing people's discontent and for providing government and business with a stable base from which to escape the economic recession. There is, too, more dissatisfaction with the functioning of social systems such as the community, the workplace, the family, and so on.

A difficulty in this situation is that whilst there is growing consciousness about social and political structures, individual and corporate energies become exclusively concerned with economic regeneration. If this succeeds, concern about the social and political will ebb away and the chance to achieve a more balanced development between these two spheres and the economic will be lost. If economic regeneration fails, we are exposed to the risk that social and political problems will be dealt with through harsh measures that herald the start of a more authoritarian approach to social and political relationships.

A major problem of our cities today is that people in their communities are starved both of material resources and of rewarding and satisfying relationships. Men and women are living as 'prisoners of an unbearable insularity', as Fanon described it. The attenuation of participative relationships is as evident between communities and those in authority as within them, a point made by a community worker interviewed by Alston:

> I feel that this lack of response is partly a result of the way in which councils have been run for years and years, and the developments that have resulted. Tenants do voice opinions from time to time, but the only way that they can be heard is to be very aggressive, and the same can be said for any community group or individual with issues to raise with council . . . There has not been any well organised, popular opposition to the cuts and I feel that this stems from the fact that the community has never had a say in the organisational change and development of council policies, so you can't really expect the community to suddenly become aware of changes and the ramifications of these changes. Council has a heritage of being shrouded in mystery, with a remote provision of services . . . no particular political party is to blame for this situation, they have all been responsible in some way. (1982)

In other words, political interests and involvement are part of an *interactive* process; they are affected by people's judgement of what they will get out of participation, and whether they are likely or not to have an impact on decision-making. Both of these will be influenced by the scale of the political environment in which people may wish to get involved, and part of the rationale for the decentralisation of local authority services and decision-making is to make them more comprehensible to, and more amenable to the influence of, local people. The diffusion of these processes may reinvigorate local politics, and enhance, in particular, the participation and influence of the most marginal groups.

The planned, purposeful development of communities as social units has not been a major concept in local administration and planning, though it was more apparent in the growth of new towns and in the earlier visions of the garden city movement. Urban communities in particular have been regarded in a laissez-faire manner; there have, of course, been interventions to provide services to individuals and groups, and to regulate matters such as land-use, transportation, public health, and so on, but such interventions have been designed to meet specific problems and do not, even cumulatively, amount to a plan of development for the community as a social unit. One of the most pronounced failures has been the inability of the planning profession to move beyond territorial planning, and Harvey has drawn attention to the failure amongst geographers, architects and planners to find general theories that relate social processes in the city to its spatial forms (1975). Even alternative or radical planning initiatives have largely been confined to advocacy planning on behalf of neighbourhood organisations and minority groups.

This brings us to a further meaning in de Chardin's statement: we must make the passage to conceiving of communities as social systems, though it would be foolish to think that in the past community workers have been any better in doing this than workers in other occupations. Indeed, Head has suggested that

> community development thus far has not dealt with the lack of a vital sense of community, if by that word we mean a society in which individuals can achieve their maximum growth within a warmly supportive social environment. The practitioners of community development . . . face the choice of continuing to seek through various pressure tactics, increasing levels of benefits from the welfare state, or conversely, they can begin the far more difficult task of attempting to change the nature of the power relationships existing between the various groups, including the new elites, who dominate and control the structures and allocations of resources of post-industrial societies. This requires a thorough analysis of these relationships, the expertise necessary to compete on a level of equality and a realistic vision of an attainable and meaningful society. Perhaps one of the most significant inadequacies in community development today is its lack of a vision of a humane and meaningful future and how to get from here to there . . .
>
> The unwillingness or inability of community development workers to tackle the task of defining the type of society required for human well-being, and to attempt the difficult task of achieving human liberation in post-industrial society represents a failure of extreme proportions. Community development in post-industrial society therefore is presently more myth than reality. Its challenge is to find ways to move beyond the present situation. (1979)

Part of the difficulty of meeting this challenge is apparent in Head's own words: it is seldom that one finds a discussion of community that avoids both vague, and often romantic, description ('warmly supportive social environment') and grand abstractions ('attainable and meaningful society'; 'achieving human liberation'). My own general statements about the need for a holistic approach to communities as social units fall into the same trap, and need to be given the hard edge of people's experiences of the areas in which they live (see, for example, the quotations from residents in the book by Knight and Hayes, 1981) and their sense of powerlessness to influence decisions being made about their well-being. It is hoped that the emphasis on networks, roles and knowledge of others that is part of the definition of communal coherence offers more concrete expressions of what is needed for the development of community. Another example of a middle-range explanation of development is provided in a paper by Sugata Dasgupta about the emergence of what he calls 'the community society'. His vision is of communities rich in sub-systems, often in conflict, and with considerable overlap between clusters of networks and relationships. Welfare in the community society is based in and on small communities, where 'the producers of welfare will also be its consumers' (1979).

Perhaps one of the most specific accounts of the community as social system was produced as long ago as 1963 by Roland Warren in his book *The Community in America*. The tasks of the community as a social system are the provision of certain 'locality-relevant functions'. These are

- production, distribution and consumption of goods and services
- socialisation
- social control
- social participation
- mutual support

I shall refer to the first as the 'economic function' and to the other four as the 'welfare functions'.

Part of the meaning of 'the community society' or 'development of community' or 'the community as a social system' is that these five functions are carried out in some kind of effective and balanced relationship with each other. When a community worker interviewed by Alston says that 'communities have broken up and it's bloody hard to pull them together in any way', the worker is referring to a number of sociological and economic factors that have made it impossible for these locality-relevant functions to be effectively fulfilled. One of the effects of the long postwar boom is that the development of communities was distorted by the economic function. Not only did it become less and less likely that people would go to work within the area in which they also lived, but energies were given up almost totally to work and to the consumption of an expanded range of goods and services. Because of this, communities have developed more in response to the imperatives of the economy than to the social and personal needs of their members. People's homes and life-styles were set to carry out economic roles in the production, distribution and consumption of goods, and the four welfare functions have become progressively less salient in shaping people's expectations of their community and their relations with neighbours, friends, and so forth. Indeed, not only have communities become dominated by the production and consumption ethic, but welfare functions have been taken over more and more by bureaucracies of the local and central state, a welfare industry, argues Dasgupta, built on the ashes of the community as an adjunct to the economic system. The problem that has been created in allowing welfare functions in the community to atrophy and to become concentrated in state welfare agencies is that welfare has become narrowly defined as a series of services to particular groups and individuals; it has lost the richness and wholeness of the meaning of well-being suggested, for example, in Warren's four functions.

The location of work opportunities outside the place of residence, the preoccupation with the consumption of goods and more privatised forms of leisure, and the attenuation of interest in, and responsibility for, the four welfare functions have all helped to reduce the extent and variety of networks present in a community. This is what is often meant when we refer to the loss of a sense of community; Head sees the development of a sense of community as a necessary counter to the domination of people's lives by 'big business, big government and big labour' and as a means to emphasise the idea of people as human beings. He is alarmed at the new breed of utopians bearing labels such as 'systems engineers', 'computer programmers', 'data processing specialists' and 'systems designers', concerned with non-people and people substitutes, and the creation of a perfect society, like that described by Skinner in *Walden Two,* in which behaviour modification is used to programme individuals to be happy, productive and creative. The fact that the alternatives are too horrendous to contemplate should galvanise our efforts to develop the community, even in the face of the structural factors that affect communities and the divisions of race, age, gender and class that are present within them.

Community workers have an important part to play in all this; indeed, Littlejohn has argued (in a paper that was ahead of its time in 1972 and which received little attention) that

It may be that we are now at the outset of a phase of full recognition, in which the structure of the social services, and the whole framework of social administration and social planning, are so inter-related that unless we regard the processes inherent in community work as being the foundations upon which they are built, it may be impossible to move forward into a new and essential phase of integrated policy-making and implementation.

This is a matter of great urgency. There is still a tendency in central and local government to think in terms of the community in a series of convenient categories – young, old, disabled, immigrants, school-children under-fives and so on – with all of us forced into unreal stereotyping and conditioned to display Pavlovian reflexes when any of these words are mentioned. Without overstating the case, it may be said that the only person within the social work/further education/social administration nexus who can break through this stereotyping process will be the community worker . . . in other words, community workers are the new all-purpose workers in community settings who are taking over from social case workers the innovatory role which they played in the personal social services twenty years ago.

These references to casework and the social services bring us close to some of the issues discussed in the wake of the Barclay report's concern with 'community social work'. The development of community, including the renewal of the four welfare functions identified by Warren and the growth of networks and roles available to people, is to be pursued as a major good on its own right; its legitimacy is not dependent on decisions taken about the nature of the functions of welfare agencies. Whether all or some of the responsibilities of the staff of social services departments, for example, should be located in the community; whether or not more community care and self-help are necessary or desirable for people who are presently dependent on professional social workers – these are matters on which it would be unwise to predicate the necessity for the development of community as discussed in this and other chapters of the book. Clearly, the efforts of social services departments to develop effective forms of community social work will depend for their success on the outcome of other efforts towards development of community; but the case for development of community is much broader, and is concerned with more important issues of politics and welfare, than the functioning of welfare agencies, and the ways in which they choose to organise their services.

The place of community work in the development of community was discussed in Chapters 2 and 3, and was set alongside the contribution of other occupations and social movements. The task of restoring urban communities to function effectively as social units with some kind of balance between economic and welfare functions may be profoundly influenced by those concerned to create what Hoch calls 'a livable environment' in our cities. He writes:

The most encouraging developments of late have been the gradual coming together of the ecology movement with both a feminist movement that can potentially contribute much to its consciousness of the disastrous effects of the present masculine emphasis on the domination of the natural world, and also with a worker's movement more and more sensitive to the dangers of occupational disease. In my judgement this ecological crisis is the present system's weakest link and may well provide the rallying ground for a broad-based coalition of working people threatened in their occupational and living environments (since most of them live in the most environmentally damaged central city areas) with ecologically-minded student and professional groups, feminists, socialists, and all those who care about the health of themselves and their children . . . Despite the social class difficulties in the way of such an alliance (for example, between industrial workers concerned about keeping their jobs and middle class groups hitherto primarily concerned about the rural and suburban environment), it does have a rational basis in the joint interest of all these groupings in maintaining a livable environment and resisting the social forces . . . that are destroying it. (1979)

I believe Hoch is making an important point here, though perhaps its impact is lessened by the fanciful way in which he writes, and by the fact that he conceives of the process he describes only in terms of alliances between certain interest groups and political factions. It may be that the interest in the safety and health of the environment has the potential to raise awareness of some of the inadequacies in the social functioning of urban communities. The growing recognition in urban communities about health hazards at work, chemical and noise pollution on the streets, transportation facilities, repairs and maintenance on public housing estates, and the level of violence especially against women, old people and ethnic groups represent, together with other issues, what might be called the 'de-greening' of the conservation movement. This refers to a direction of the energies and resources of those concerned with conservation towards the deteriorating urban environment, using the experience and knowledge gained in fighting on environmental issues in the countryside. Urban conservationists, stuck fast in the more limited task of defending buildings and open spaces, will be forced to consider broader environmental issues. Members of the peace movement, largely concerned at the moment with nuclear armaments, may find it difficult to resist the logic of extending their concerns to the level of peacelessness on the streets. We might expect that these movements, together with some of the interest groups mentioned by Hoch, will find that their work to create a livable urban environment will necessarily lead them to consider the social functioning of communities; that is, the extent and quality of relationships between people and groups in the locality in which they live. The fact that changes in the economy will mean that more people will be spending more time in their communities rather than in a place of work will add considerable urgency to the task of making these communities places that offer rewarding opportunities for participation in a range of roles and responsibilities. What will people do with the time, energy and creative talents that were previously spent at the workplace? If we assume that we want to avoid a society in which large sections of the population are either conscripted into the armed forces or sedated permanently through alcohol, drugs, television, and so forth, then it is difficult to see how these energies and talents can be productively used other than within the locality of residence.

The occupation of community work has much to offer to the regeneration of the social processes of urban communities. A danger is that too much will be expected of it because, as Head has acknowledged in writing about community development, 'the concept of community development still possesses the power to arouse the hopes and aspirations of mankind for a better world. The terms "community" and "development" contain connotations which evoke strong emotional reactions in many people, possibly because both have been so systematically undermined in modern industrial societies.' Certainly, a sense of optimism and hope about people's abilities is one of the gifts offered by community work to fellow occupations who have been preoccupied with using resources to build up large administrative structures and a corps of professional staff in fields such as welfare, health and education. So many of these resources have been devoted to providing crisis-orientated services at minimum definitions of well-being. These services may be necessary but they are not sufficient; the additional, more challenging task from which social welfare has turned aside in the past in favour of administrative development is the development of community. There is much talk about structural imperatives, such as the influence of the economy, undermining what the 'helping professions' are trying to achieve in their work with individuals, families and groups; the community in which people live out most of their lives is no less a structural factor that influences efforts to improve the well-being of particular individuals, groups, and so forth. (Community workers have been as neglectful of this fact as other occupations.) What we all have to face up to is the need to change the way in which we *think* about communities, and then about the strengths, resources, needs and problems within them. We must begin to see communities as more than the back-drop or milieu to the delivery of services; we must see that it is necessary and possible to intervene to improve a community as a system, and that this way of thinking need not degenerate into rural idealism or nostalgia. Neither does this ability to evaluate a community's functioning as a system depend on the presence in the people who live there of an identification with their locality. It is possible and desirable to intervene, for example, to develop networks and roles for various people in an area without wanting them to identify with that area as 'their community', though such an identification may turn out to be a side effect of the intervention.

Such changes in thinking about communities must be accompanied by an awareness of the scale of resources and political will that are needed to sustain communities as viable social systems; some of the risks may be as great as the benefits to be achieved. But the promise is there of restoring political significance and competence, and of creating communal coherence, and in achieving both, to release an enormous store of human talents and values. Community work has the potential to contribute to this process; the roots of effective practice have been laid down in the last decade which one correspondent saw as 'a growing period from which the flowers may or may not come in the eighties'. In the years ahead, we may dare to believe the promises we have heard and made about developing new social and political relationships through which people make the passage 'from being, to being more' that is the theme of the poem with which this book ends.

You brought me daffodils
In the quiet ward, where I lay razed,
Shrunken, docile, dazed.
The buds modestly sealed, like all your messages
Unfolded only after you were gone –
And then their fearless yellow sang aloud
And last year's shuffling stalks fell silent
And winter's deadweight clods began to break
And seeds beneath them, long resigned to burial
Dared to believe the promises they heard
Of warmth and air to leaf in.

Stevie Krayer

References

ACW (Association of Community Workers) (1975), *Knowledge and Skills for Community Work* (London: ACW).

ACW (1978), *Unemployment: What Response from Community Work?* (London: ACW).

ACW (1981*a*), *Community Work on CQSW Courses,* Talking Points No. 27 (London: ACW).

ACW (1981*b*), *Resourcing Community Groups,* Talking Points No. 31 (London: ACW).

ACW (1981*c*), *Towards a Definition of Community Work* (London: ACW).

Alston, J. (1982), 'Community work – threatened or strengthened by financial cuts?', unpublished paper, National Institute for Social Work.

Baldock, P. (1974), *Community Work and Social Work* (London: Routledge & Kegan Paul).

Baldock, P. (1977), 'Why community action? The historical origins of the radical trend in community work', *Community Development Journal,* vol. 12, no. 2 (April).

Baldock, P. (1979*a*), 'An historical review of community work 1968–78', *Community Development Journal,* vol. 14, no. 3 (October).

Baldock, P. (1979*b*), 'Community action and the achievement of popular power', in D. A. Chekki (ed.), *Community Development: Theory and Method of Planned Change* (New Delhi: Vikas Publishing House).

Baldock, P. (1980), 'The origins of community work in the United Kingdom', in *Boundaries of Change in Community Work,* ed. P. Henderson *et al.* (London: Allen & Unwin).

Batten, T. R. (1957), *Communities and Their Development* (London: Oxford University Press).

Batten, T. R. (1965), *The Human Factor in Community Work* (London: Oxford University Press).

Batten, T. R. (1967), *The Non-Directive Approach in Group and Community Work* (London: Oxford University Press).

Benington, J. (1975), 'Local government becomes big business: corporate management and the politics of urban problems', in *Coventry CDP Final Report,* Vol. 2.

Biddle, W. (1968), 'Deflating the community developer', *Community Development Journal,* vol. 3, no. 4 (October).

Blackmore, M. (1981), *Community Work Training: A Study of Opportunities for Workers in the Field* (London: National Council for Voluntary Organisations).

Bolger, S., *et al.* (1981), *Towards Socialist Welfare Work* (London: Macmillan).

Booton, F., and Dearling, A. (1980), *The 1980s and Beyond: The Changing Scene of Youth and Community Work* (Leicester: National Youth Bureau).

Bryers, P. (1979), 'The development of practice theory in community work', *Community Development Journal,* vol. 14, no. 3 (October).

Butcher, H., *et al.* (1980), *Community Groups in Action: Case Studies and Analysis* (London: Routledge & Kegan Paul).

Butterworth, E., *et al.* (1982), 'The Batley battle revisited', *Community Care,* 28 January.

Calouste Gulbenkian Foundation (1968), *Community Work and Social Change* (London: Longman).

Calouste Gulbenkian Foundation (1973), *Current Issues in Community Work* (London: Routledge & Kegan Paul).

Carmichael, S., and Hamilton, C. V. (1969), *Black Power: The Politics of Liberation in America* (Harmondsworth: Penguin).

Cary, L. J. (ed.) (1970), *Community Development as a Process* (Columbia, Mo.: University of Missouri Press).

CCETSW (Central Council for Education and Training in Social Work) (1974), *The Teaching of Community Work* (London: CCETSW).

CCETSW (1979), *Council Policy on Training for Community Work within the Personal Social Services* (London: CCETSW).

CDP (Community Development Project) (1975), *Workers on the Scrap Heap* (Birmingham: CDP).

CDP (1976), *Whatever Happened to Council Housing?* (London: CDP Information and Intelligence Unit).

CDP (1977), *The Costs of Industrial Change* (London: CDP Information and Intelligence Unit).

Chekki, D. A. (ed.) (1979), *Community Development: Theory and Method of Planned Change* (New Delhi: Vikas Publishing House).

Cmnd 3702 (1968), *Report of the Committee on Local Authority and Allied Personal Social Services* (Seebohm Report) (London: HMSO).

Cockburn, C. (1977), *The Local State* (London: Pluto Press).

Colonial Office (1958), *Community Development: A Handbook* (London: HMSO).

Community Action (1980), 'Organising in the 1980s' (September–October issue).

Community Development Group, William Temple Foundation (1980), *Involvement in Community: A Christian Contribution* (Manchester: William Temple Foundation).

Community Links Report, The (1980), produced by Community Links, London E6.

Constantino, R. (1978), *Neocolonial Identity and Counter-Consciousness* (London: Merlin Press).

Corkey, D., and Craig, G. (1978), 'CDP: community work or class politics?', in P. Curno (ed.), *Political Issues and Community Work* (London: Routledge & Kegan Paul).

Coventry and other Trades Councils (1980), *State Intervention in Industry: A Workers' Inquiry* (Newcastle: Coventry and other Trades Councils).

Curno, P. (ed.) (1978), *Political Issues and Community Work* (London: Routledge & Kegan Paul).

Dasgupta, S. (1979), 'Three models of community development', in D. A. Chekki (ed.), *Community Development: Theory and Method of Planned Change* (New Delhi: Vikas Publishing House).

Davies, C., and Crousaz, D. (1982), *Local Authority Community Work – Realities of Practice,* Research Report No. 9 (London: HMSO).

Du Sautoy, P. (1962), *The Organisation of a Community Development Programme* (London: Oxford University Press).

Du Sautoy, P. (1966), 'Community development in Britain?', *Community Development Journal,* vol. 1, no. 1 (January).

Edwards, J., and Batley, R. (1978), *Politics of Positive Discrimination* (London: Tavistock).

Elliot, B., *et al.* (1982), 'Bourgeois social movements in Britain: repertoires and responses', *The Sociological Review*, vol. 30, no. 1 (February).

Frazer, H. (ed.) (1981*a*), *Community Work in a Divided Society* (Belfast: Farset Press).

Frazer, H. (1981*b*), 'Community work in the 80s', in H. Frazer (ed.), *Community Work in a Divided Society* (Belfast: Farset Press).

Galper, J., and Mandros, J. (1980), 'Community organisation in social work in the 1980s: fact or fiction?', *Journal of Education for Social Work,* vol. 16, no. 1 (Winter).

Gladstone, F. (1979), *Voluntary Action in a Changing World* (London: Bedford Square Press).

Goetschius, G. (1975), 'Some difficulties in introducing a community work option into social work training', in D. Jones and M. Mayo (eds), *Community Two* (London: Routledge & Kegan Paul).

Goodenough, W. (1963), *Cooperation in Change: An Anthropological Approach to Community Development* (New York: Russell Sage).

Grassby, J. (1978), 'What can the unemployed do?', in *Unemployment: What Response from Community Work?* (London: ACW).

Great Britain (DES) (1973), *Adult Education: A Plan for Development* (London: HMSO).

Griffiths, H. (1974), 'The aims and objectives of community development', *Community Development Journal,* vol. 9, no. 2 (April).

Griffiths, H. (1979), 'Models and strategies for participation in community development', paper given in Dublin.

Griffiths, H. (1980), 'Community work in the 80s: paid and voluntary action', in G. Poulton (ed.), *Community Work Issues and Practice in the 80s* (Southampton: Southern Council for Community Work Training).

Groombridge, B., *et al.* (1982), *Adult Education and Participation* (London: Universities' Council for Adult and Continuing Education).

Haggstrom, W. (1970), 'The psychological implications of the community development process', in L. J. Cary (ed.), *Community Development as a Process* (Columbia, Mo.: University of Missouri Press).

Hanmer, J., and Rose, H. (1980), 'Making sense of theory', in P. Henderson *et al.* (eds), *The Boundaries of Change in Community Work* (London: Allen & Unwin).

Harvey, D. (1975), *Social Justice and the City* (London: Edward Arnold).

Head, W. A. (1979), 'Community development in post-industrial society: myth or reality?', in D. A. Chekki (ed.), *Community Development: Theory and Method of Planned Change* (New Delhi: Vikas Publishing House).

Henderson, P., Jones, D., and Thomas, D. N. (eds) (1980), *The Boundaries of Change in Community Work* (London: Allen & Unwin).

Henderson, P., and Thomas, D. N. (1980), *Skills in Neighbourhood Work* (London: Allen & Unwin).

Henderson, P., and Thomas, D. N. (1981), *Readings in Community Work* (London: Allen & Unwin).

Hindess, B. (1980), 'Democracy and the limitations of parliamentary democracy', in *Politics and Power 1* (London: Routledge & Kegan Paul).

Hoch, P. (1979), *White Hero Black Beast: Racism, Sexism and the Mask of Masculinity* (London: Pluto Press).

Horowitz, I. L. (1966), *Three Worlds of Development: The Theory and Practice of International Stratification* (New York: Oxford University Press).

Huber, L., and McCartney, F. (1980), 'Community work in Belfast: a neighbourhood approach', in P. Henderson *et al.* (eds), *The Boundaries of Change in Community Work* (London: Allen & Unwin).

Hubley, J. (1978–9), 'Community education, community development and health education', *Community Education,* no. 1 (Winter).

Hubley, J. (ed.) (1980), *Community Work and Health* (Paisley: Local Government Research Unit).

Jones, D. (1977), 'Community work in the United Kingdom', in H. Specht and A. Vickery (eds), *Integrating Social Work Methods* (London: Allen & Unwin).

Jones, D., and Mayo, M. (eds) (1975), *Community Two* (London: Routledge & Kegan Paul).

Key, M., *et al.* (1976), *Evaluation Theory and Community Work* (London: Young Volunteer Force Foundation).

Kingsley, S. (1981), 'Voluntary action: innovation and experiment as criteria for funding', in *Research Bulletin,* Home Office, No. 11 (London: HMSO).

Knight, B., and Hayes, R. (1981), *Self-Help in the Inner City* (London: London Voluntary Services Council).

Kramer, R. (1979), 'Voluntary agencies in the welfare state: an analysis of the vanguard role', *Journal of Social Policy,* vol. 8, no. 4 (October).

Kuenstler, P. (ed.) (1960), *Community Organisation in Great Britain* (London: Faber).

Laski, H. J. (1930), *Liberty in the Modern State* (London: Faber).

Lees, S., *et al.* (1980), *Studies in Community Development* (London: Polytechnic of North London).

Leissner, A. (1967), *Family Advice Centres* (London: Longman).

Littlejohn, E. (1972), 'Community work and community relations', *New Community,* vol. 1, no. 2 (January).

London Council for Community Work Training (1979), *Report of the Accreditation Working Party* (London: LCCWT).

Maas, H. S. (1966), *Five Fields of Social Service: Reviews of Research* (New York: National Association of Social Workers).

Marshall, T. H. (1972), 'Value problems of welfare capitalism', *Journal of Social Policy,* vol. 1, no. 1.

Mayo, M. (1982), 'Community action programmes in the early eighties – what future?', *Critical Social Policy* (Spring).

Miliband, R., and Saville, J. (eds) (1980), *The Socialist Register 1980* (London: Merlin Press).

Miller, S. M. (1980), 'The eighties and the left: an American view', in R. Miliband and J. Saville (eds), *The Socialist Register 1980* (London: Merlin Press).

Milligan, F. (1961), 'Community associations and centres', in P. Kuenstler (ed.), *Community Organisation in Great Britain* (London: Faber).

Moseley, L. G. (1971), 'Evaluation research in community development: a missing dimension', *Community Development Journal,* vol. 6, no. 3 (Autumn).

310   *The Making of Community Work*

Murray, R., and Hubley, J. (1980), 'Housing and health', in J. Hubley (ed.), *Community Work and Health* (Paisley: Local Government Research Unit).
National Consumer Council (1977), *The Fourth Right of Citizenship: A Review of Local Advice Services* (London: NCC).
National Council of Social Service (1963), *Community Organisation: Work in Progress* (London: NCSS).
National Institute for Social Work (1982), *Social Workers: Their Role and Tasks* (London: Bedford Square Press).
Non-Violence Study Group (1980), *In and Out of the Muck: An Introduction to Non-Violence* (Sydney: NVSG).
Ohri, A., *et al.* (eds) (1982), *Community Work and Racism* (London: Routledge & Kegan Paul).
Perlman, R., and Gurin, A. (1972), *Community Organisation and Social Planning* (New York: Wiley).
Pringle, R. (1981), 'Training for the eighties: some pointers', *Community Development Journal,* vol. 16, no. 3 (October).
Prior, M., and Purdy, D. (1980), *Out of the Ghetto* (London: Spokesman).
Purdy, D. (1980), 'The left's alternative economic strategy', in *Politics and Power 1* (London: Routledge & Kegan Paul).
Rivera, F. G., and Erlich, J. L. (1981), 'Neo-*Gemeinschaft* minority communities: implications for community organisation in the United States', *Community Development Journal,* vol. 16, no. 3 (October).
Rosenthal, H. (1980), *Health and Community Work: Some New Approaches* (London: King's Fund Centre).
Ross, M. G. (1955), *Community Organisation: Theory, Principles and Practice* (New York: Harper & Row).
Rothman, J. (1974), *Planning and Organising for Social Change* (New York: Columbia University Press).
Rothman, J. (1979), 'Macro social work in a tightening economy', *Social Work* (July).
Sainsbury, E. (1982), review article in *International Social Work,* vol. 15, no. 2.
Schler, D. (1970), 'The community development process', in L. J. Cary (ed.), *Community Development as a Process* (Columbia, Mo.: University of Missouri Press).
Seebohm Report (1968), see Cmnd 3702 (1968).
Senghor, L. S. (1964), *On African Socialism* (New York: Praeger).
Sharman, N. (1978), 'The economic crisis and the community's response', in *Unemployment: What Response from Community Work?* (London: ACW).
Sills, P. (1980), *Community Work: An Introduction to Current Approaches and Issues* (Berkhamsted: Volunteer Centre Talk).
Smith, I. (1980), *Community Work and 'Qualifications',* Talking Points No. 19 (London: ACW).
Smith, L., and Jones, D. (eds) (1981), *Deprivation, Participation and Community Action* (London: Routledge & Kegan Paul).
Smith, M. (1979), 'Concepts of community work: a British view', in D. A. Chekki (ed.), *Community Development: Theory and Method of Planned Change* (New Delhi: Vikas Publishing House).
Specht, H. (1975), 'The dilemmas of community work in the United Kingdom', repr. in *Readings in Community Work,* ed. P. Henderson and D. N. Thomas (London: Allen & Unwin).

Specht, H. (1978), 'The grass roots and government in social planning and community organisation', *Administration in Social Work,* vol. 2, no. 3 (Fall).

Specht, H., and Vickery, A. (eds) (1977), *Integrating Social Work Methods* (London: Allen & Unwin).

Stiles, J. (1982), 'Opening employment and training opportunities in community work', in A. Ohri *et al.* (eds), *Community Work and Racism* (London: Routledge & Kegan Paul).

Streatfield, D. R. (1980*a*), 'Neighbourhood information centres and community workers', *Community Development Journal,* vol. 15, no. 3 (October).

Streatfield, D. R. (1980*b*), 'Information and community workers', MA thesis, University of Sheffield.

Symons, B. (1981), 'Promoting participation through community work', in L. Smith and D. Jones (eds), *Deprivation, Participation and Community Action* (London: Routledge & Kegan Paul).

Tasker, L. (1980), 'Practice and theory in community work: a case for reconciliation', in P. Henderson *et al.* (eds), *Boundaries of Change in Community Work* (London: Allen & Unwin).

Taylor, G. (1980), 'The Marxist inertia and the labour movement', in *Politics and Power 1* (London: Routledge & Kegan Paul).

Taylor, M. (1979), *Managing Community Resources,* Talking Points No. 13 (London: ACW).

Thomas, D. N. (1978), 'Community work, social change and social planning', in P. Curno (ed.), *Political Issues and Community Work* (London: Routledge & Kegan Paul).

Thomas, D. N. (1980), 'Research and community work', *Community Development Journal,* vol. 15, no. 1 (January).

Thomas, D. N., and Warburton, W. (1975), *Community Workers in Social Services Departments: A Case Study* (London: National Institute for Social Work/Personal Social Services Council).

Twelvetrees, A. (1976), *Community Associations and Centres: A Comparative Study* (Oxford: Pergamon).

Twelvetrees, A. (1982), *Community Work* (London: Macmillan).

United Nations (1958), *Training for Social Work* (New York: UN).

Waddington, P. (1979), 'Looking ahead – community work into the 1980s', *Community Development Journal,* vol. 14, no. 1 (October).

Warren, R. L. (1963), *The Community in America* (Chicago: Rand McNally).

Worthington, T. (1980), 'Is local community self-help a viable policy for local government to encourage?', paper given at an SCSS conference (November).

Younghusband, E. L. (1959), *Report of the Working Party on Social Workers in the Local Authority Health and Welfare Services* (London: HMSO).

Younghusband, E. L. (1978), *Social Work in Britain 1950–75: A Follow-Up Study,* Vol. 2 (London: Allen & Unwin).

Appendix 1: *The Members of the Advisory Committee*

Paul Curno	*Calouste Gulbenkian Foundation*
Paul Henderson	*National Institute for Social Work*
David Jones	*National Institute for Social Work*
Sister Mary McAleese	*Parish Mission Sisters*
Richard Mills	*Calouste Gulbenkian Foundation*

Appendix 2: *The Panel of Readers*

The following people kindly agreed to join the panel of readers. A first draft of the manuscript was sent to them for their advice and comments.

F. J. C. Amos — *Senior Fellow, Institute of Local Government Studies, University of Birmingham*

John Armstrong — *Student Supervisor, The Community Work Training Unit, Leicester*

Peter Baldock — *Principal Community Worker, Family and Community Services Department, Sheffield*

John Benington — *Chief Officer, Employment Department, Sheffield*

Phil Bryers — *Assistant Regional Community Development Officer, Strathclyde*

Sebastian Charles — *Canon of Westminster*

Pushpinder Chowdhry — *Community Worker, London*

Malcolm Cross — *Senior Research Fellow, Research Unit on Ethnic Relations, The University of Aston in Birmingham*

Ann Curno — *Lecturer in Community Work, Goldsmiths College*

David Donnison — *Professor, Department of Town and Regional Planning, University of Glasgow*

Chris Elphick — *Unit Coordinator, Community Education Training Unit, Oldham*

Ross Flockhart — *Director, Scottish Council of Social Services*

Hugh Frazer — *Director, Northern Ireland Voluntary Trust*

Hywel Griffiths — *Director, The Council of Social Service for Wales*

Jalna Hanmer — *Lecturer, Department of Applied Social Studies, University of Bradford*

John Harrison — *Community Chaplain, Stockton YMCA*

Stephen Hatch — *Senior Research Fellow, Policy Studies Institute, London*

John Lambert — *Lecturer, Department of Social Administration, University College of Cardiff*

Felicity McCartney — *Administrative College, Boroko, Papua New Guinea, formerly Community Worker, Belfast*

Basil Manning — *formerly Ethnic Adviser, Lewisham Social Services Department, London*

Marg Mayo	*Research Officer, Polytechnic of Central London*
Mike Newman	*Warden, the Working Men's College, London*
Pat Sills	*Lecturer, Department of Social Administration and Social Work, University of York*
Roger Smith	*Director, Nottingham Community Project*
Teresa Smith	*Lecturer, Department of Social and Administrative Studies, University of Oxford*
Linbert Spencer	*Deputy Director, Greater Manchester Youth Association*
Jenny Stiles	*General Secretary, Southwark CVS*
Laurence Tasker	*Head of Department, Department of Administrative and Social Studies, Teeside Polytechnic, Middlesbrough*
Marilyn Taylor	*Researcher, Community Projects Foundation, London*
Pat Taylor	*Lecturer in Social Work, University of Bristol*
Paul Waddington	*Senior Lecturer, Department of Sociology and Applied Social Studies, City of Birmingham Polytechnic*
Gerry Williams	*Senior Community Worker, Cambridge House and Talbot Settlement, London*
Anne Wright	*Community Worker, Voluntary Action Westminster*

Comments on all or part of the text were also made by John Haines, Jim Jackson and Peter Kuenstler.

Appendix 3: *The Participants in the Delphi Exercises*

TRAINING IN COMMUNITY WORK

Brian Astin	*Barton Project Student Unit*
Alan Barr	*University of Glasgow*
Philip Bryers	*Strathclyde Social Work Department*
Hugh Butcher	*Ilkley College*
Roger Cartlidge	*University of Durham*
John Harrison	*Stockton YMCA*
Keith Jackson	*Northern College*
David Jones	*Southampton Social Services Department*
Charlie McConnell	*Dundee College of Education*
Geoff Poulton	*University of Southampton*
Florence Rossetti	*University of Bath*
David Sawdon	*York Community Council*
Laurence Tasker	*Teeside Polytechnic*
David Thomas	*National Institute for Social Work*
Jenny Tremeer	*Bradford*
Alan Twelvetrees	*University College of Swansea*
Lionel van Reenan and colleagues	*Goldsmiths College*
Gerry Wheale	*University of Manchester*
Mike Winwood	*University of Bristol*

RESEARCH AND COMMUNITY WORK

Maria Blackmore	*London*
Dave Burghley	*National Youth Bureau*
Jim Cowan	*Wandsworth Social Services Department*
Carolyn Davies	*Department of Health and Social Security*
Mike Fleetwood	*Community Worker, Cardiff*
Leo Jago	*National Council of Voluntary Organisations*
Sue Kingsley	*Researcher*
Adrian Lanning	*West Midlands Social Planning Unit*
Ray Lees	*Polytechnic of Central London*
Areyeh Leissner	*University of Keele*
Patrick Sills	*University of York*
Ann Sloan	*Community Forum, Belfast*
Marilyn Taylor	*Community Projects Foundation*
David Thomas	*National Institute for Social Work*

Index

accreditation schemes 204–6, 208, 211, 220
administrative politics 74
  problems of 77
'administrative self-expression' 23
adult education
  and participative democracy 84–5, 232
  low priority of 27
  relationship to community work 29, 232
advice and information centres 37, 65, 136, 230
affluence
  and decline of political significance 78–9
Albany Settlement 39
Albermarle Report 27
animation 32
apprenticeship schemes 203–4, 206, 208, 220, 227
Association of Community Workers 14, 36, 38, 45, 52, 221, 278
  and development of training 223, 280
  and professionalisation issue 146
  definition of a community worker 127
  failures of 54–5, 57
  literature 250
  views of training 55–6, 185, 197, 198, 206, 211–12, 220
Association of London Housing Estates 21

Baldock, P. 18, 29
  and Athene Fallacy 121
Barclay Report 197, 231, 291, 302
Batten, R. 20, 25, 28, 29, 30
  non-directive approach 91
Benington, J. 45
Beresford, P. 111
Biddle, W. 33
Birmingham Polytechnic 193
Blackmore Report 217, 218, 219, 222, 223
Bradford University 193
Brinson, P. 20
British Council of Churches 243

Calouste Gulbenkian Foundation 20, 38
  advisory committees 52
  Community Resource Unit 40, 280
  proposals on a national body 280–1
  support for community work in voluntary sector 39–40, 57
  see also Gulbenkian Reports
Carmichael, S. 60, 294, 296

case-studies
  as method of studying practice 248–9
Central Council for Education and Training in Social Work
  and community work qualifications 211
  and community work training 31, 56, 146, 187, 193–4, 212
  research listings 268
  study into community work teaching 25
central government
  and franchisal development 71–3, 81–9
  attitudes to participation 66, 69, 81–2
  inability in management 77–8
  relationship with trade unions 63
Centreprise 39
Certificate in Youth and Community Work 209, 210
Certificate of Qualification in Social Work
  as community work qualification 209, 210
  community work content and teaching 194–7
child care services 20–1
  and development of community work 22
Children & Young Persons Act 1963
  and development of preventive work 21
Children & Young Persons Act 1969
  proposals on prevention and community development 22
Clark, G. 46
class
  and community 90–2, 96, 258–60
  see also middle classes; working classes
Cockburn, C. 46
collectivism
  and community work 126, 130, 289–90
Colonial Office
  handbook on community development 26
communal coherence 96–100, 102, 114, 174–5, 305
community (as a concept) 91, 299–300
  as a social system 46, 115, 296, 298–9, 300–1
  as world of residence 93–4
  networks 82–3, 94–5, 96, 301
  organising culture of 86–7, 296
  realising potential of 171–7, 304–5
  reconstruction of 154–68
  see also communal coherence

see also adult education; informal
    education
Educational Priority Areas Project 27
elderly
    as a focus for community work practice
        169, 170, 171
electoral politics 74
    effects of radicalisation 148
    subordination of 75–9, 80
employment
    and role of community work 156–61
    of community workers 225–9
    see also unemployment
environmental issues
    and the community 303
European Regional Clearing House for
    Community Work 38, 279
evaluation 266–7

Family Advice Centres 21
family life
    'privatisation' of 78, 176
Federation of Community Work Training
    Groups 14, 36, 52, 84, 146, 219, 220,
        221, 280
    and training reforms 211–12, 223
    and development of community work
        287
    as national promotion body 281
    history of 224
    in-action training 201, 208
Federation of Independent Advice Centres
    information services 277
feminism
    and development of community work
        theory 46, 255, 261, 297
franchisal development 71–3, 81
    and 'political modernisation' 294–5
    means of 81–9
    see also political responsibility
fraternity 175, 176
funding
    and central government departments 40,
        56, 235–6
    and employment strategy 234
    and local authorities 230, 241–3, 244
    Gulbenkian 40
    indirect 242–3
    joint 41, 242
    of a national body 285
    policies 236–8
    research 269–70
    'short-term' 238–40
    special funds 243–4

Goetschius, G. 191
Goldsmiths College 27, 193
government see central government; local
    government
Griffiths, H. 25, 28, 30, 140–1
group processes
    and community work 260
    and community work skills 137
    and resource allocation 64–5
Gulbenkian Foundation see Calouste
    Gulbenkian Foundation
Gulbenkian Report 1968 20, 24, 29, 38, 92
    ideas on national body 279
    on theory development 253
    training recommendations 186–7, 210,
        217
Gulbenkian Report 1973 92
    ideas on national body 279
    on theory development 253
    training recommendations 187–9, 217
    views on funding 243
Gulbenkian Study Group 1966 28–30
    see also Gulbenkian Report 1968
Gurin, A. 30

Hatch, S. 46
health care
    and community work involvement 162–5
Heath, E. 63, 77
Hodge, P. 28
Home Office
    and community work projects 56, 236
Home Office, Children's Department
    proposals for CDPs 22–3
housing
    issues and community work practice
        161–2
    problems and early community work 90,
        91

indigenous workers
    problems of employment 226–7
industrial politics 74, 80
informal education
    and community development 33–5
    and franchisal development 81, 86
    and the unemployed 160
    as a goal of community work 31–2,
        84–5, 128, 130–1
    see also skills development
information
    needs of community workers 274–8
Ingleby Committee Report 20–1
Inlogov
    research listing 268